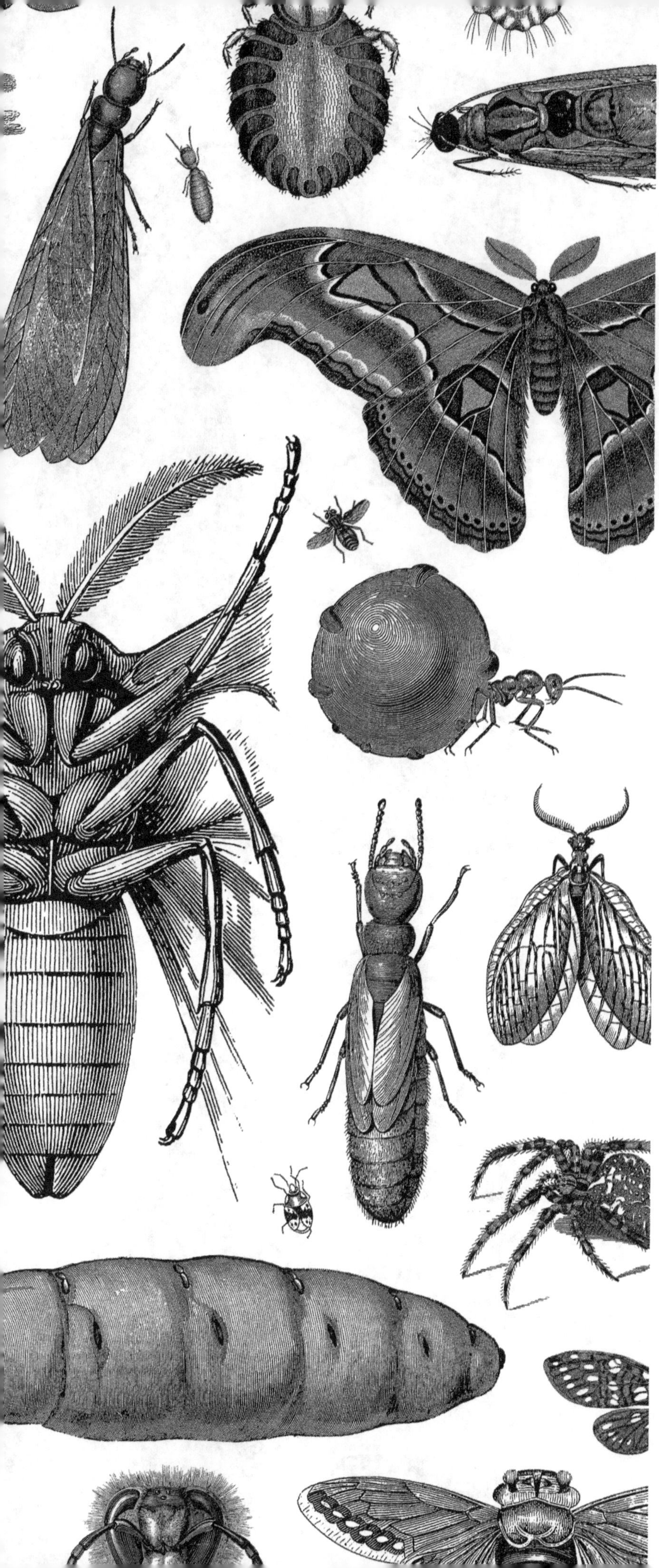

VOLUME NUMBER ONE

AF224966

INSECTS
REFERENCE
BOOK

AN IMAGE ARCHIVE FOR
ARTISTS *And* DESIGNERS

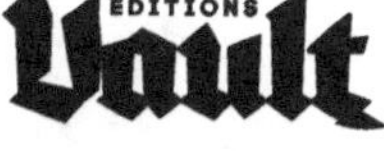

EDITIONS VAULT

INTRODUCTION

Insects have long been a source of inspiration
for artists and designers. Their intricate patterns
and striking colours have been the starting
point for many works of art and were one of the
primary sources of inspiration for the art nouveau
movement. They are a popular source of inspiration
for contemporary artists, designers, and even
architects. Insects' unique form and function
have provided endless opportunities for creative
interpretation; from delicate jewellery to large-
scale sculptures and industrial design, insects
have inspired some fascinating works of art. As we
continue to explore our surroundings and expand
our understanding of the natural world, insects will
likely continue to serve as an important source of
inspiration for artists and designers.

VAULT EDITIONS

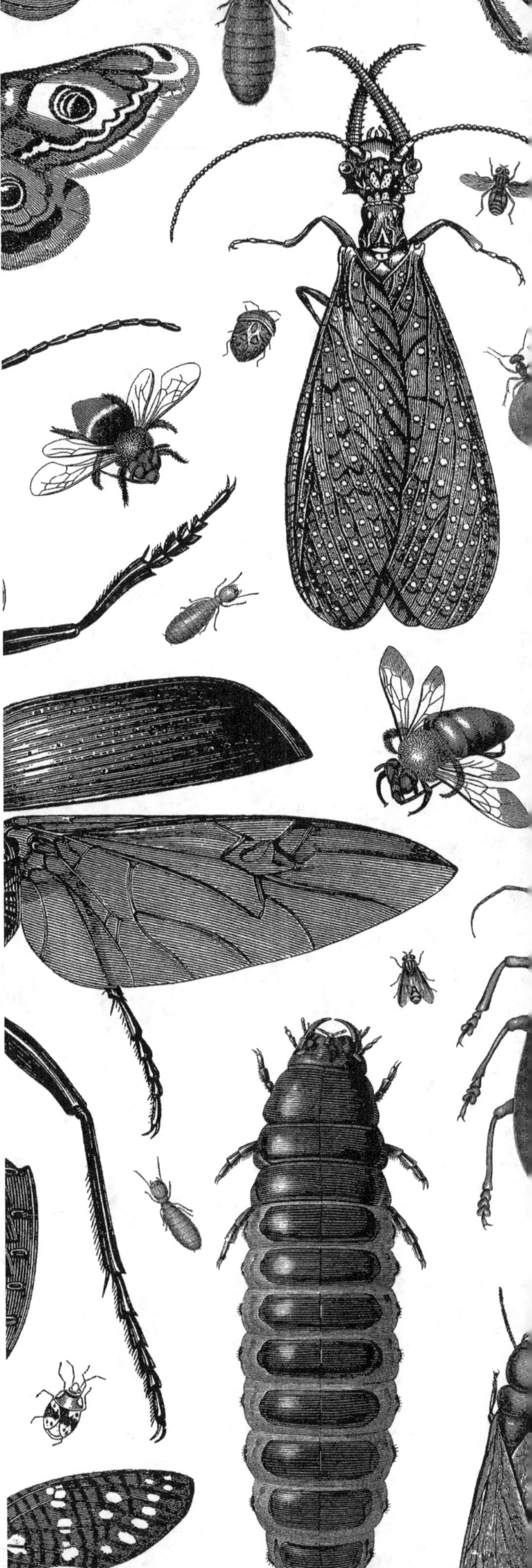

TABLE OF CONTENTS

Moths	01-20
Butterflies	21-28
Various genus of winged insects	29-35
Locusts, Crickets & Grasshoppers	36-41
Mantises	42
Flies	43-50
Bees, Wasps & Hornets	51-58
Dragonflys	59
Aphids and insects of the order Hemiptera	60-61
Beetles	62-80
Ants	81-82
Centipedes, Scorpions & Spiders	83-96
Fleas & Lice	97-100
List of illustrations	101-102
Image download instructions	103

DOWNLOAD YOUR FILES

Downloading your files is simple. To access your digital files, please go
to the last page of this book and follow the instructions.

For technical assistance, please email:
info@vaulteditions.com

Copyright
Copyright © Vault Editions Ltd 2022.

Bibliographical Note

This book is a new work created by Vault Editions Ltd.

ISBN: 978-1-925968-97-2

INSECTS REFERENCE BOOK

VAULT EDITIONS

INSECTS

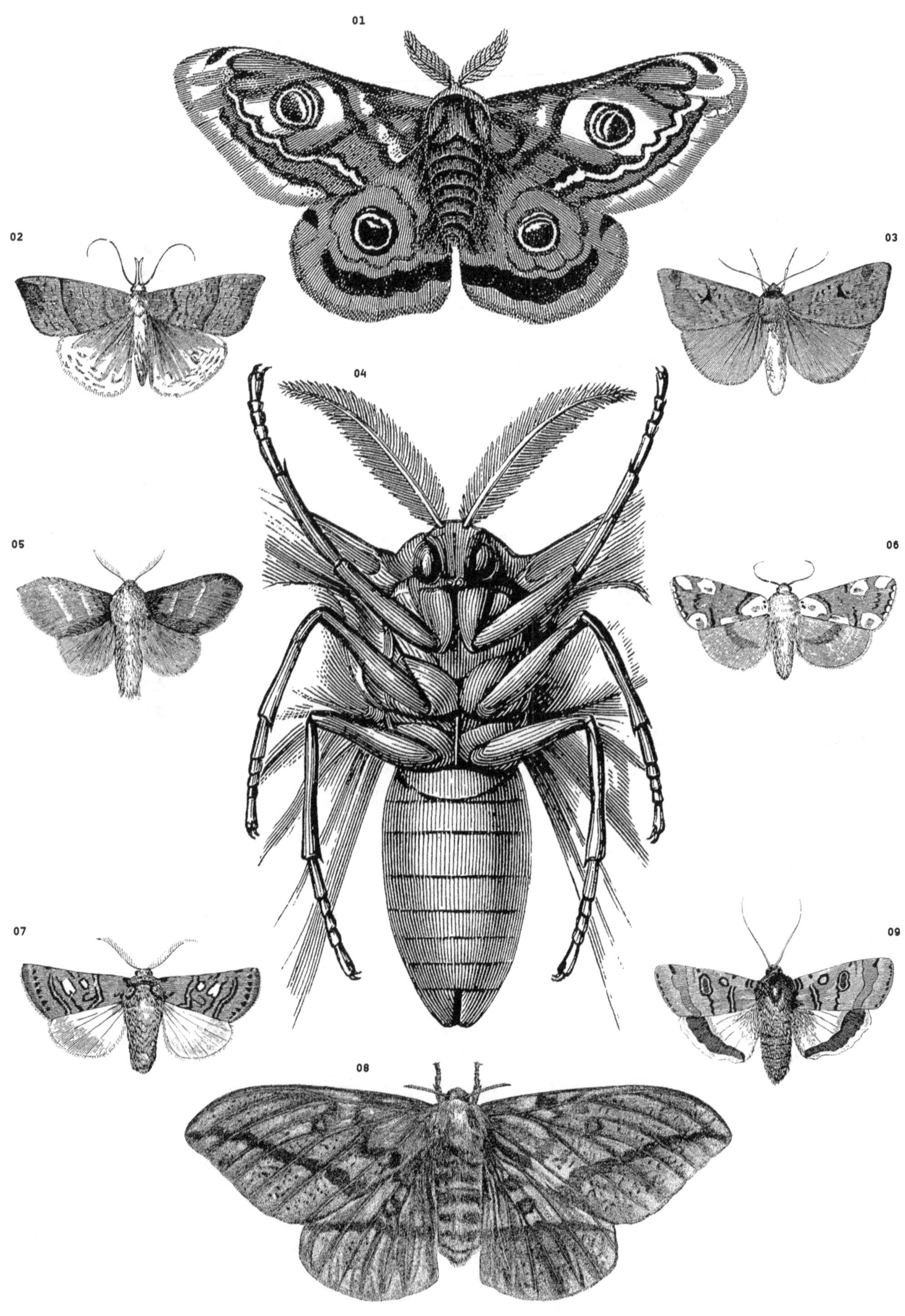

MOTHS

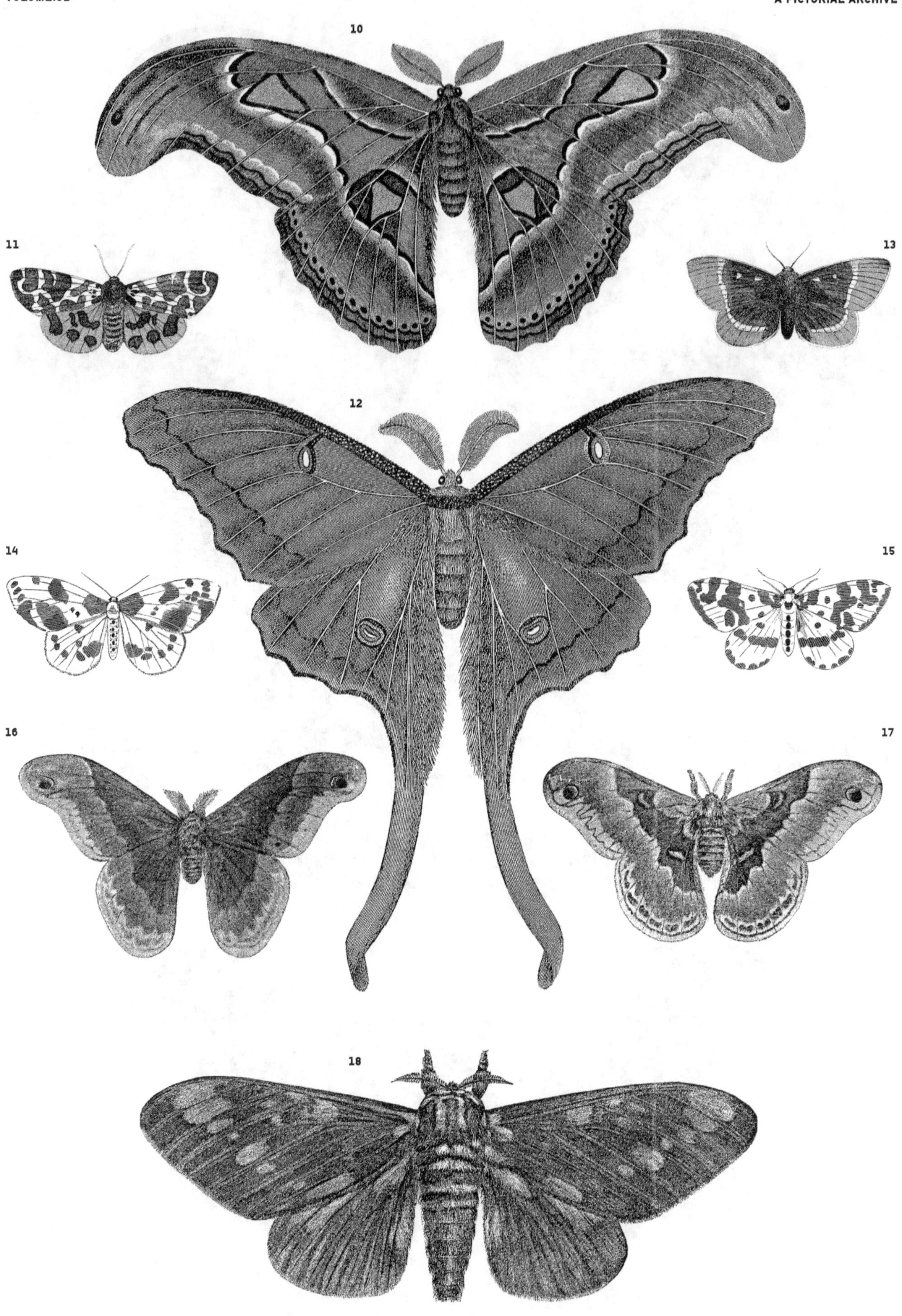
10
11
13
12
14
15
16
17
18
INSECTS

INSECTS

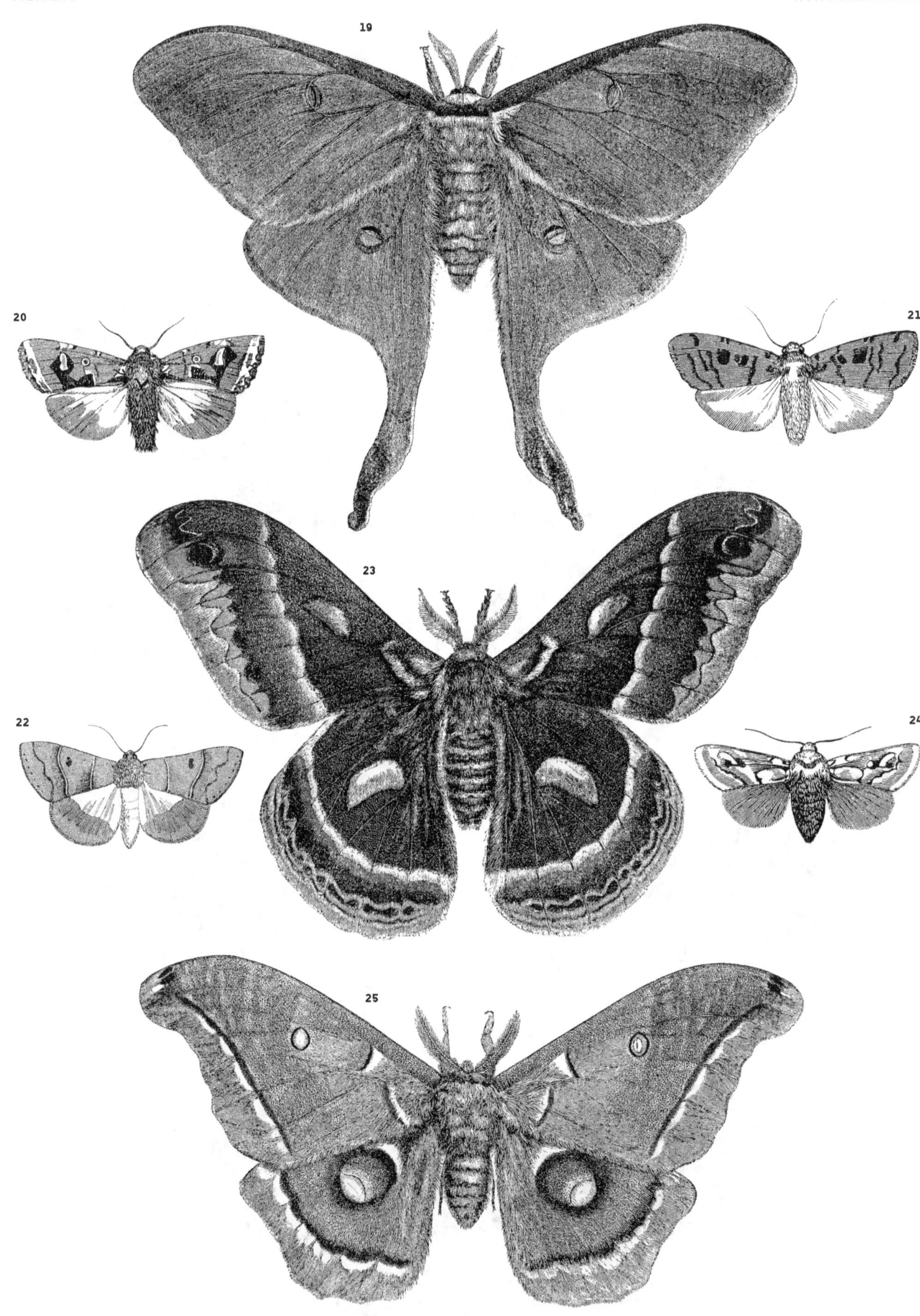

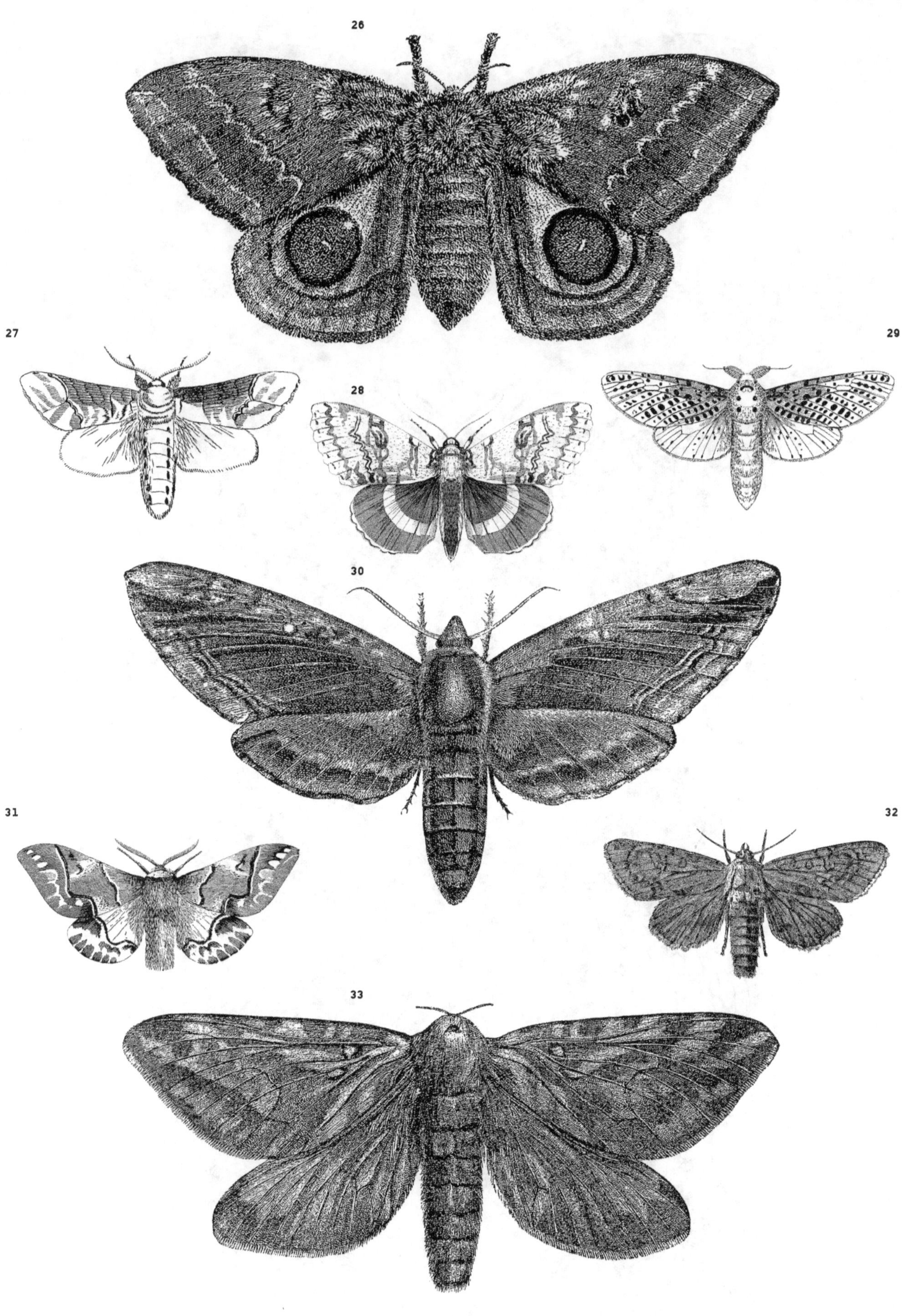

MOTHS

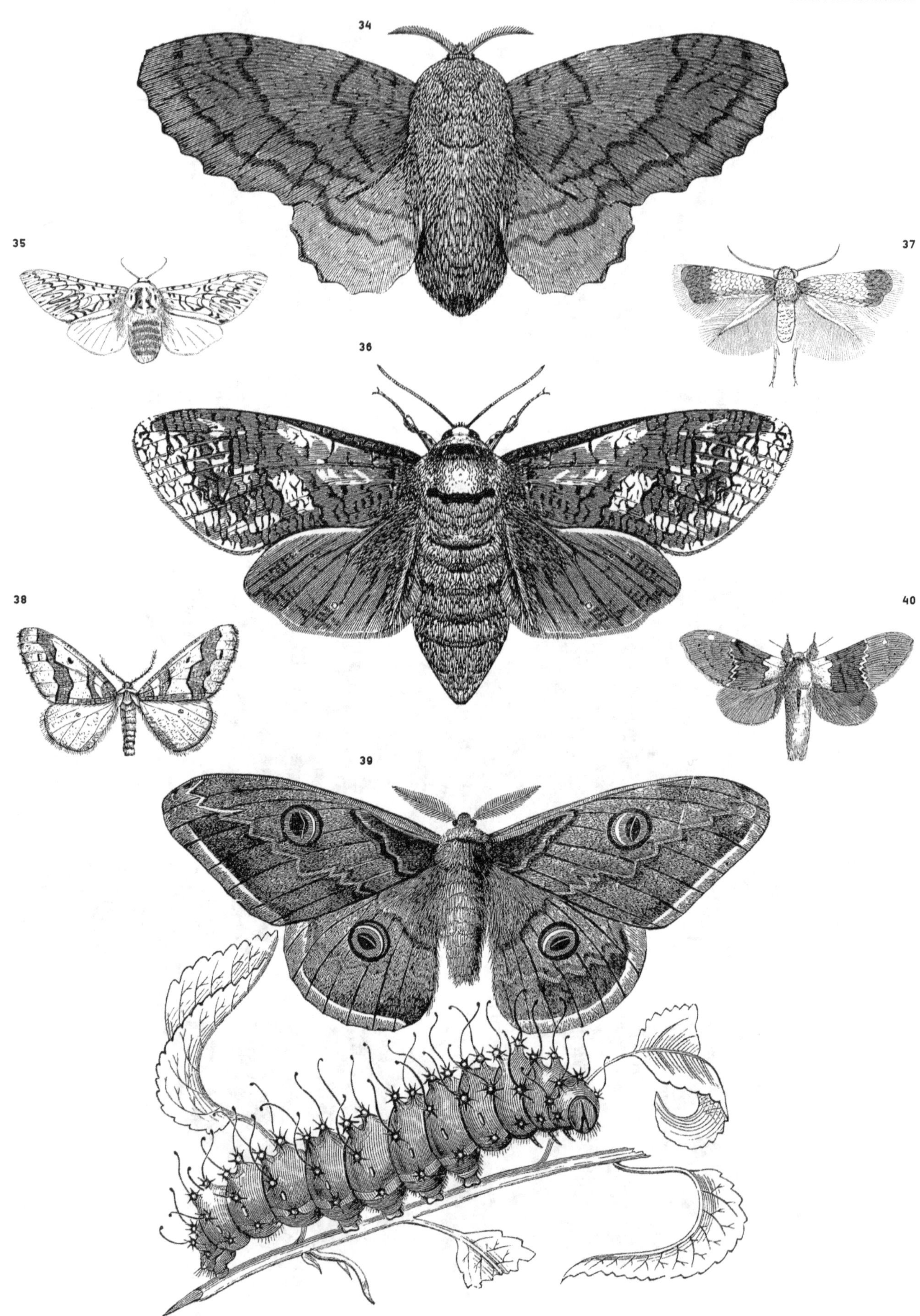

MOTHS

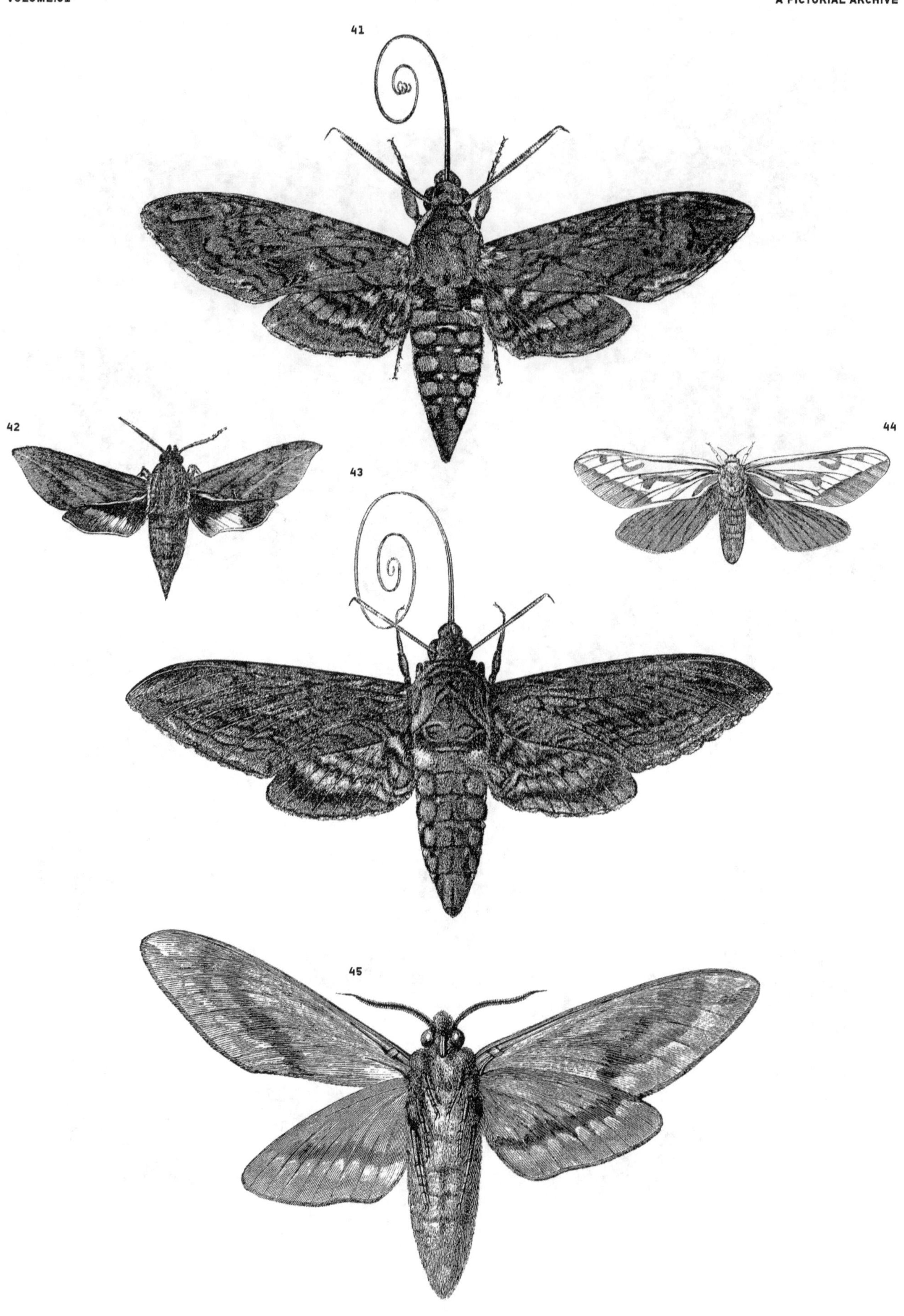

41
42
43
44
45
INSECTS

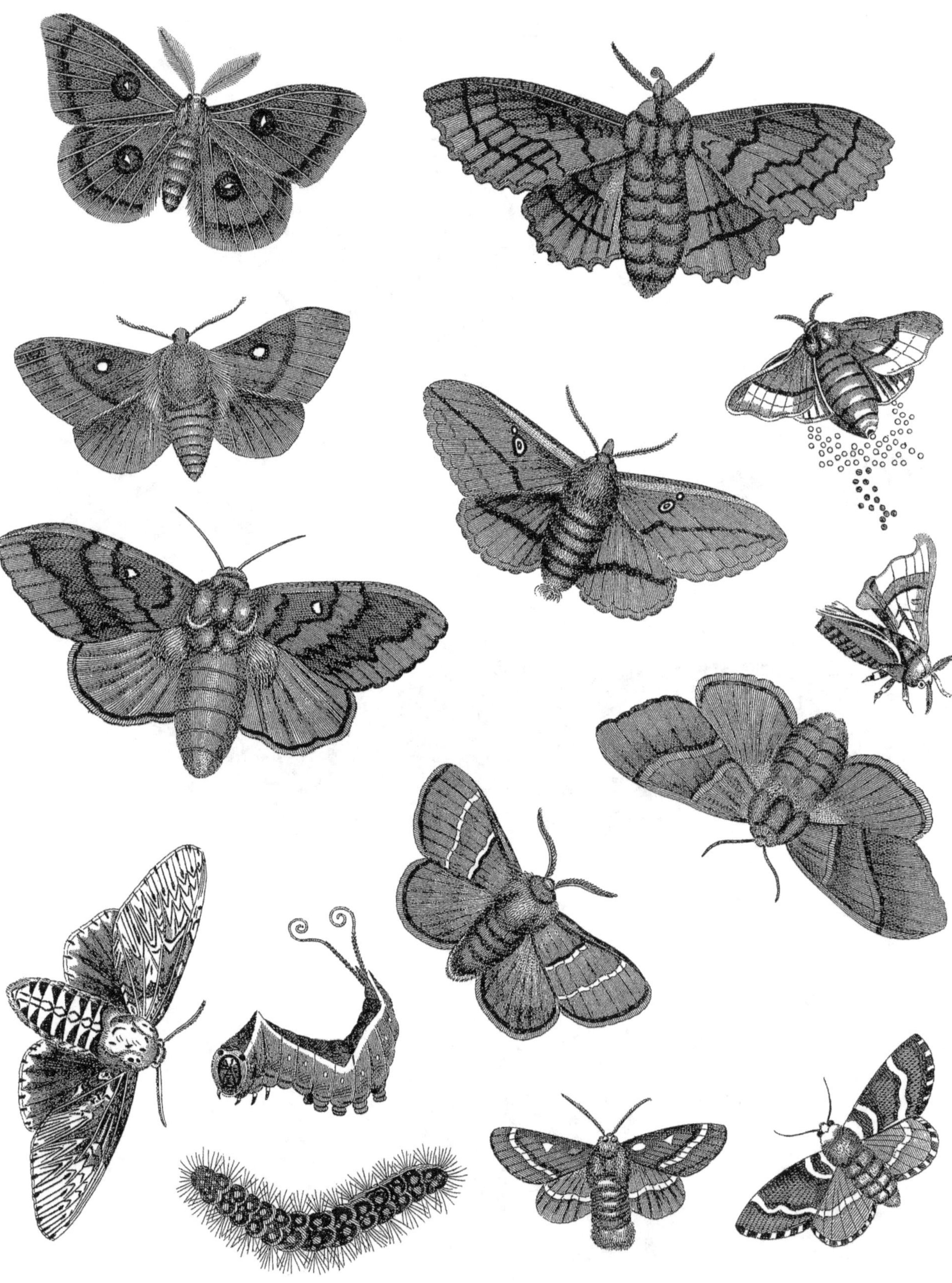

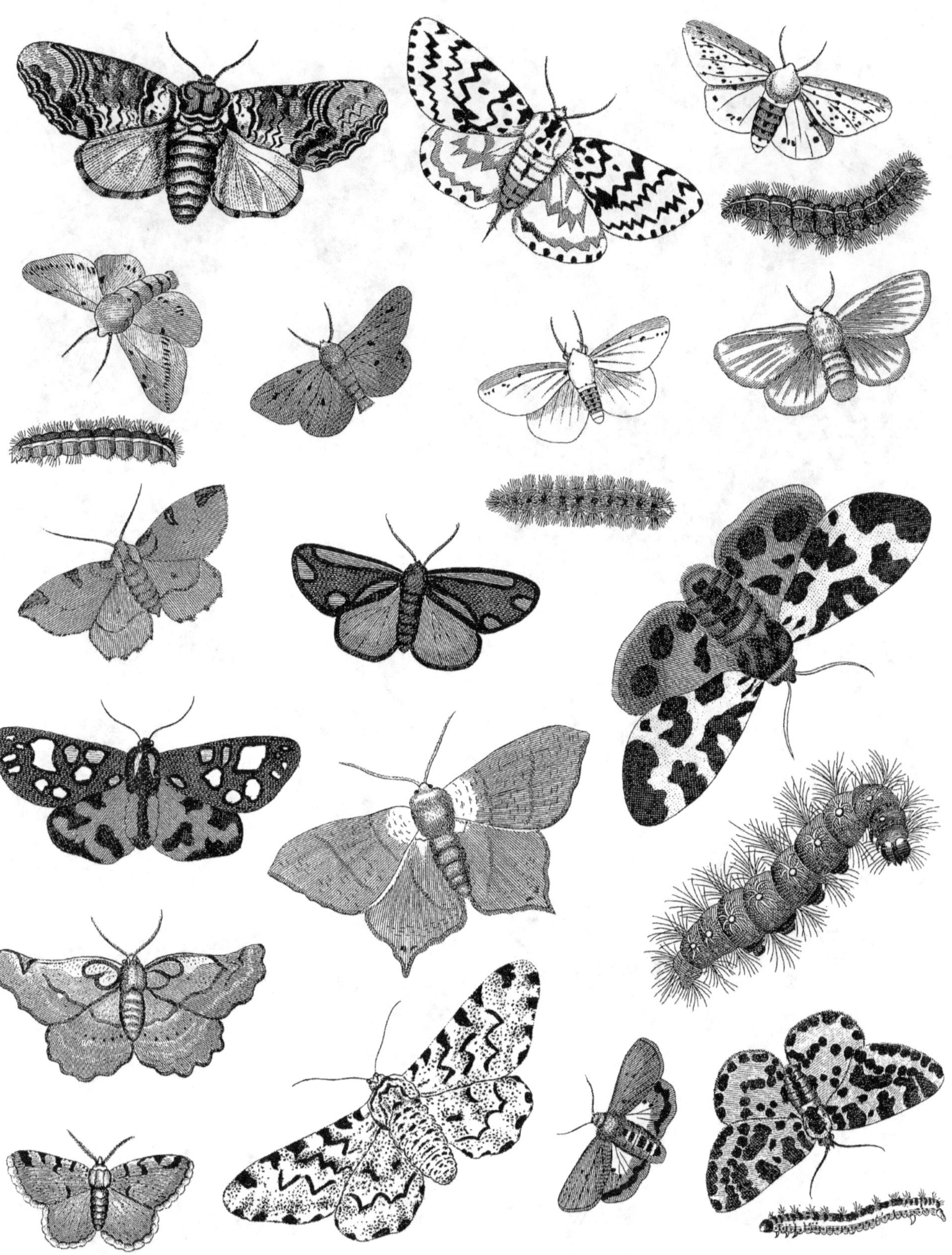

INSECTS

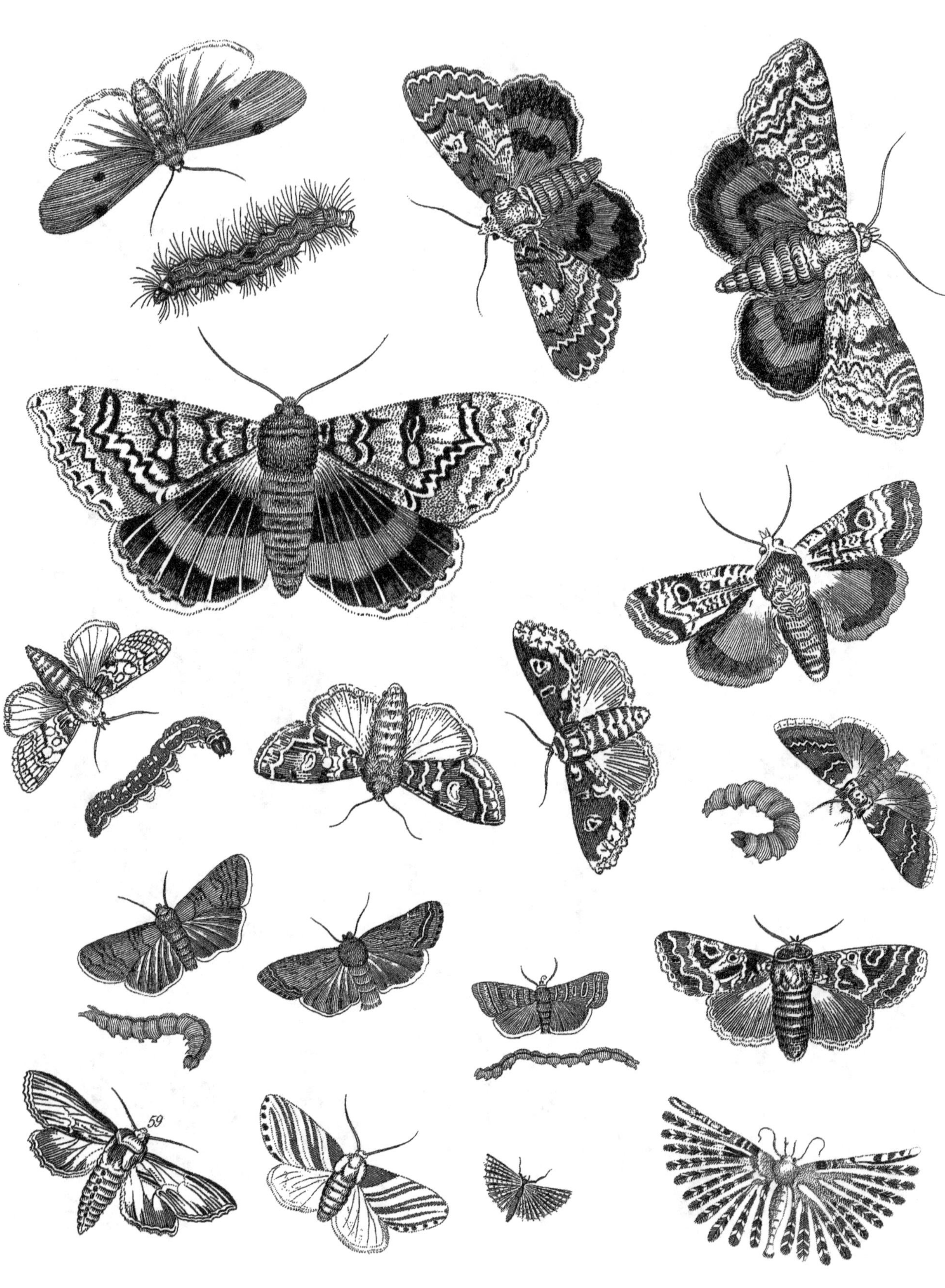

INSECTS

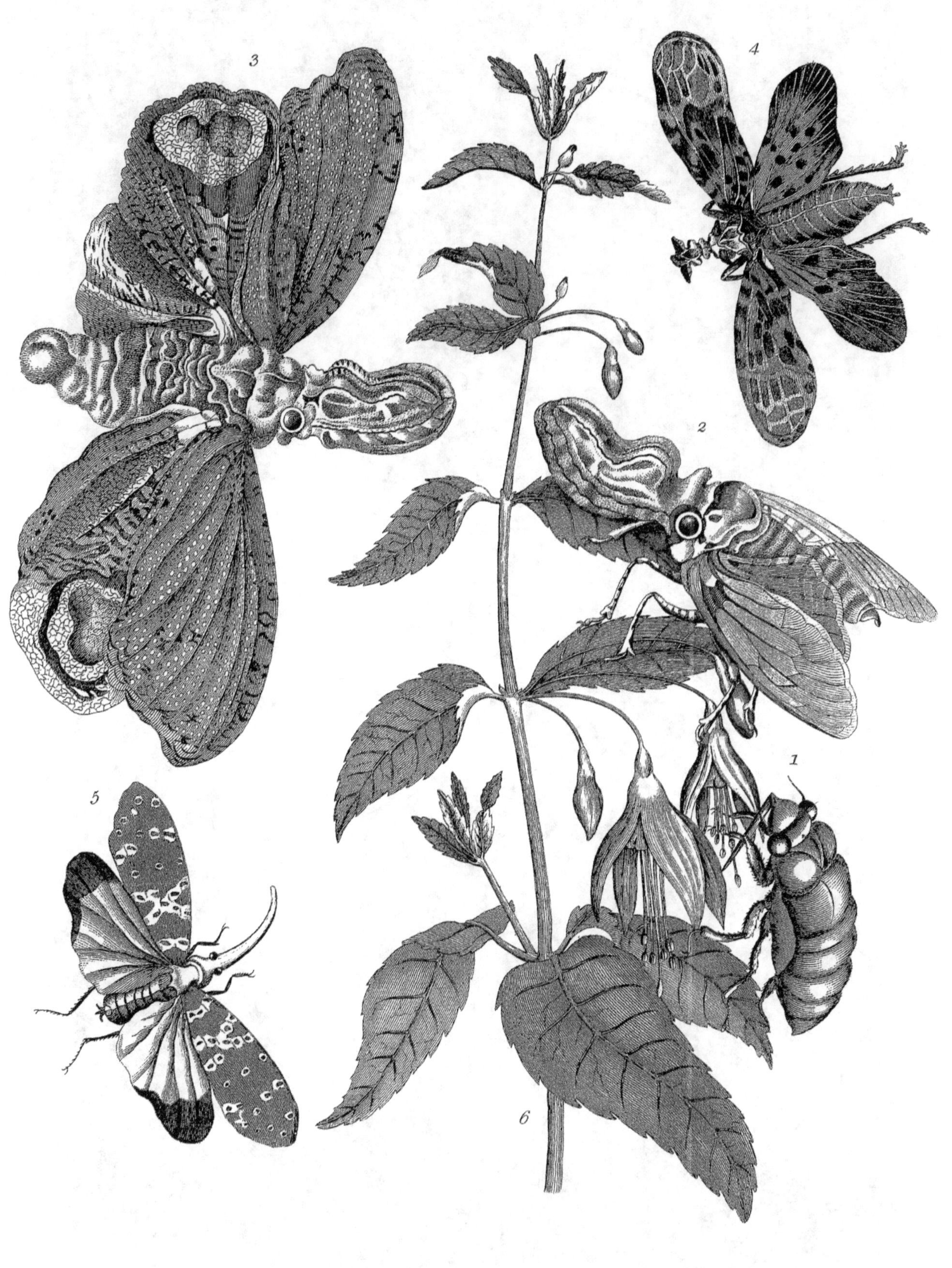

MOTHS

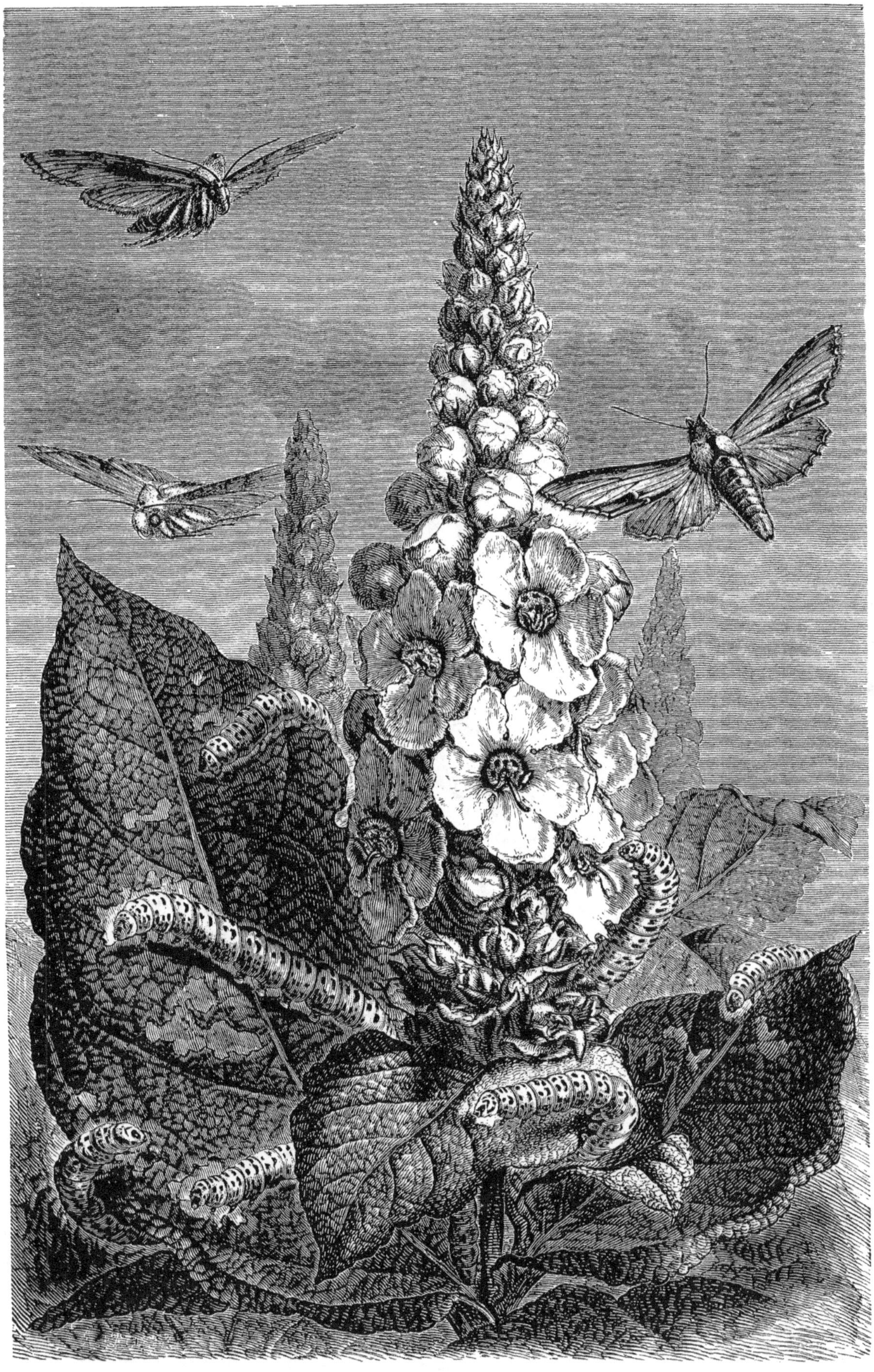

50

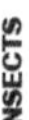

51
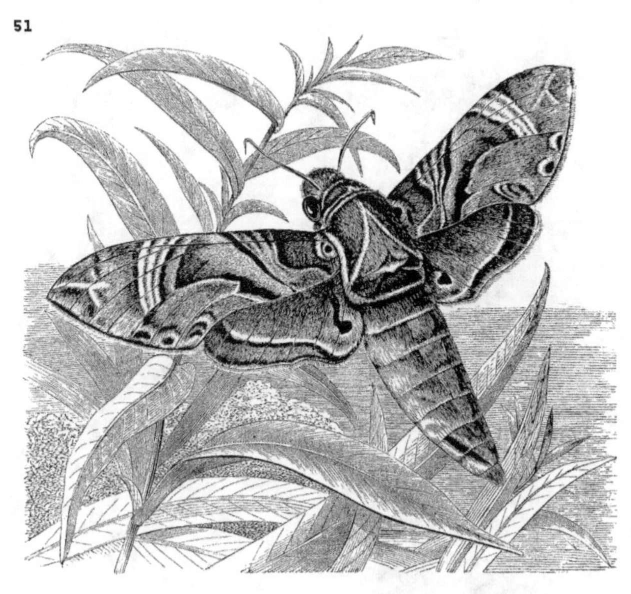

52
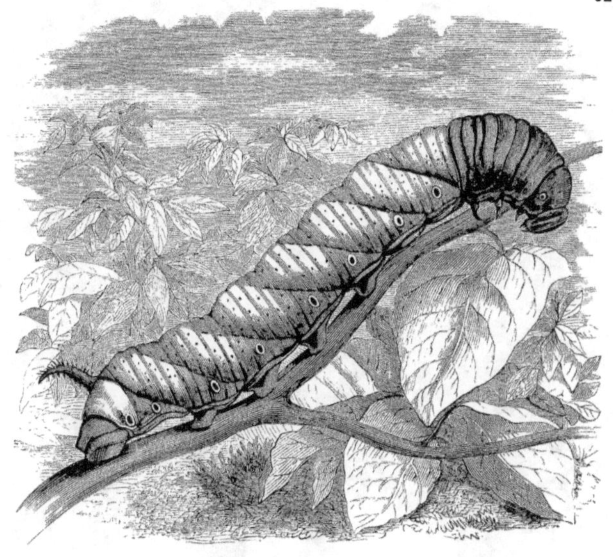

53
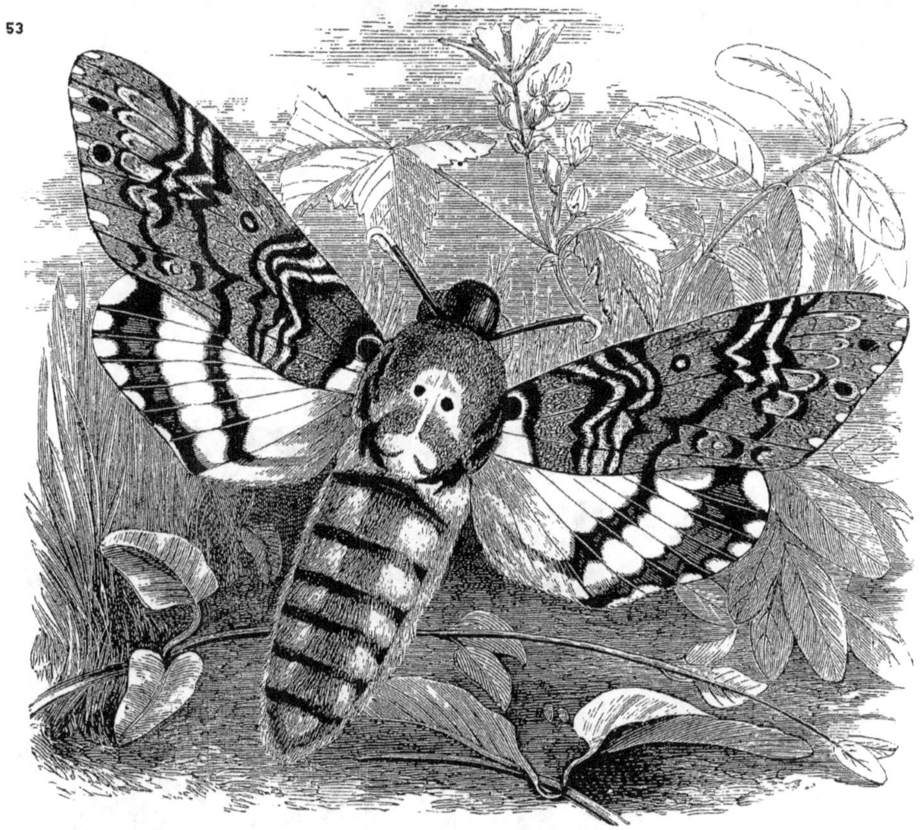

54
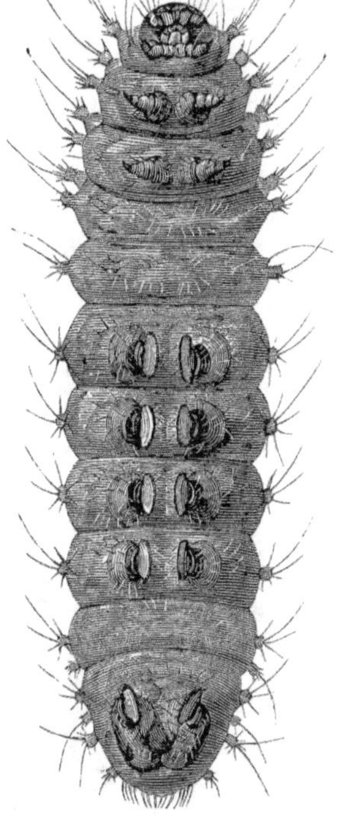

INSECTS

55
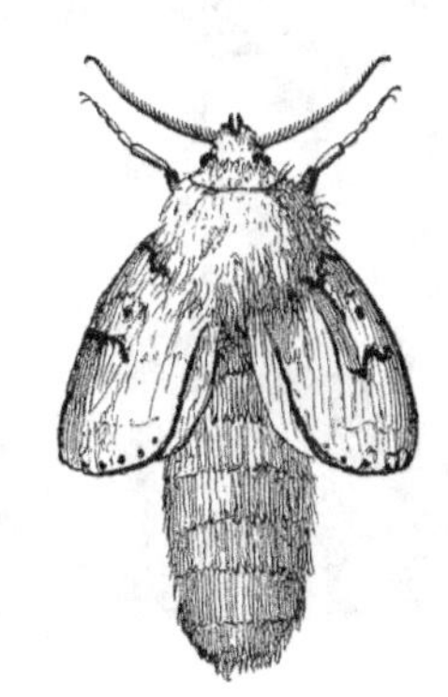
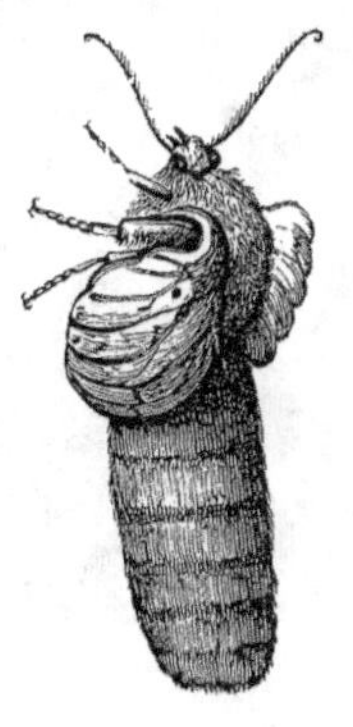

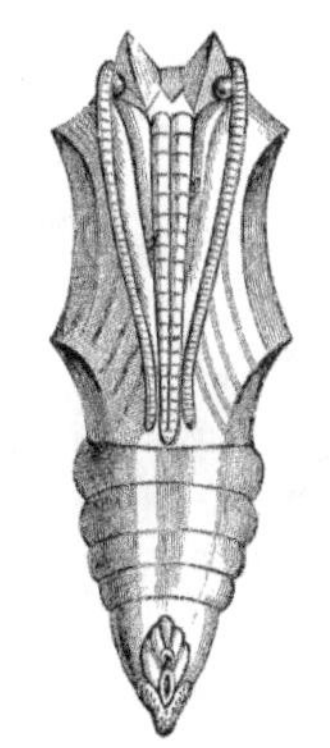
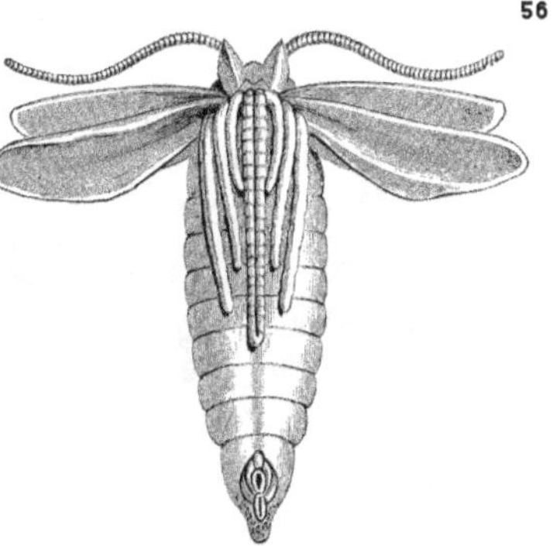
56

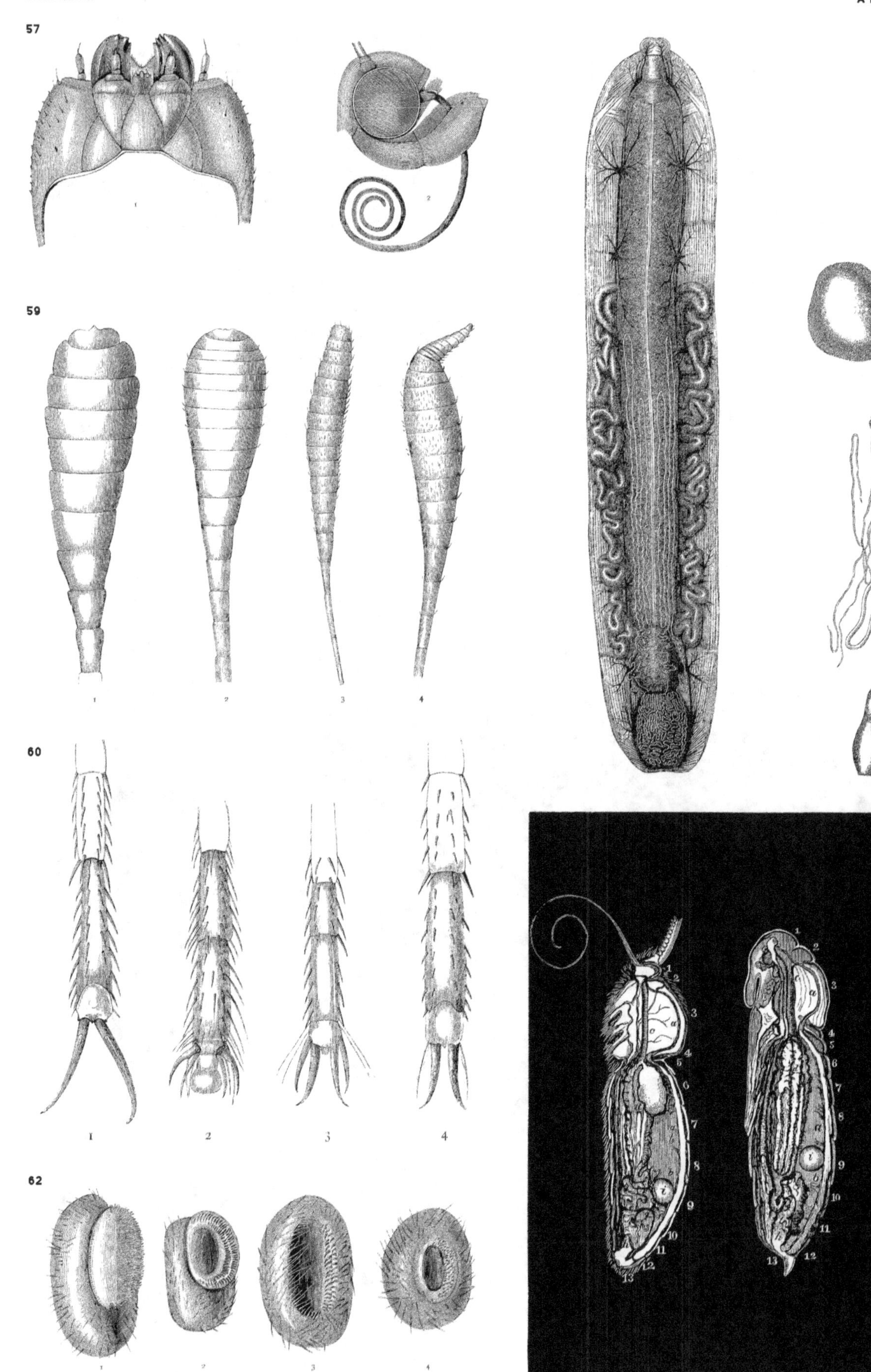

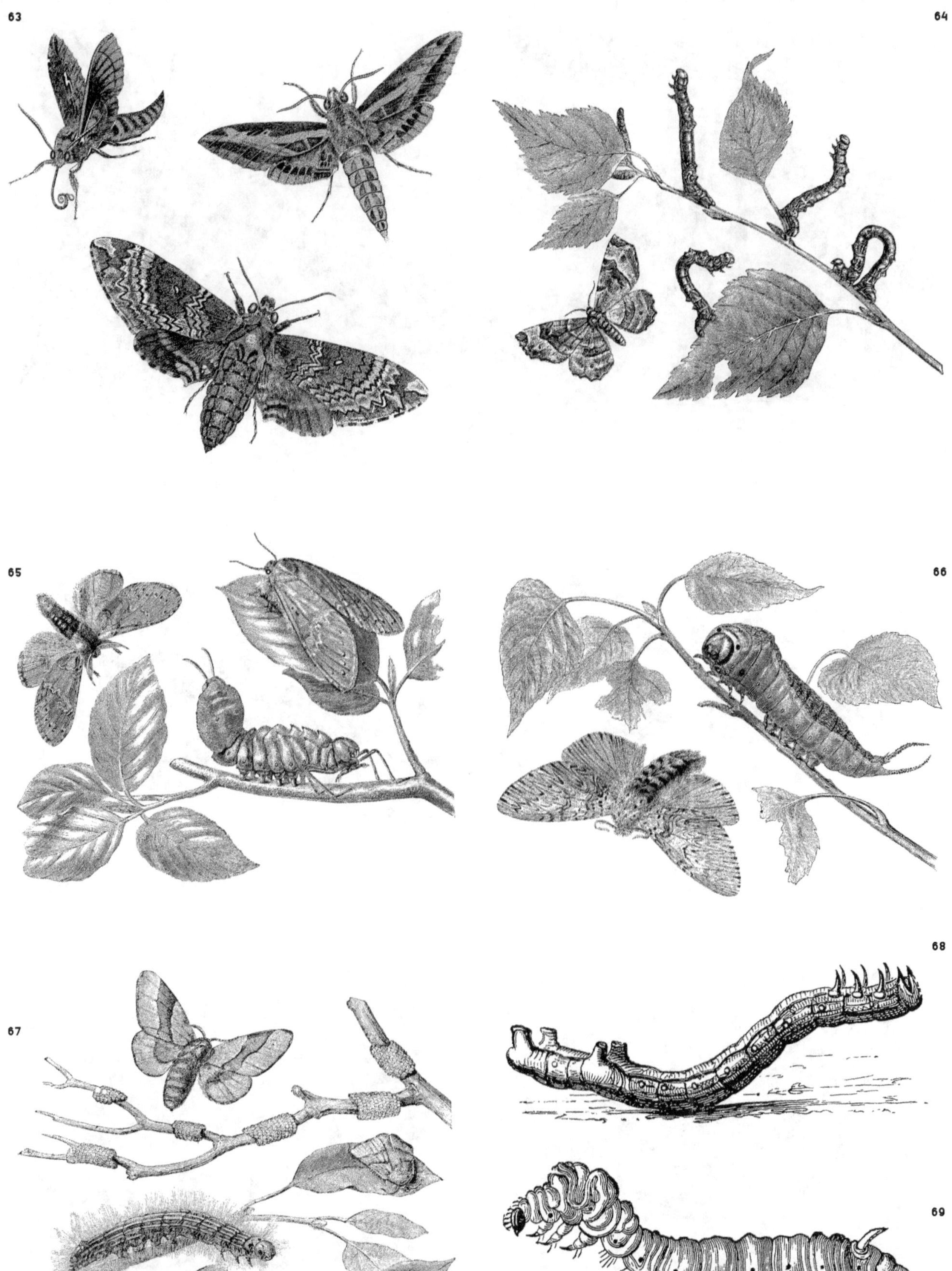

63
64
65
66
67
68
69
INSECTS

70

71

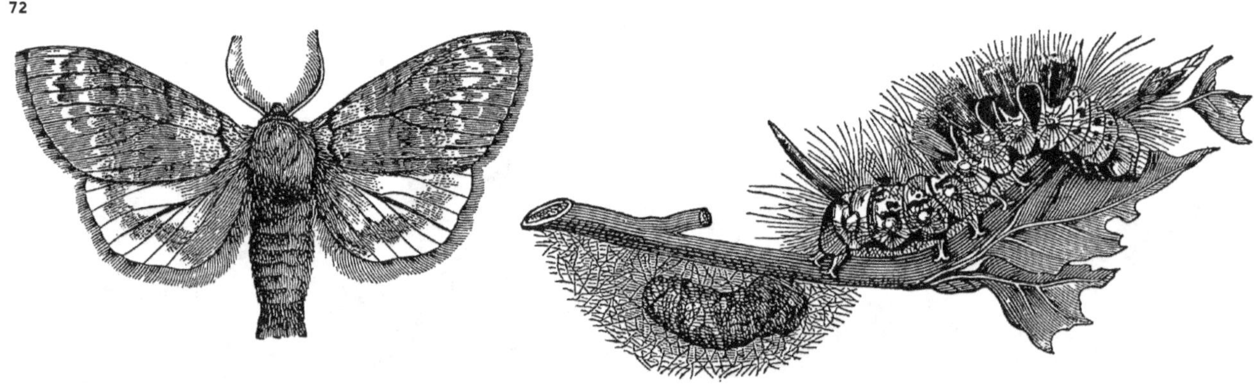

72

73

74

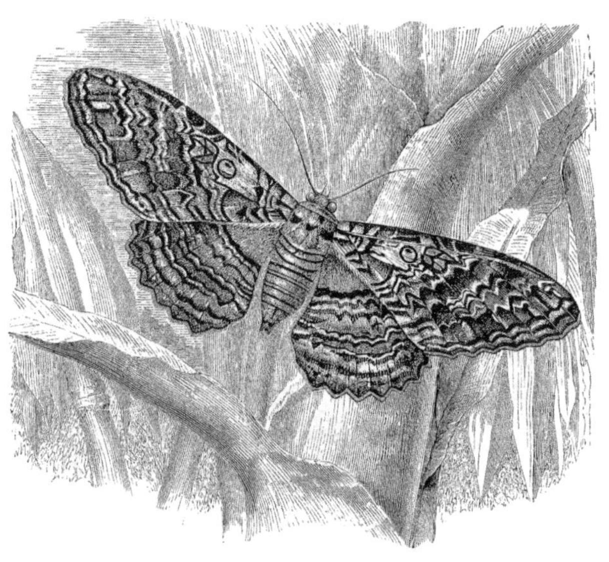

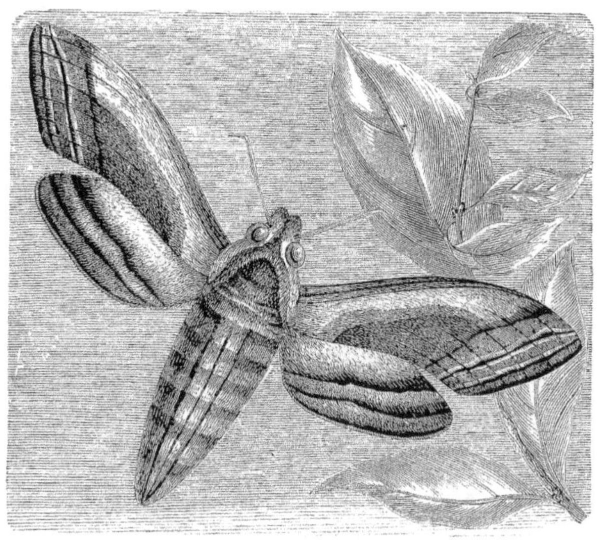

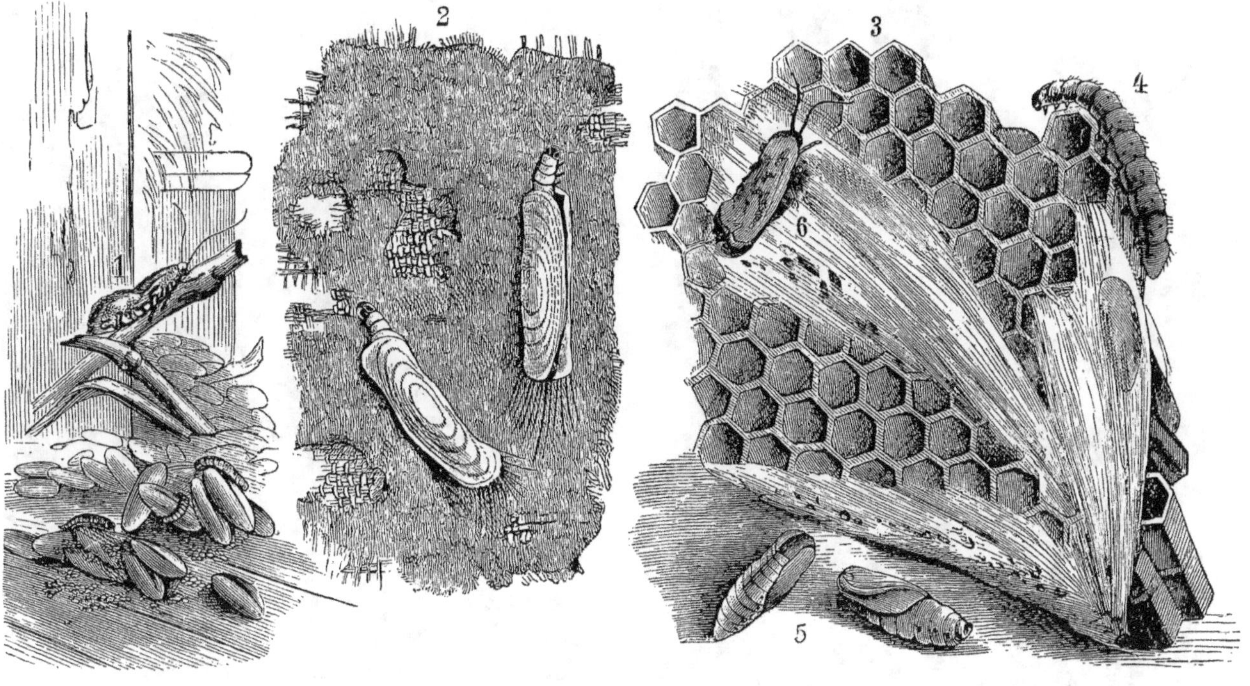

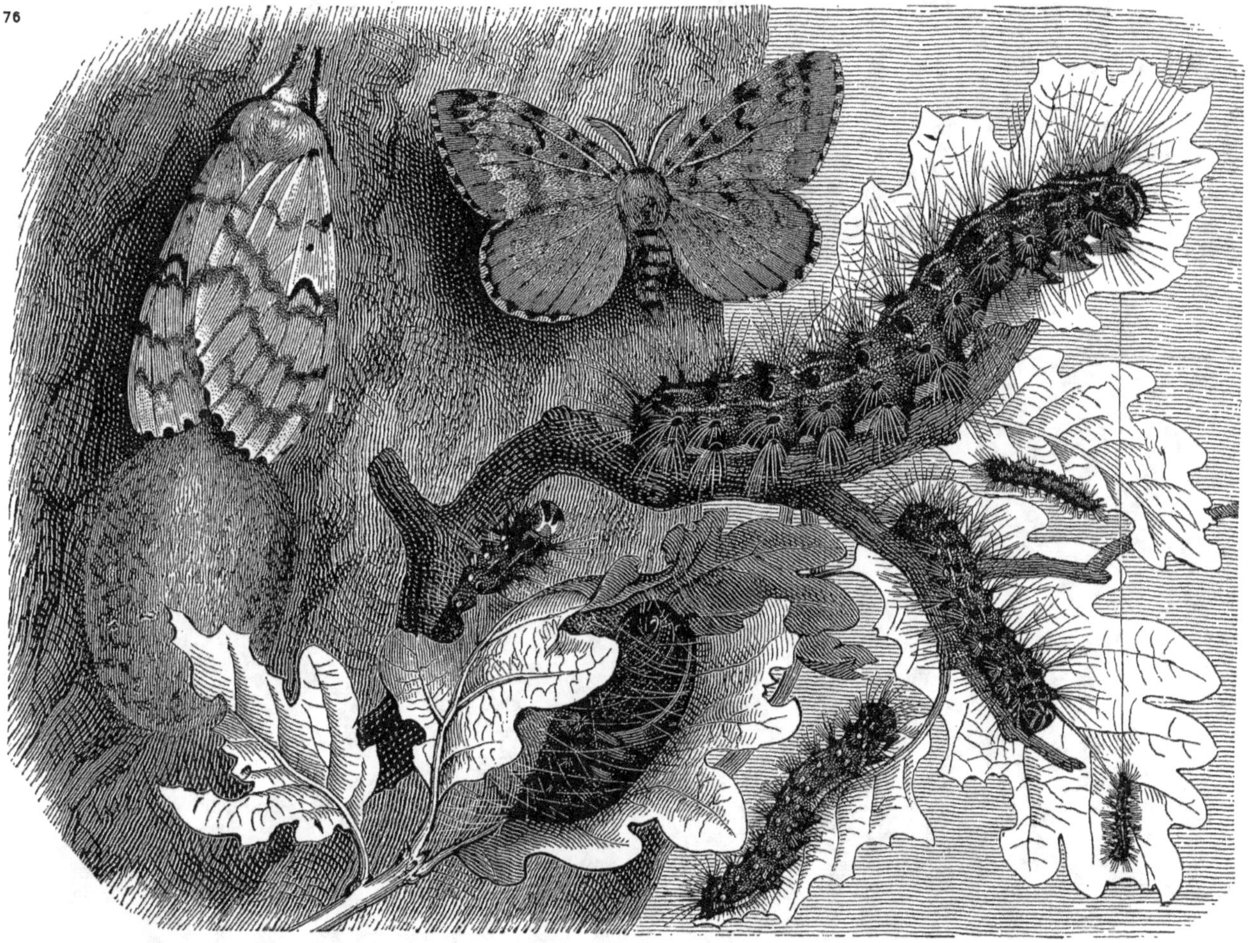

77

78

INSECTS

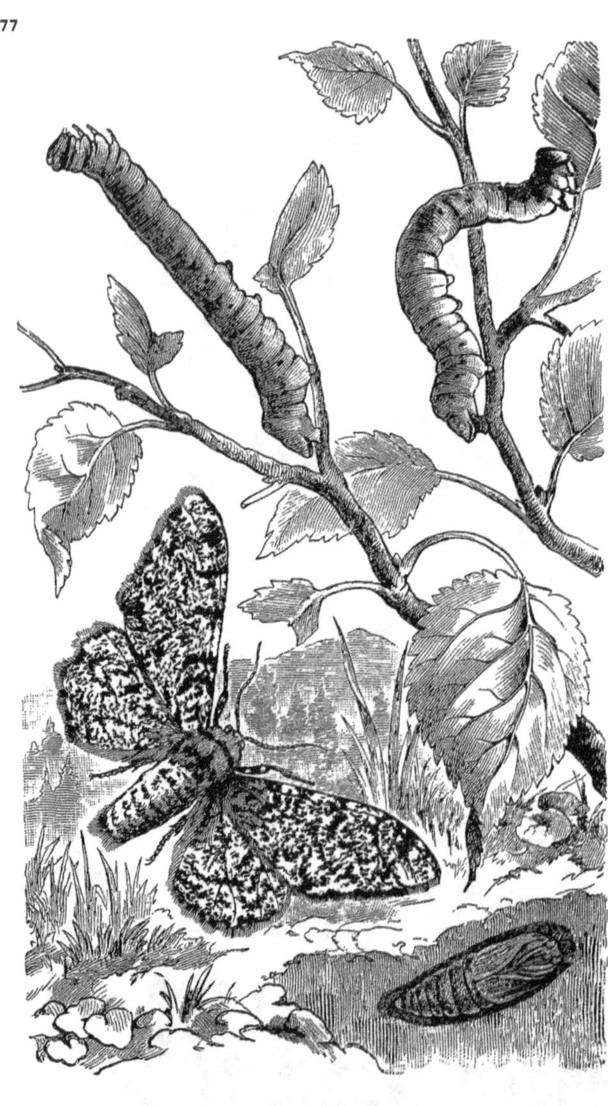

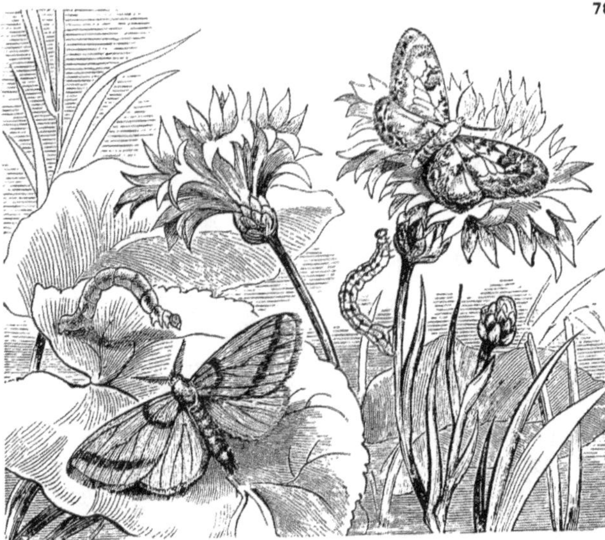

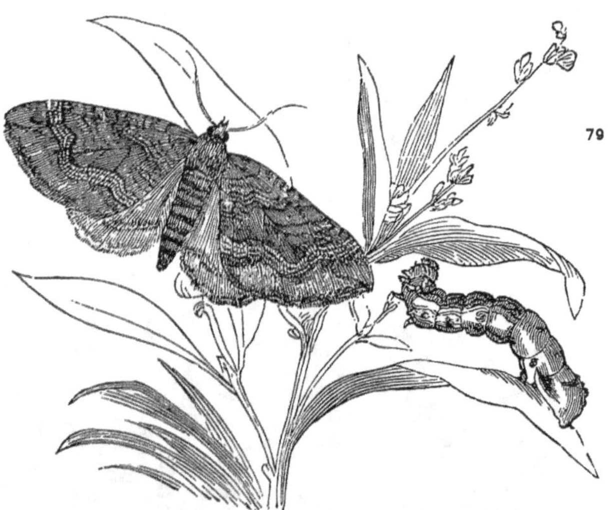

79

80

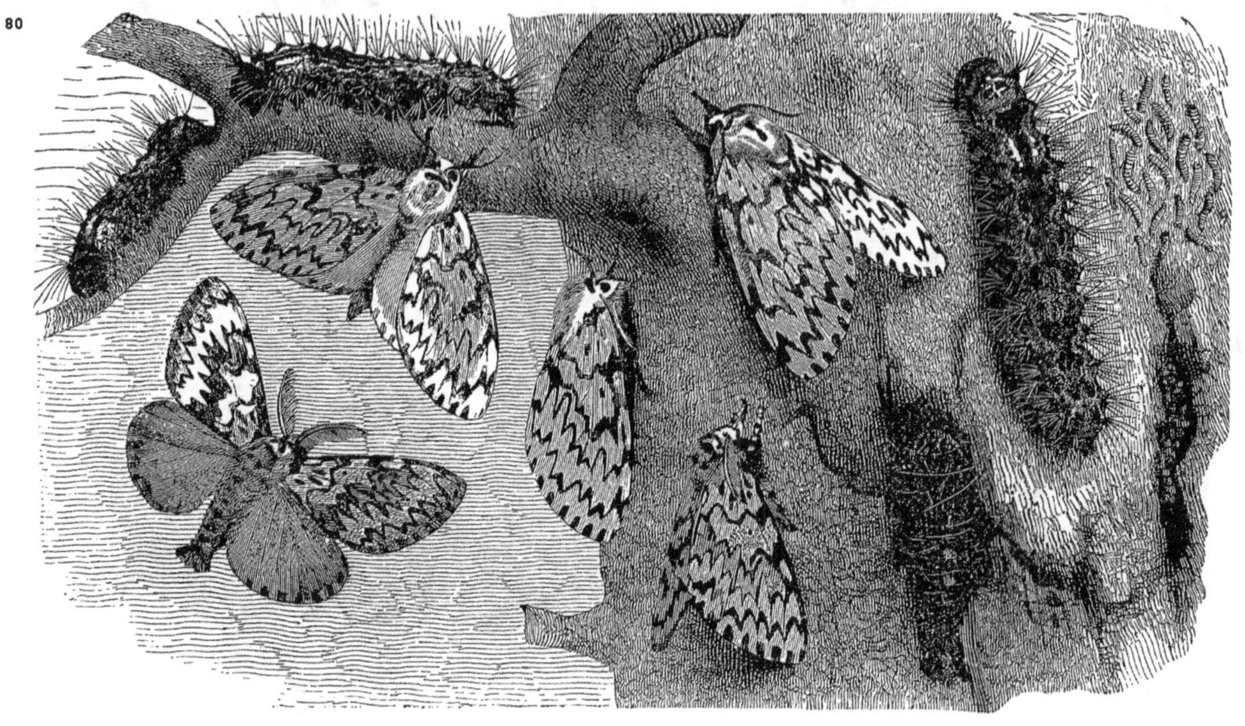

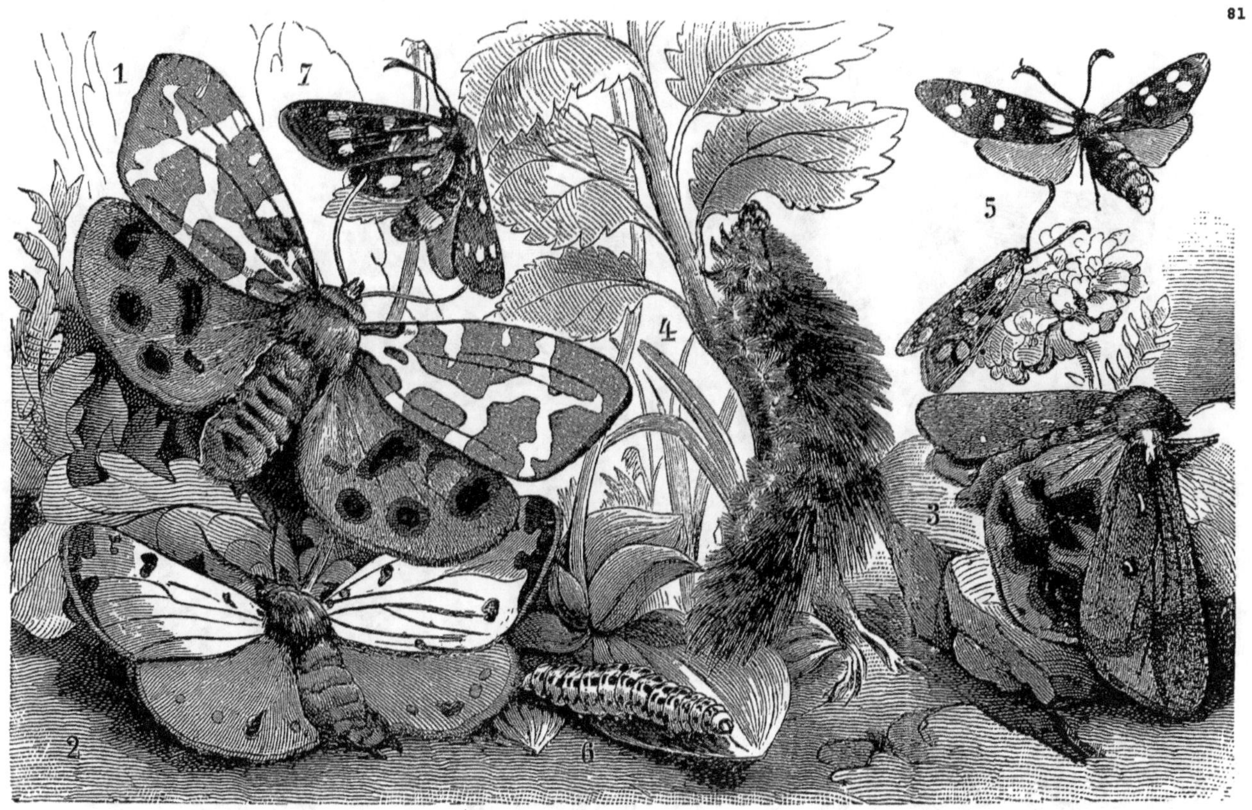
1
7
5
4
3
6
2
82
INSECTS
1
7
9
4
6
8
3
2
5

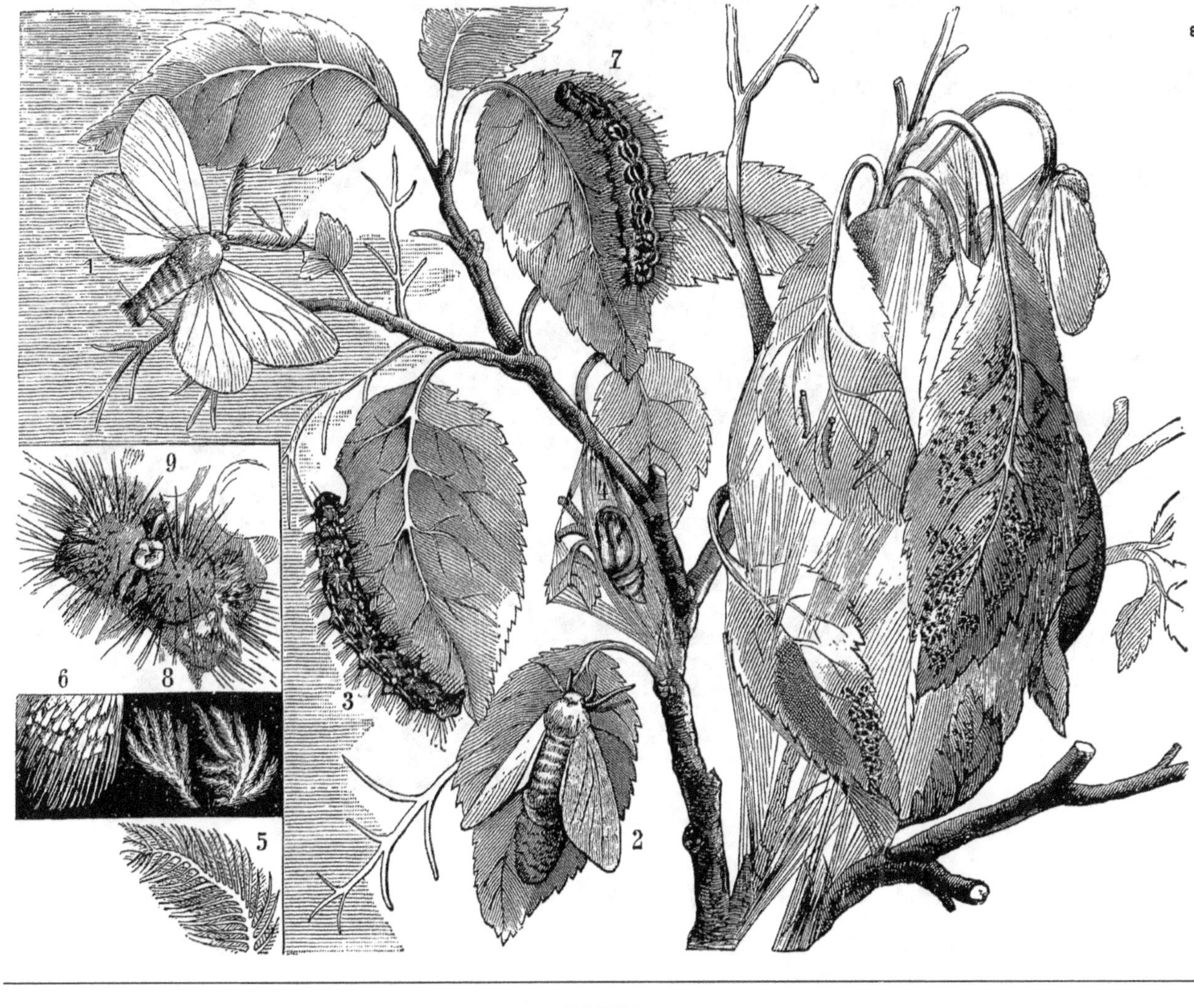

INSECTS

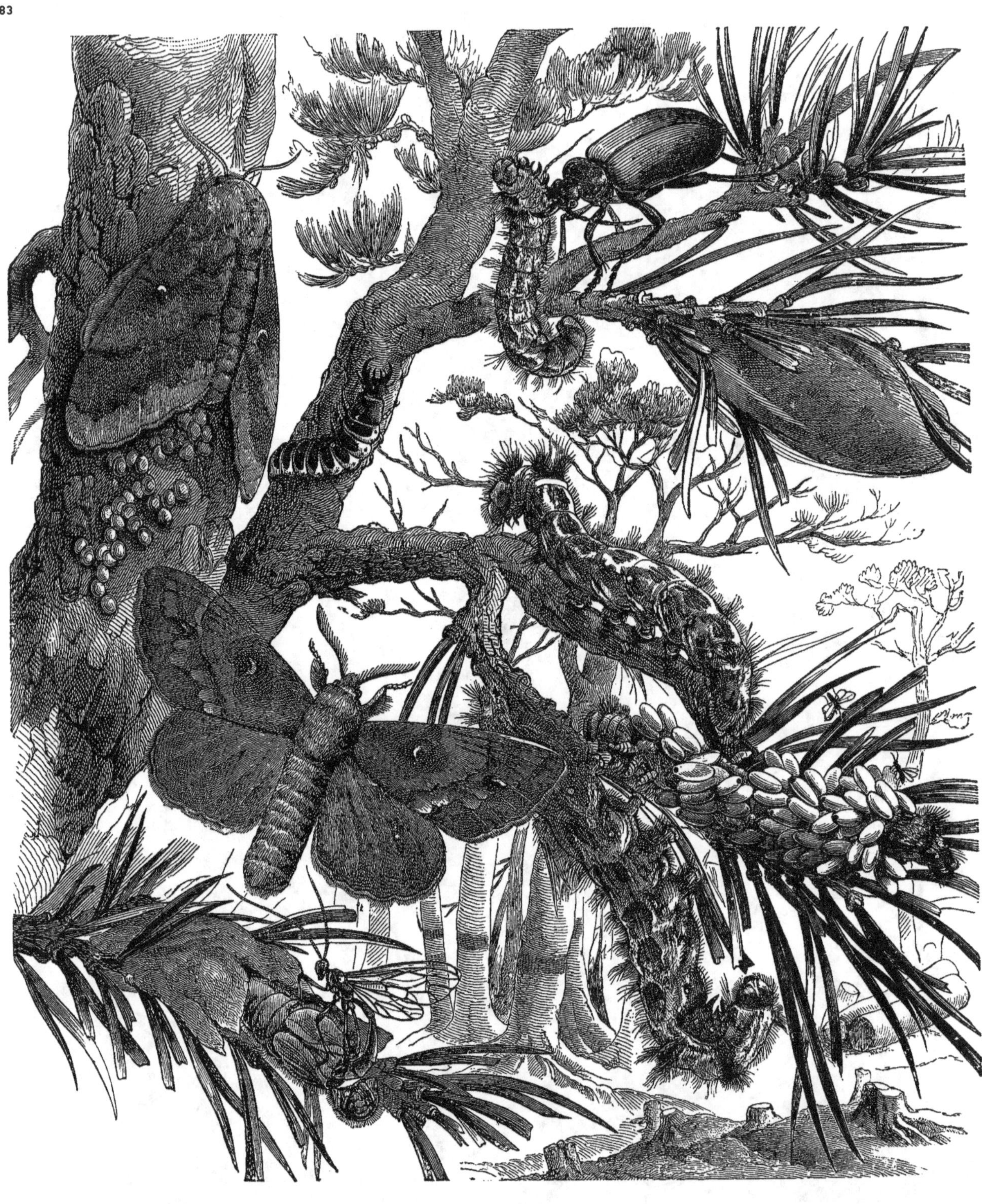

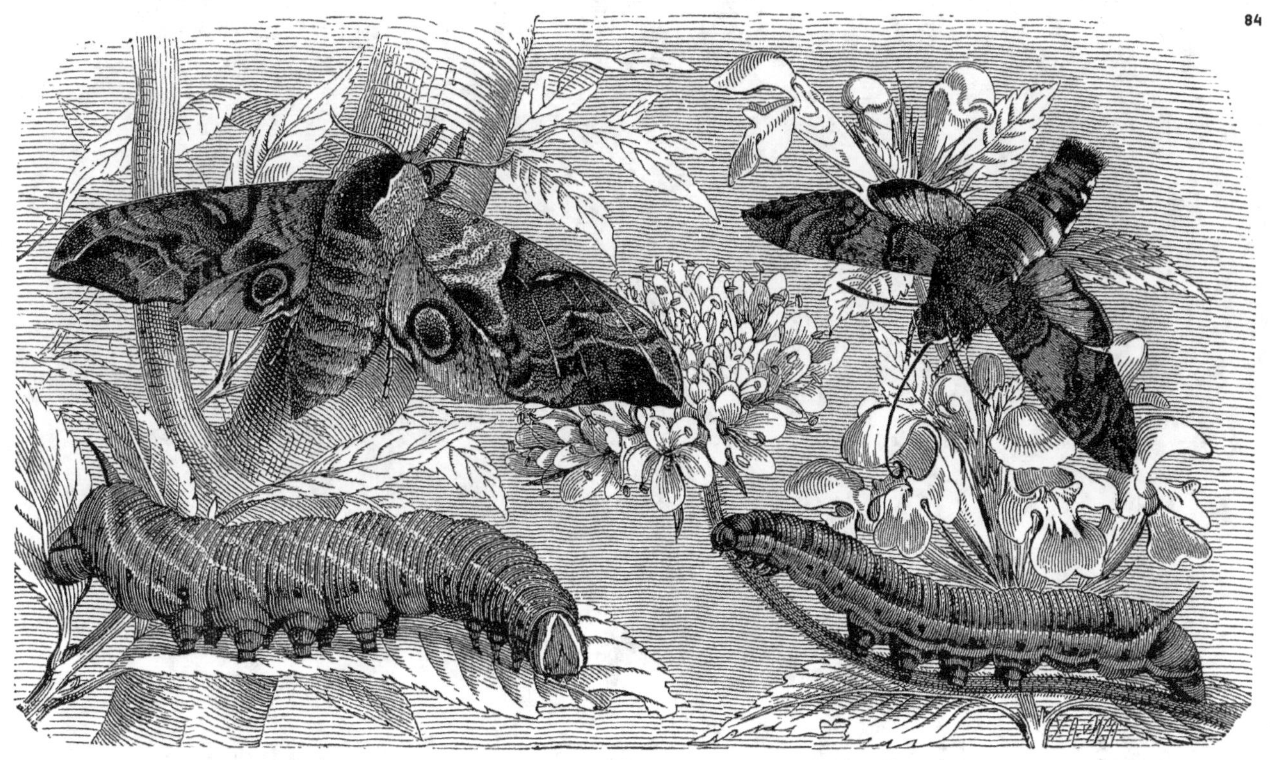

84

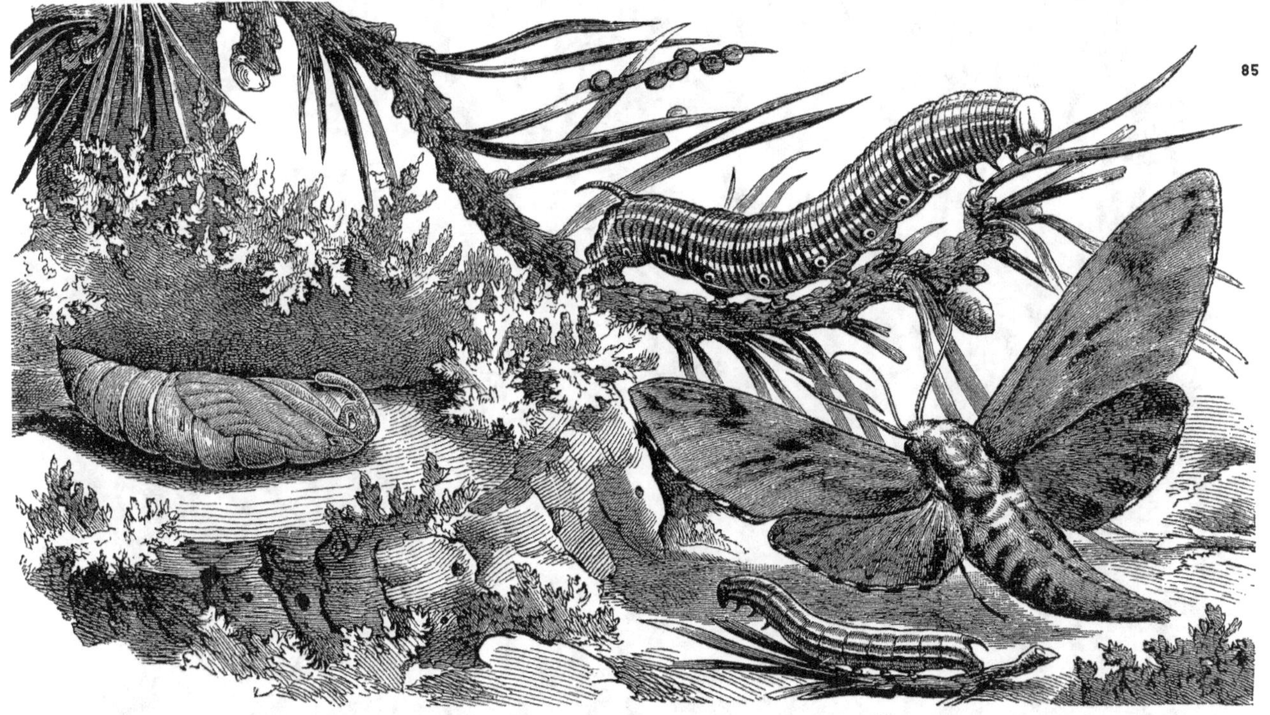

85

86

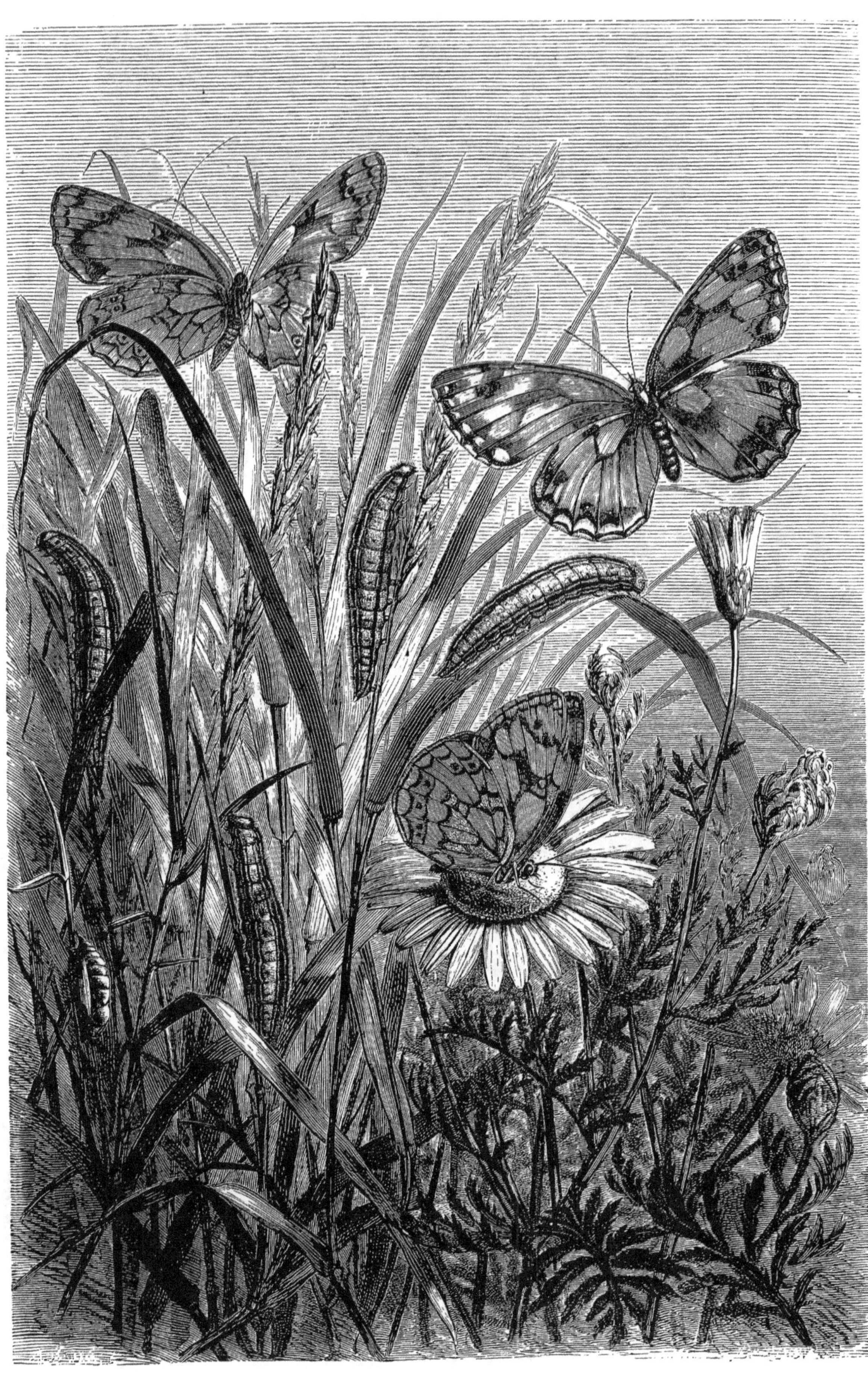

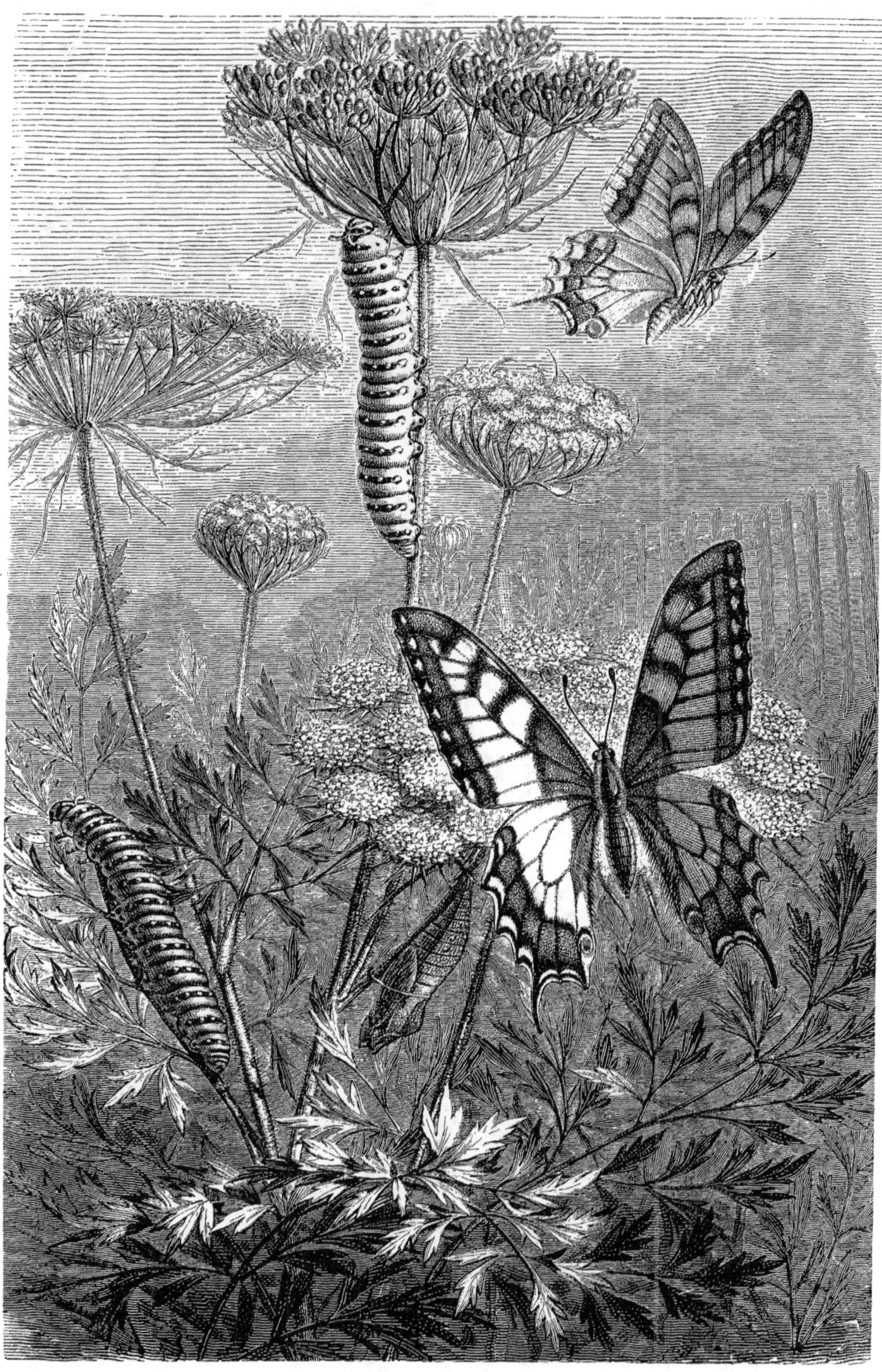

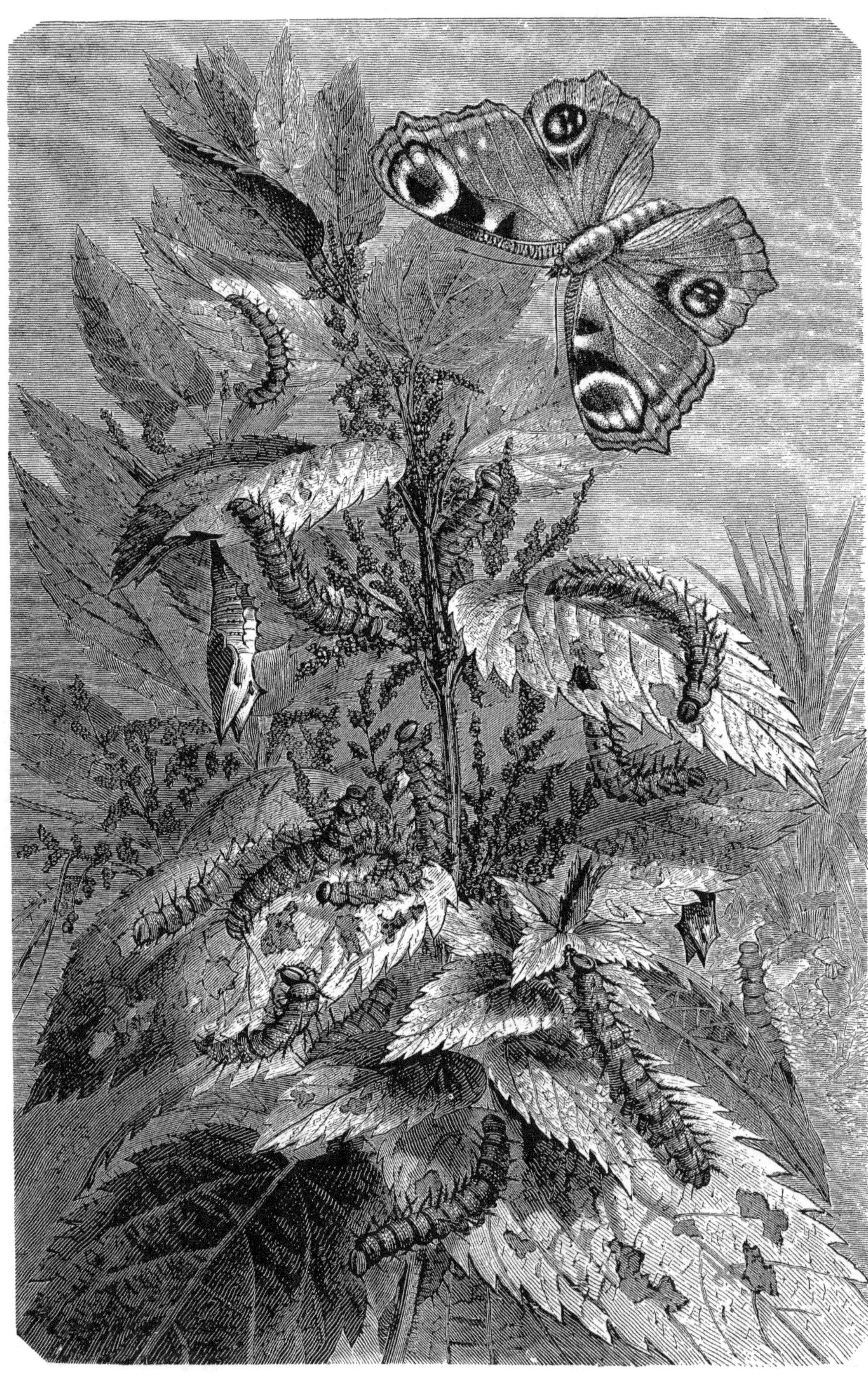

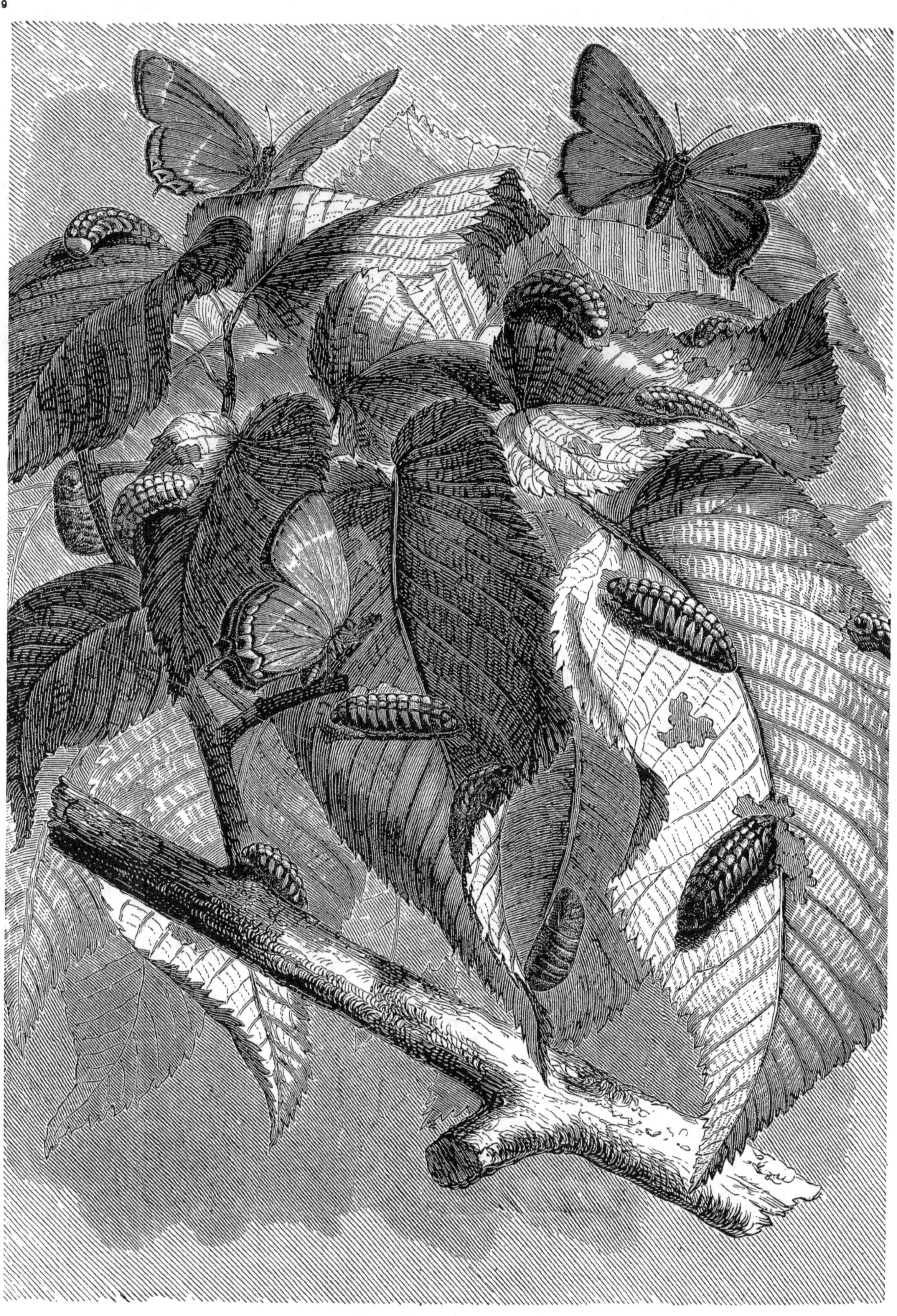

INSECTS

90

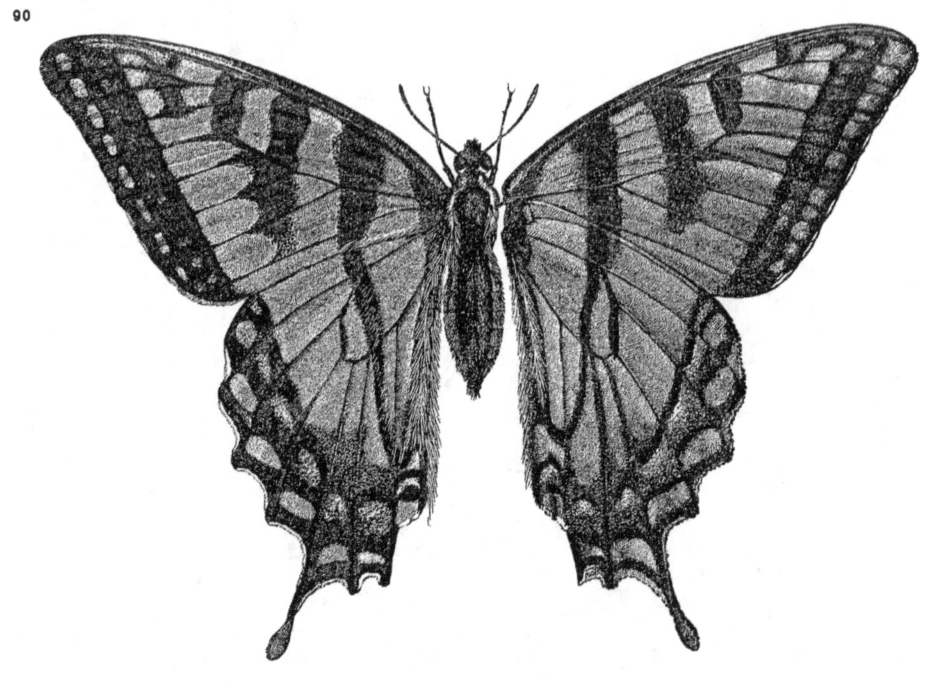

91

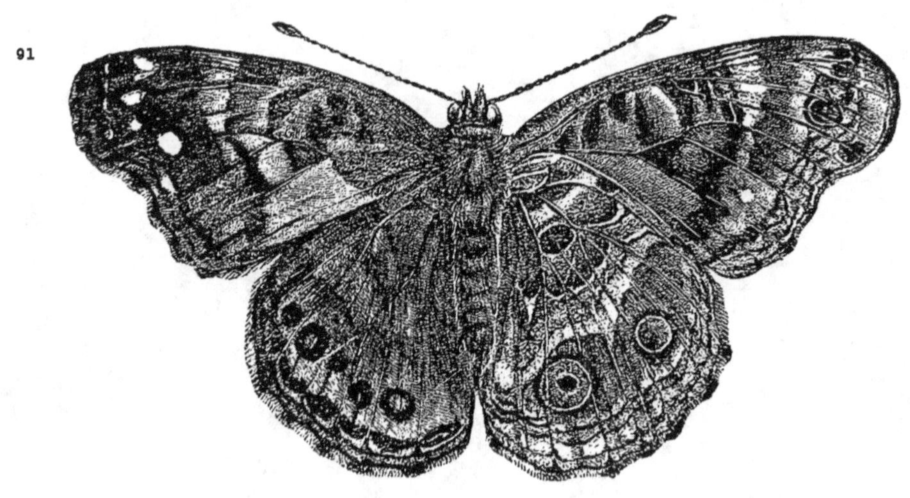

92

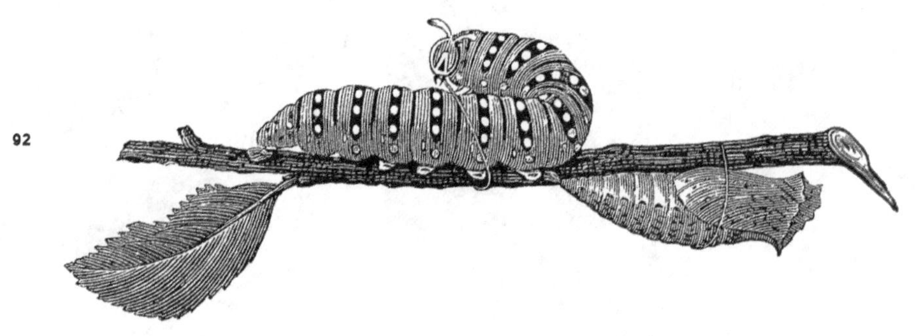

93

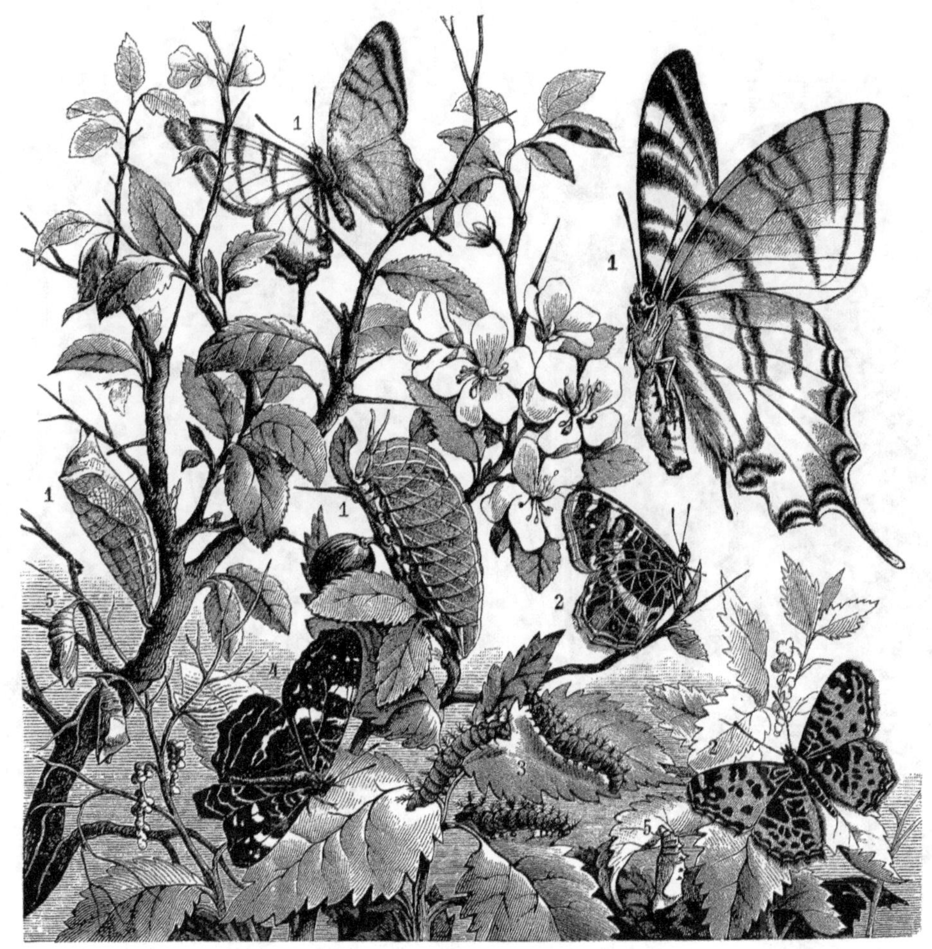

94

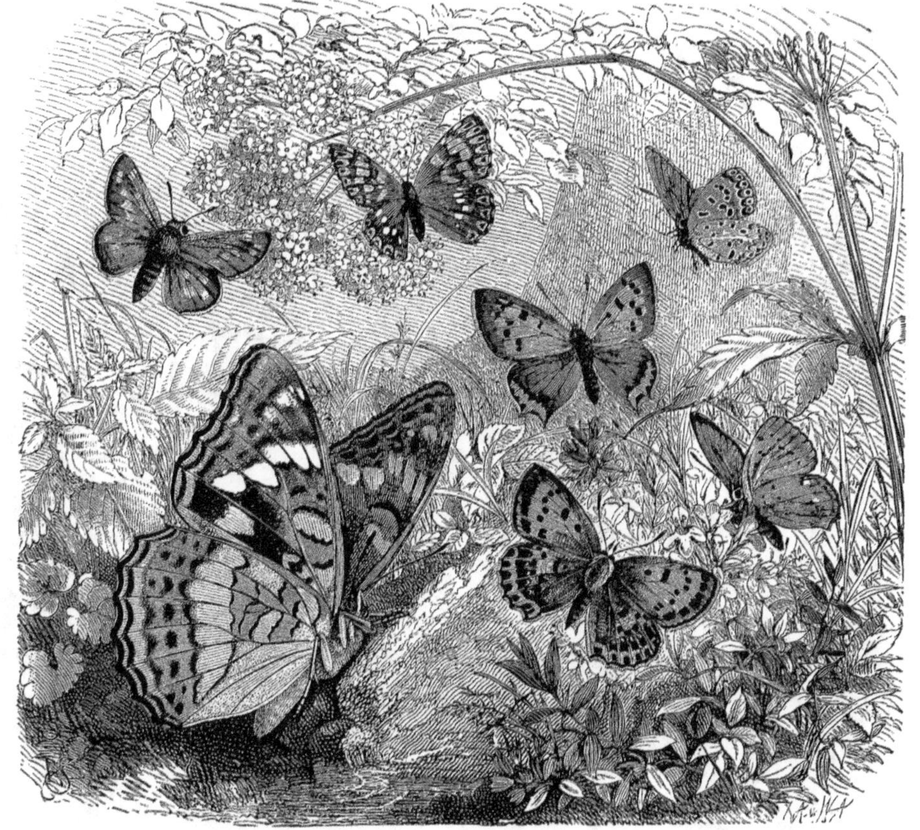

BUTTERFLIES

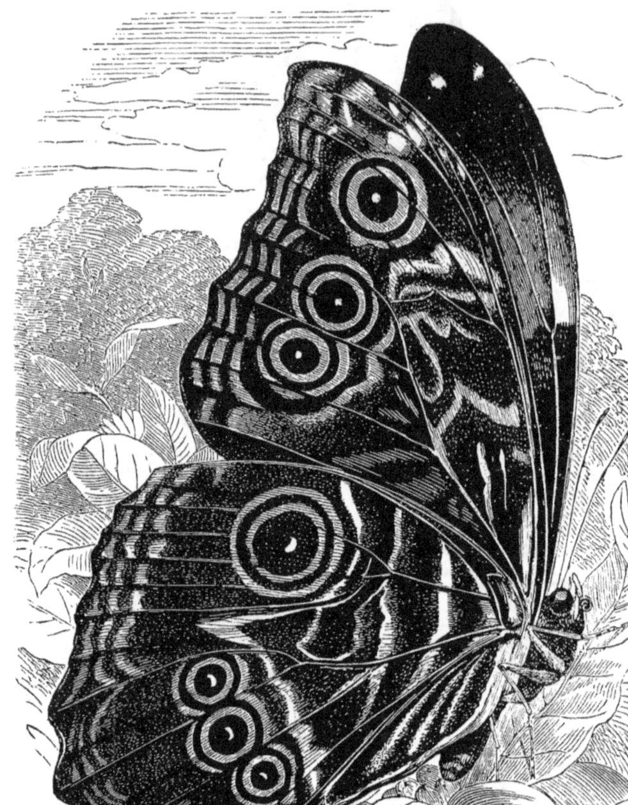

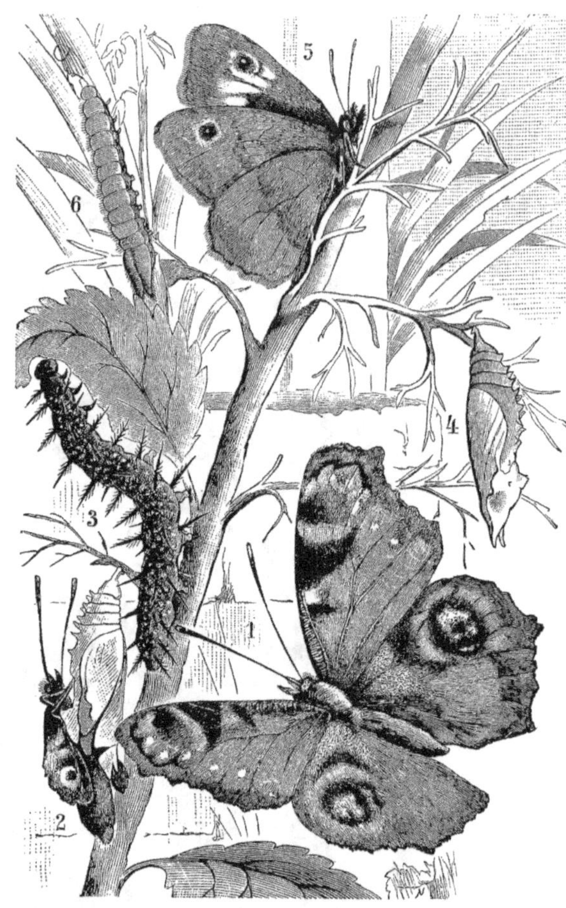

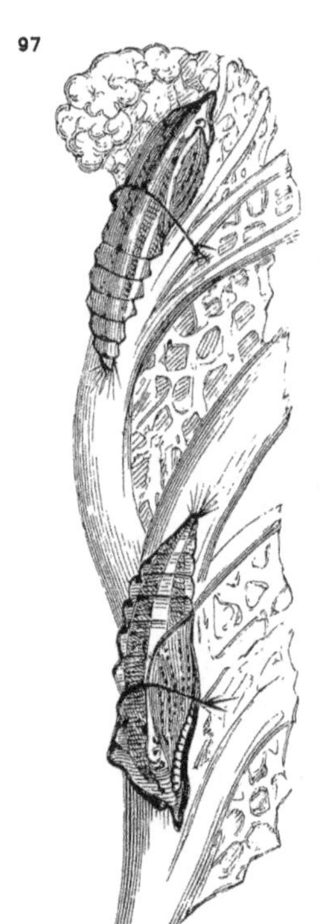

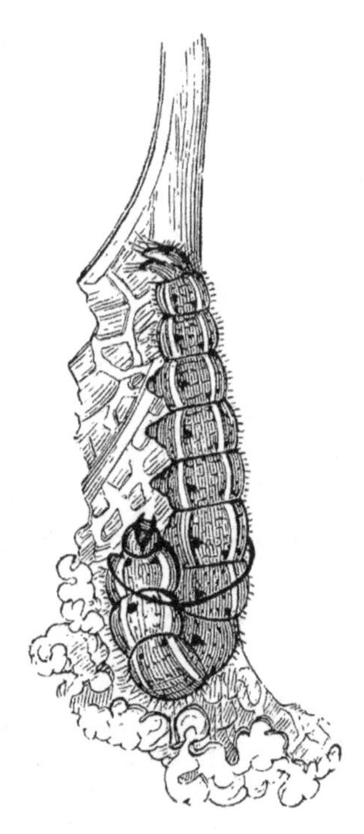

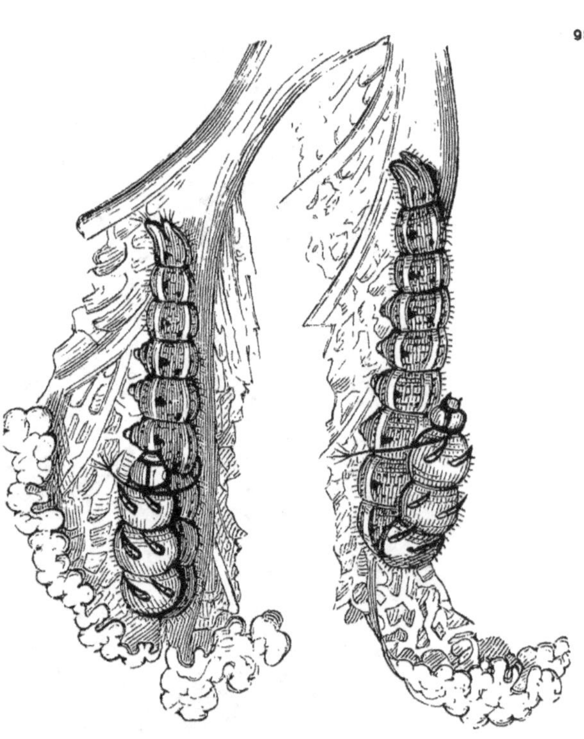

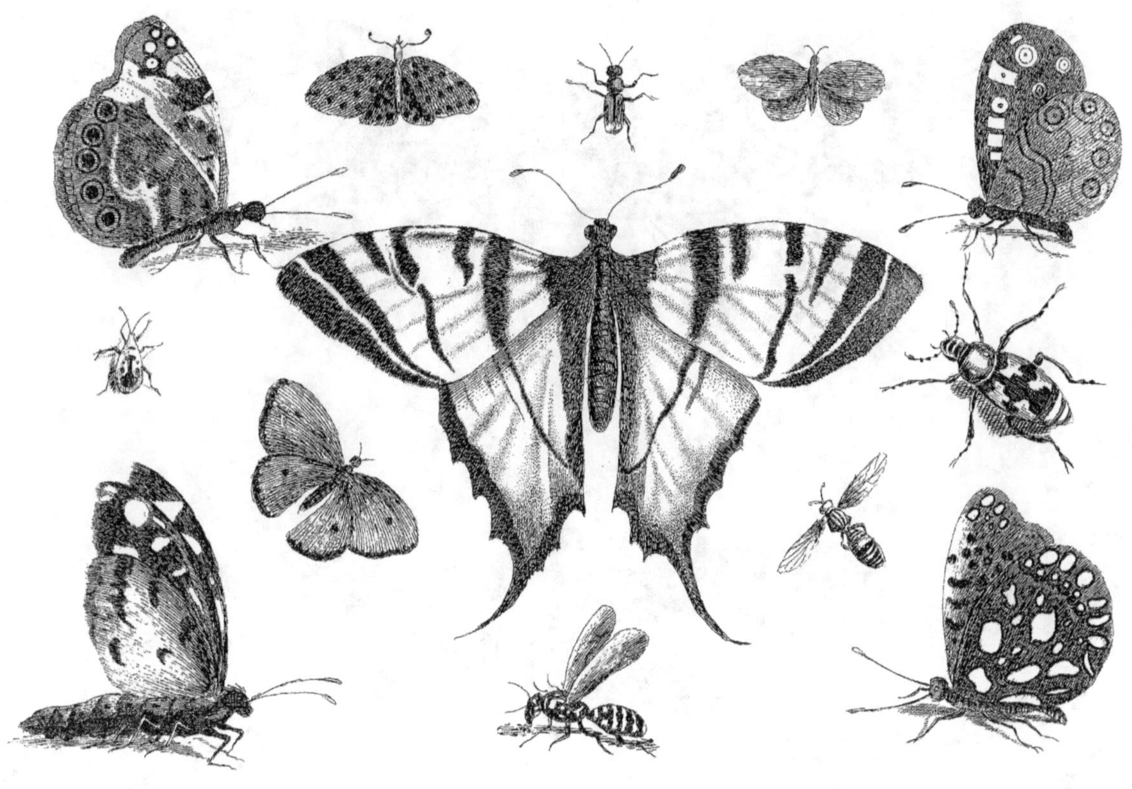

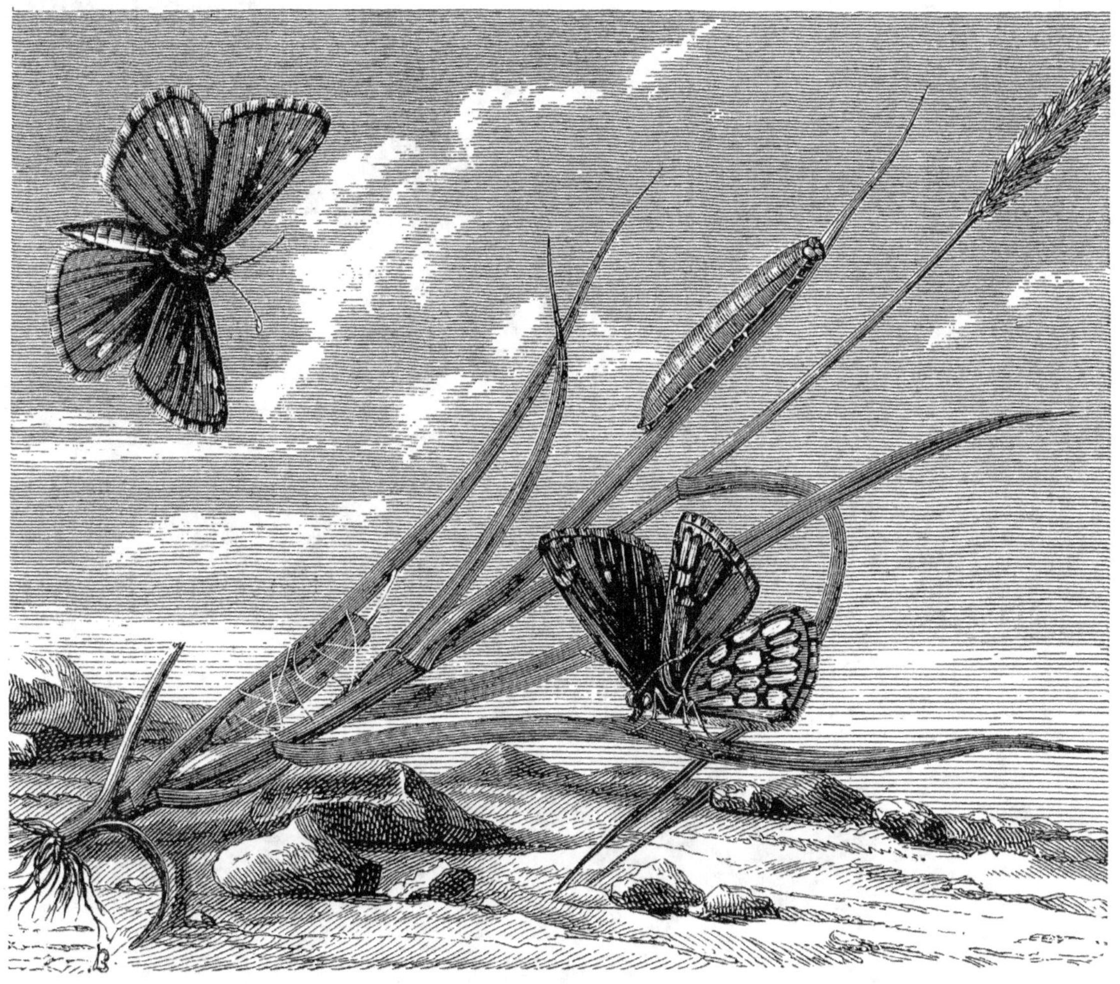

101

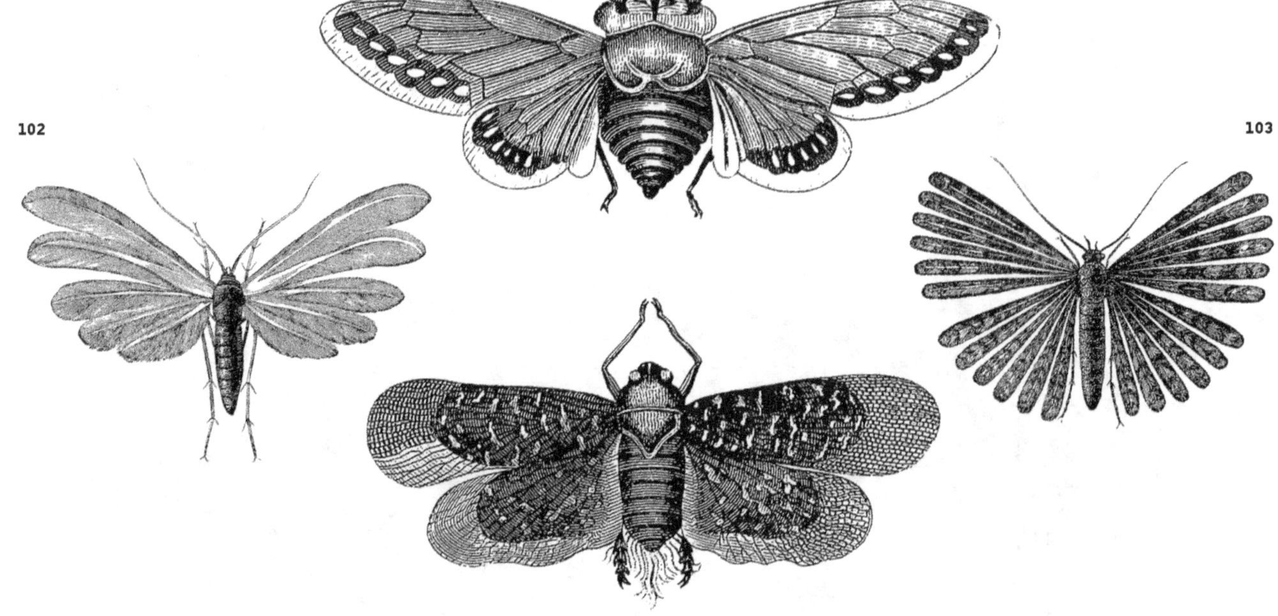

102

103

104

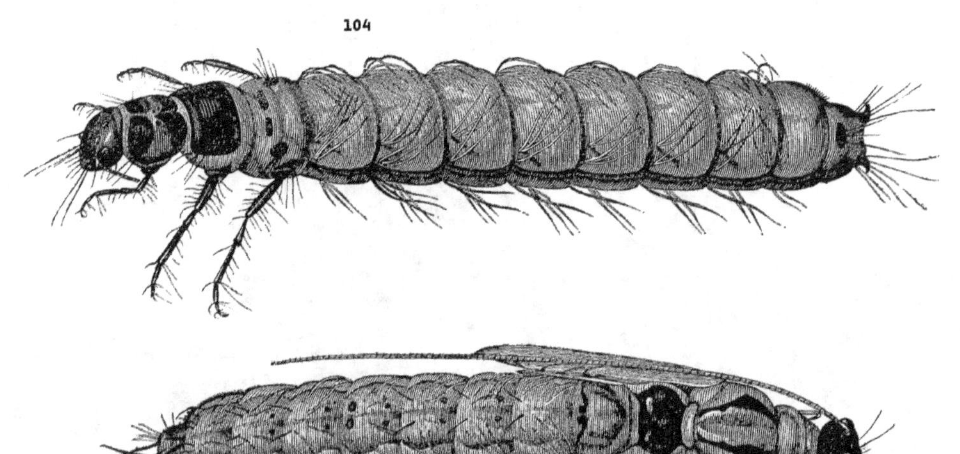

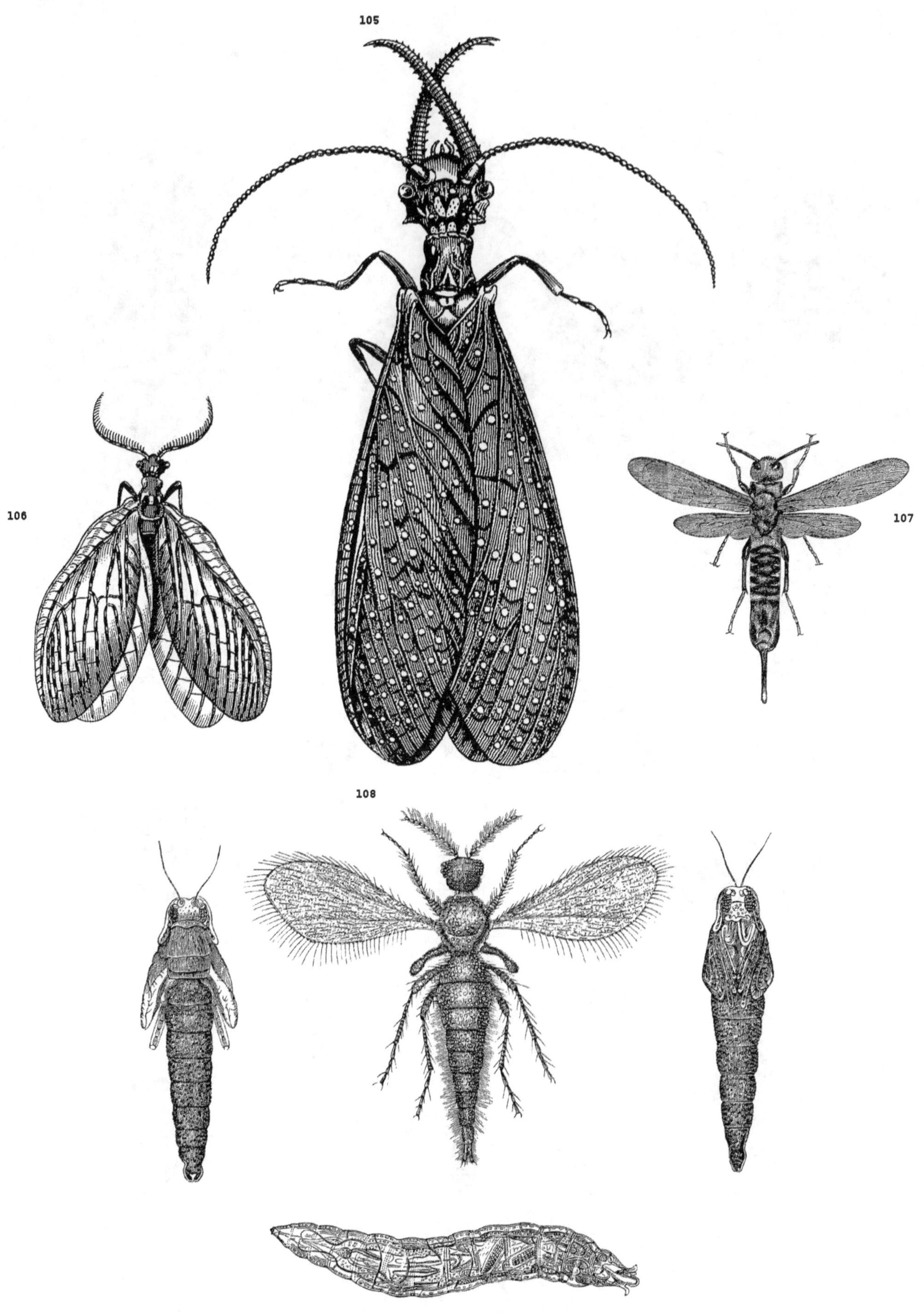

VARIOUS WINGED INSECTS

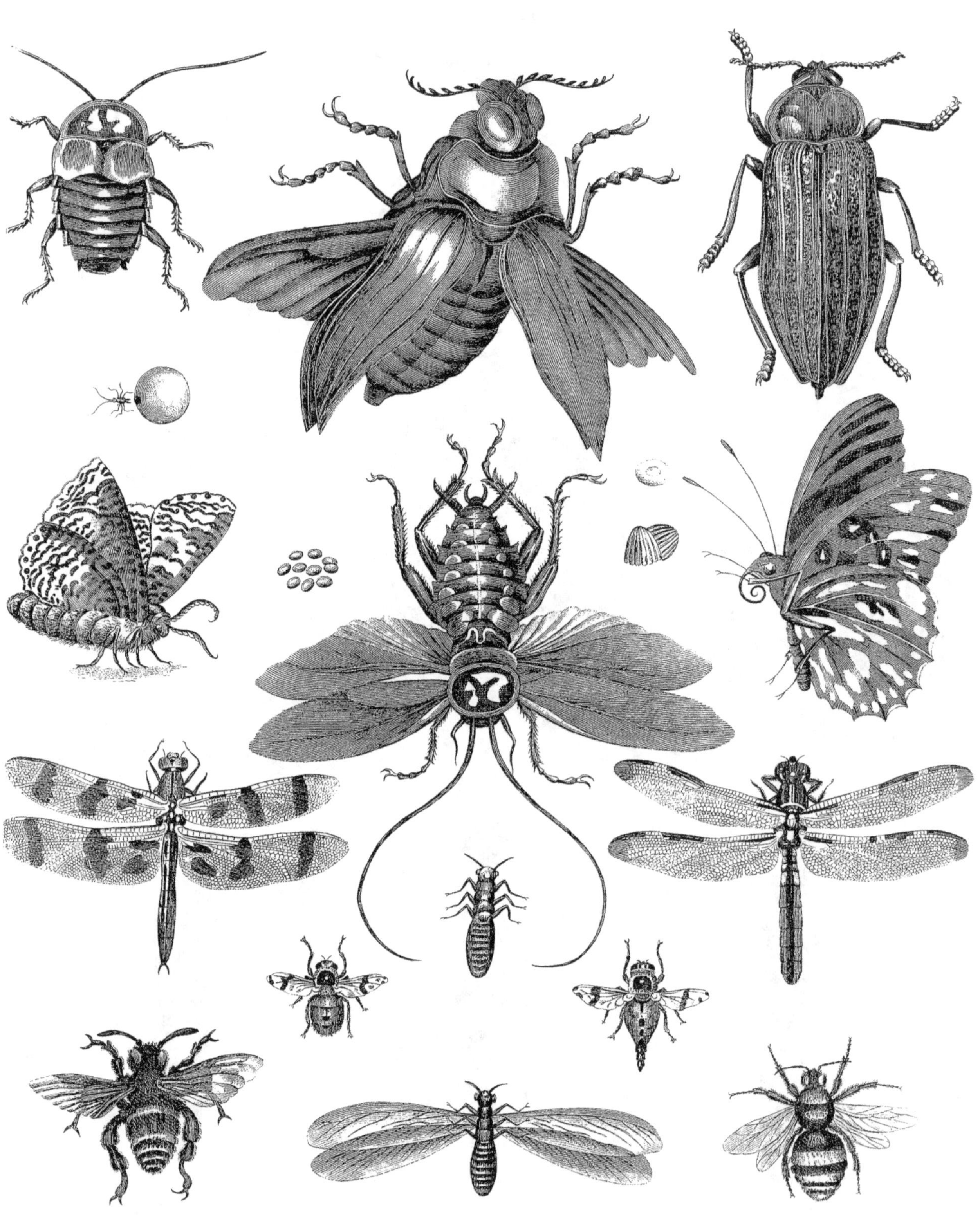

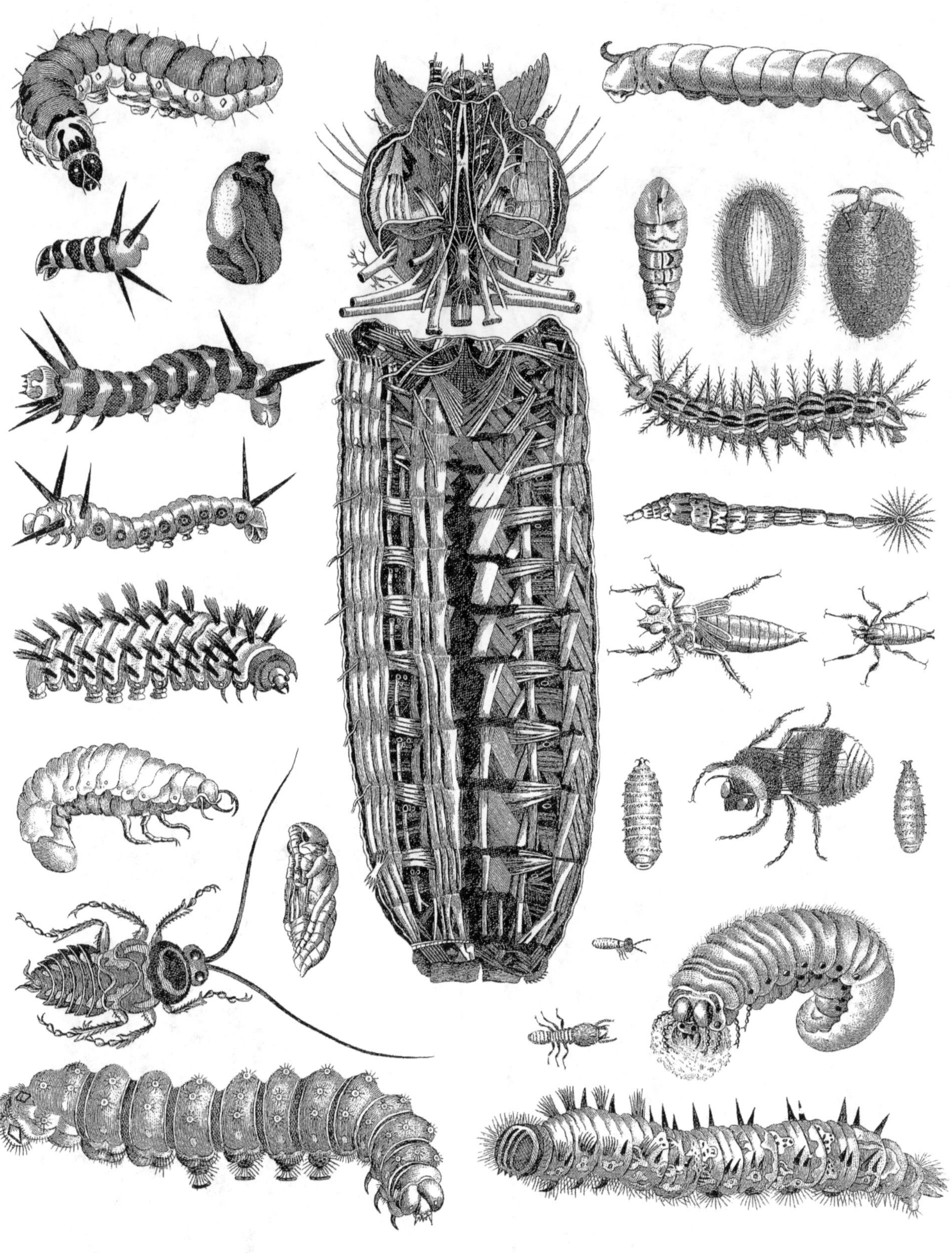

VARIOUS WINGED INSECTS

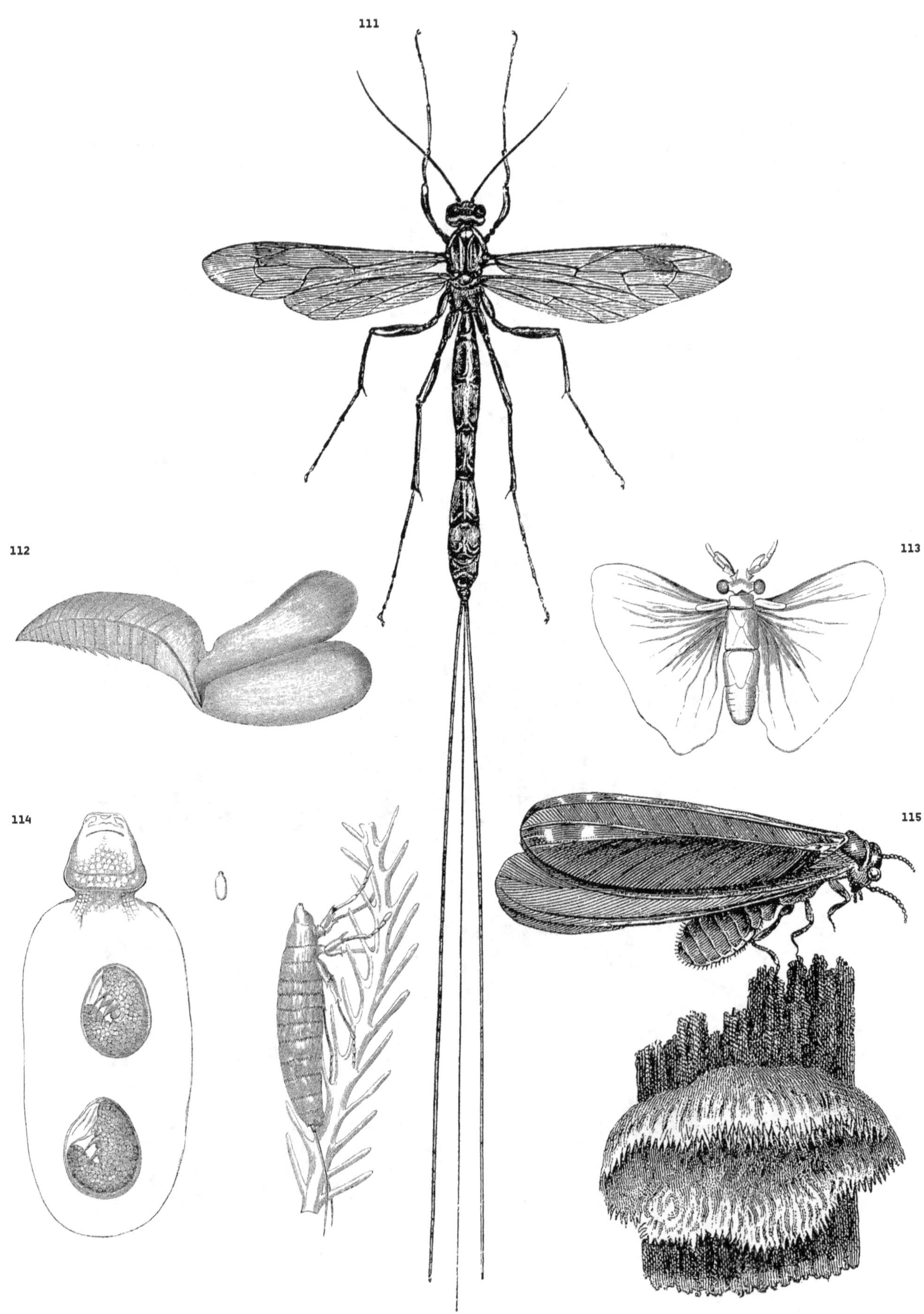

VARIOUS WINGED INSECTS

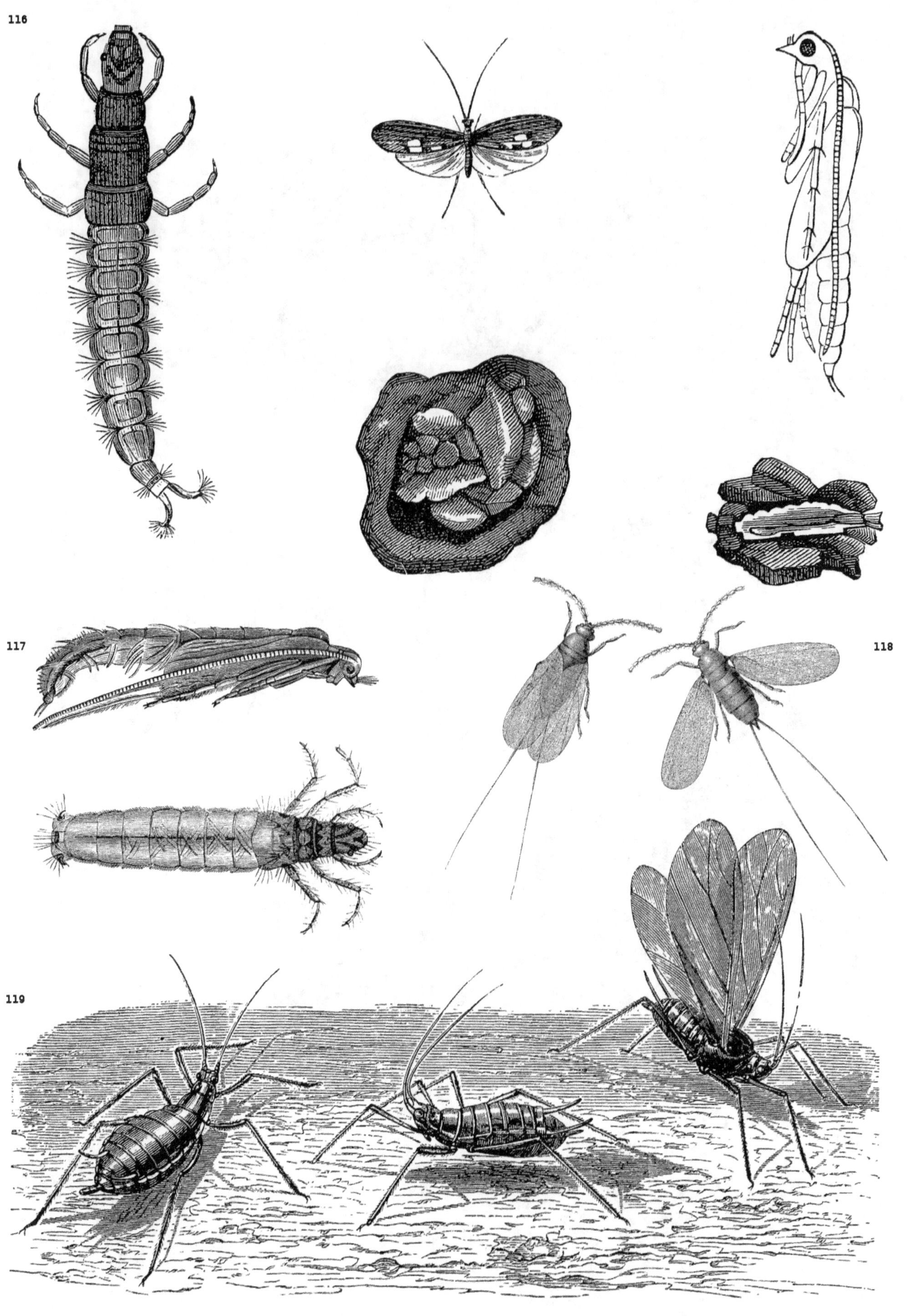

VARIOUS WINGED INSECTS

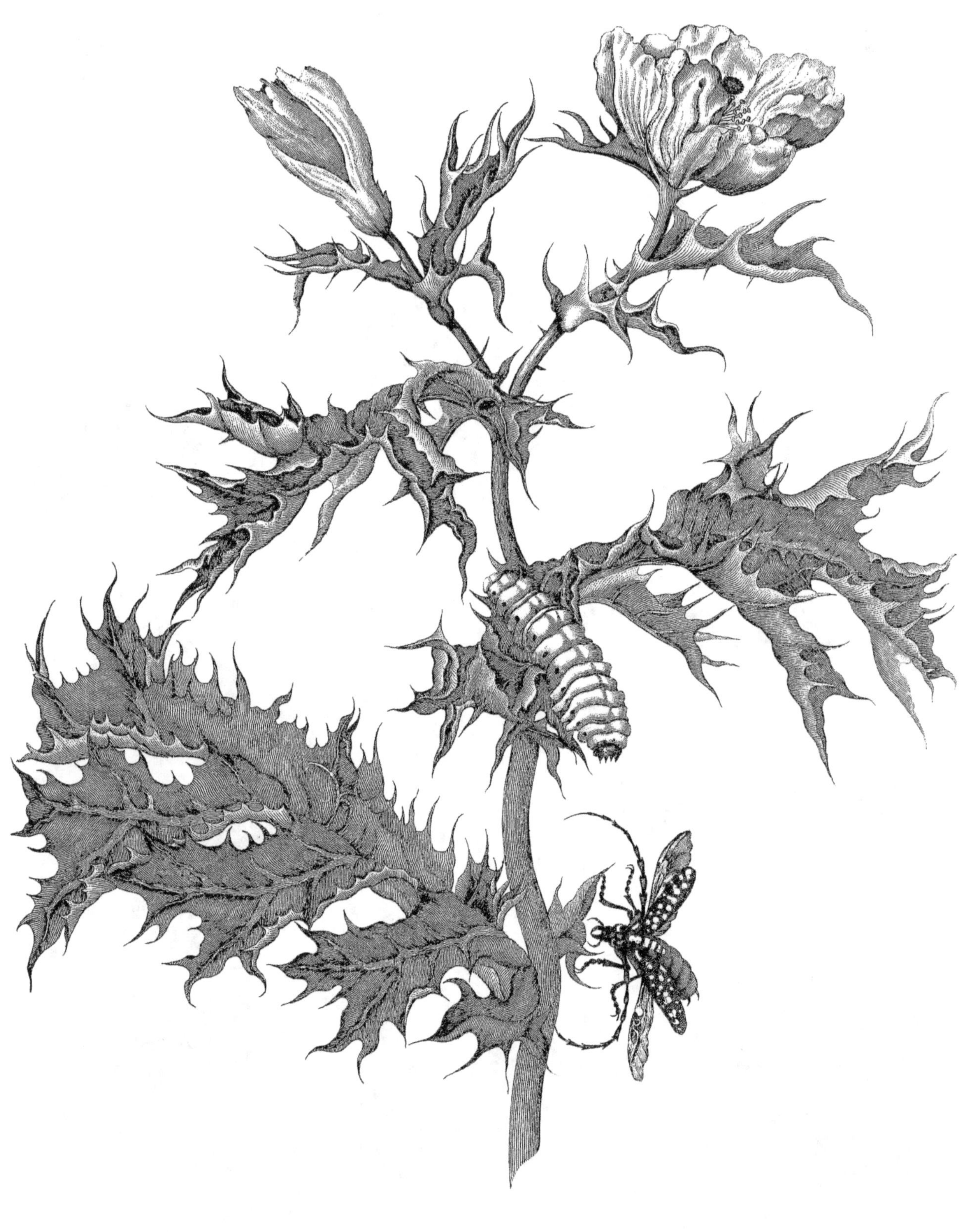

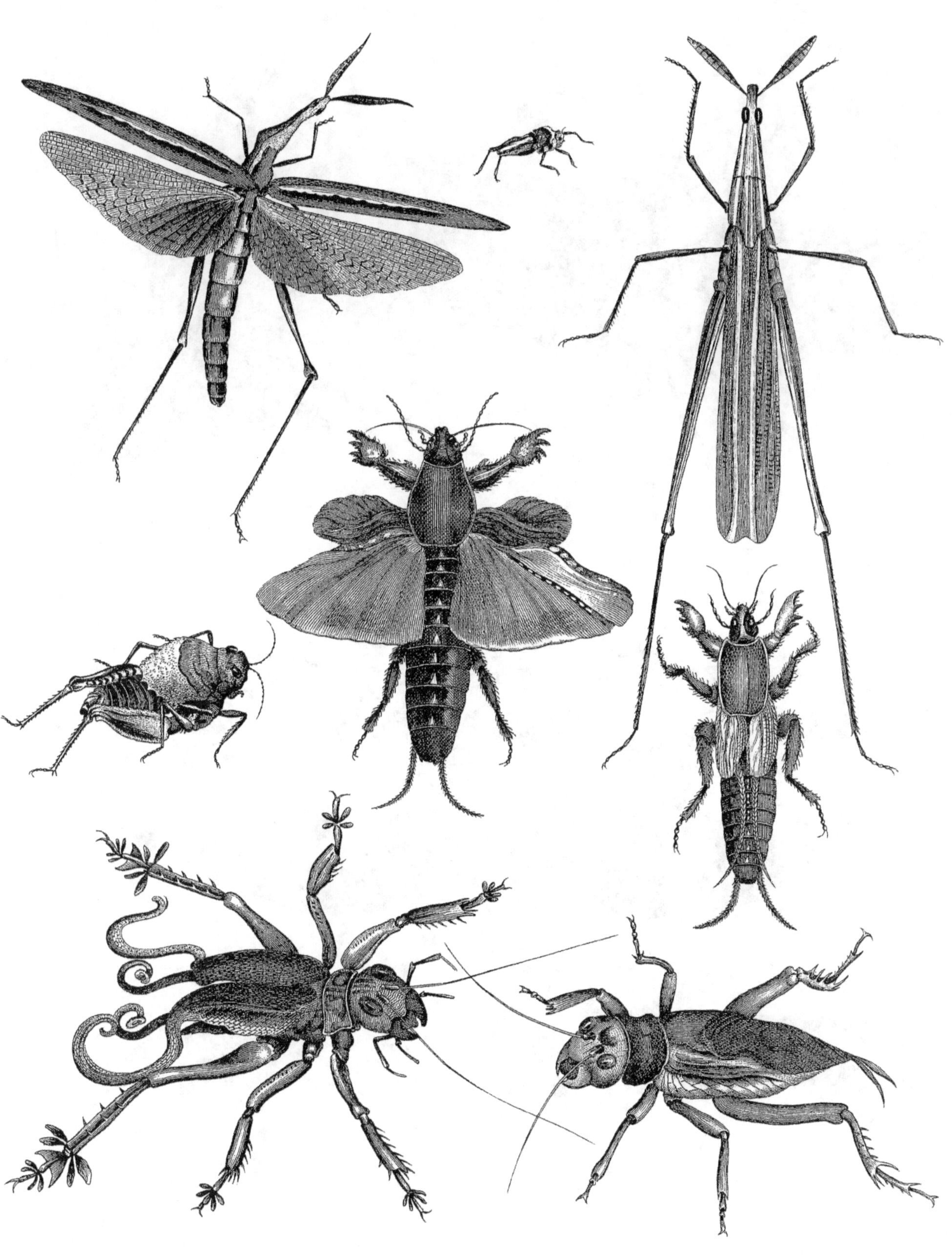

INSECTS

122

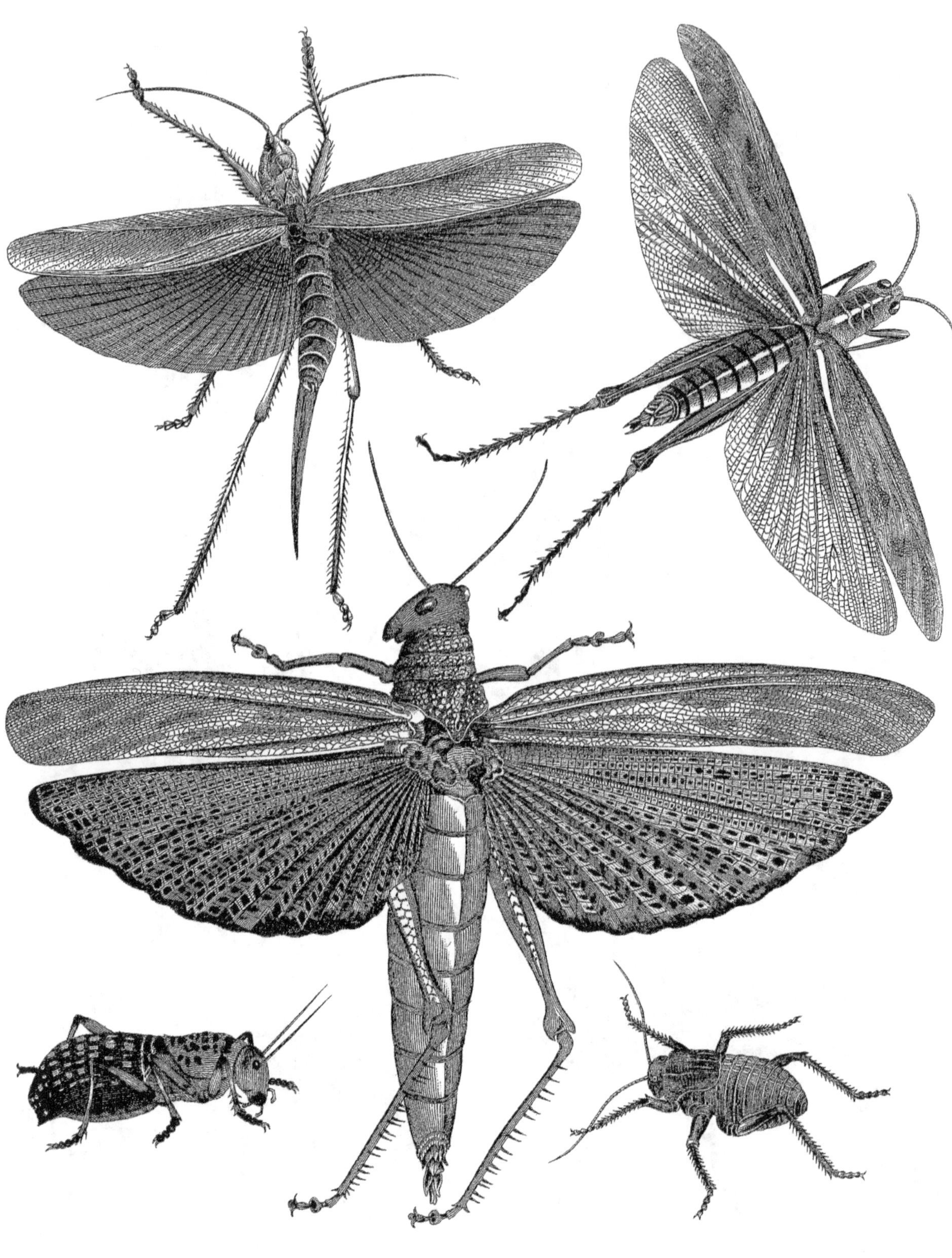

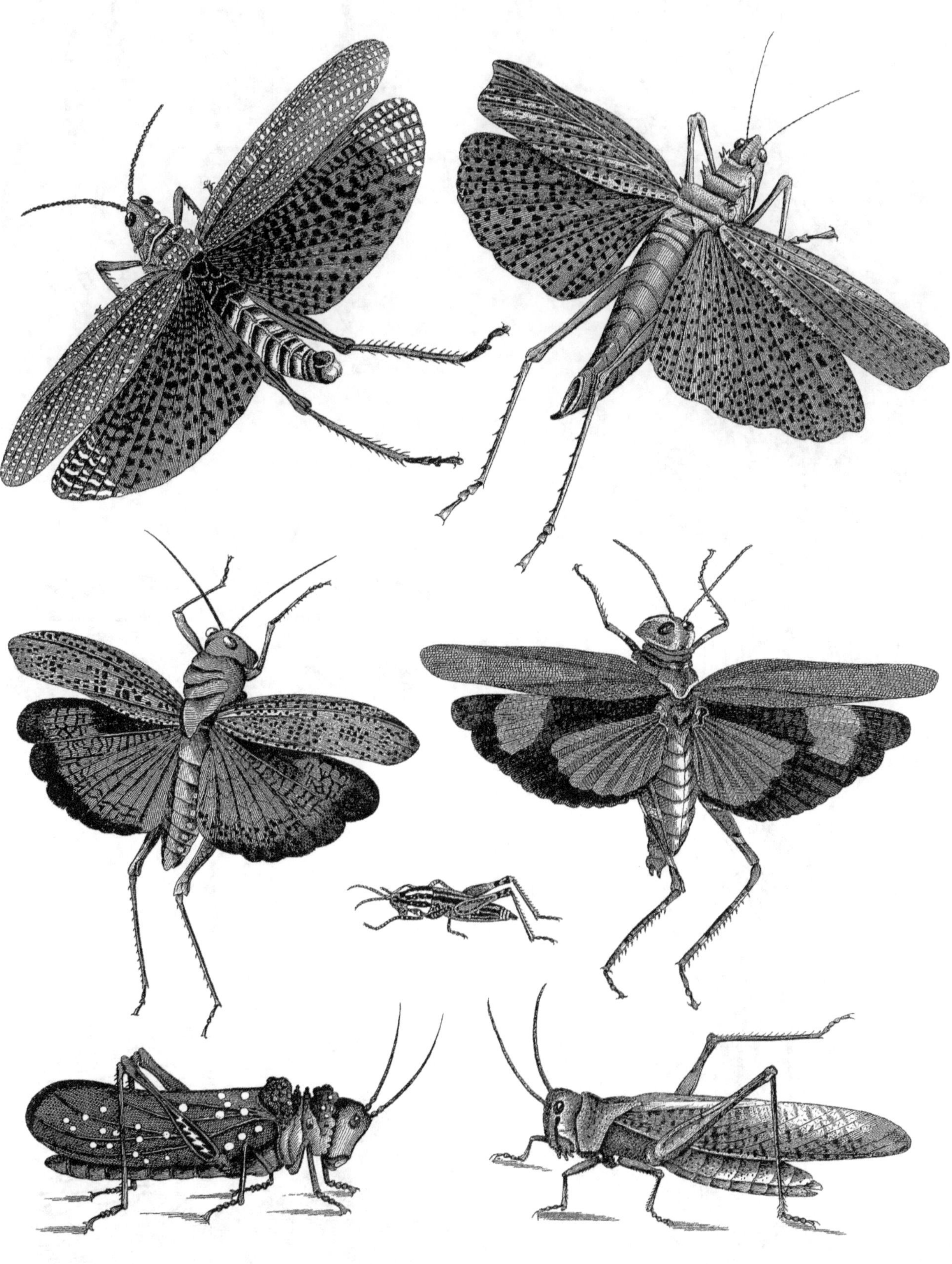

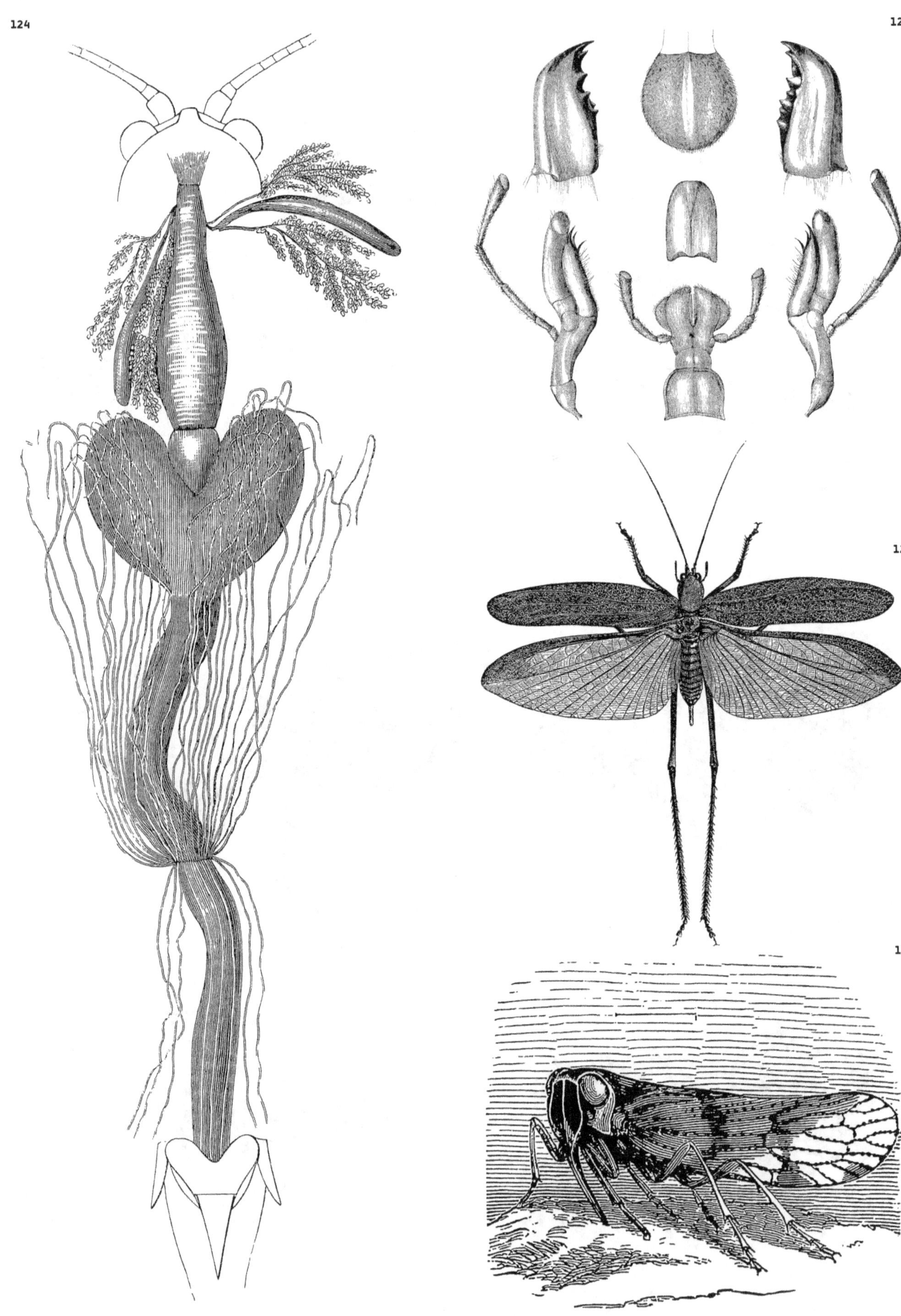

124

125

126

127

INSECTS

128

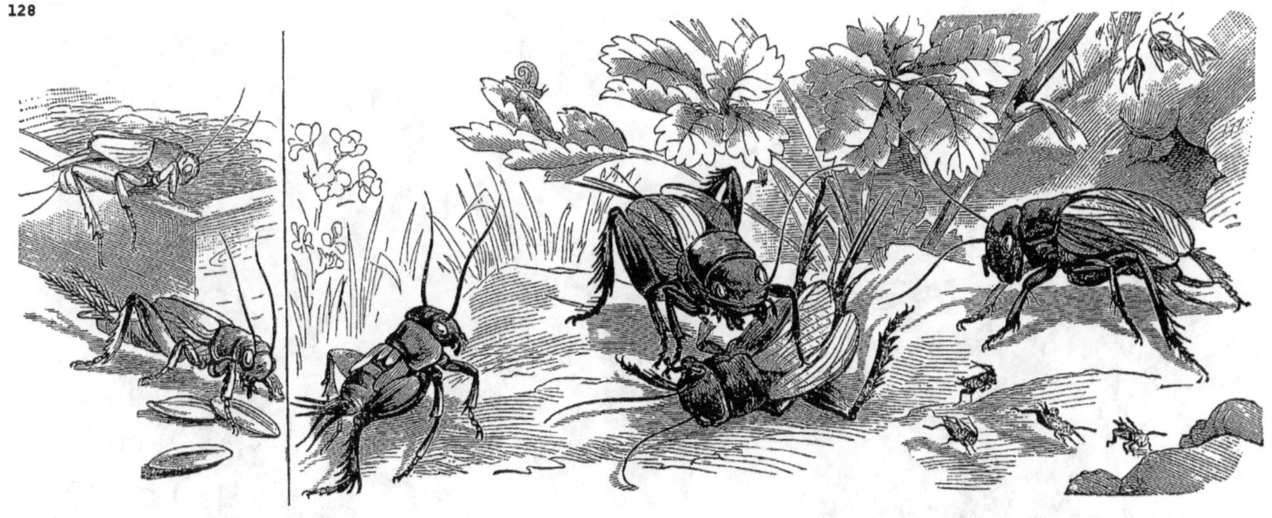

129

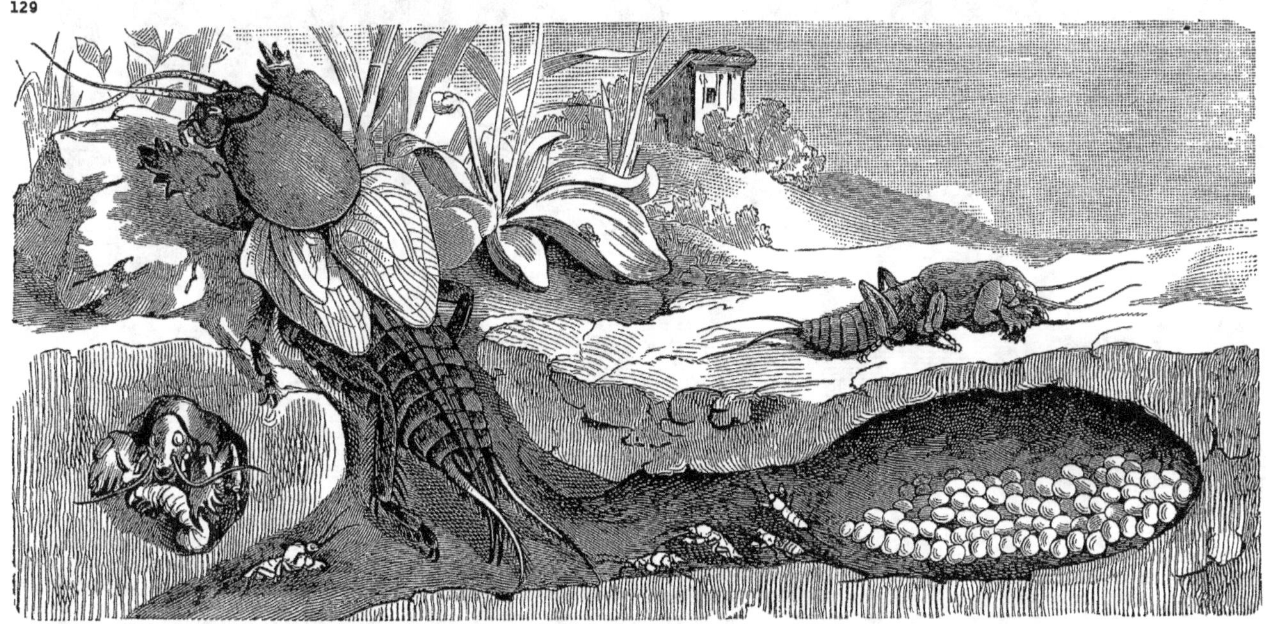

130

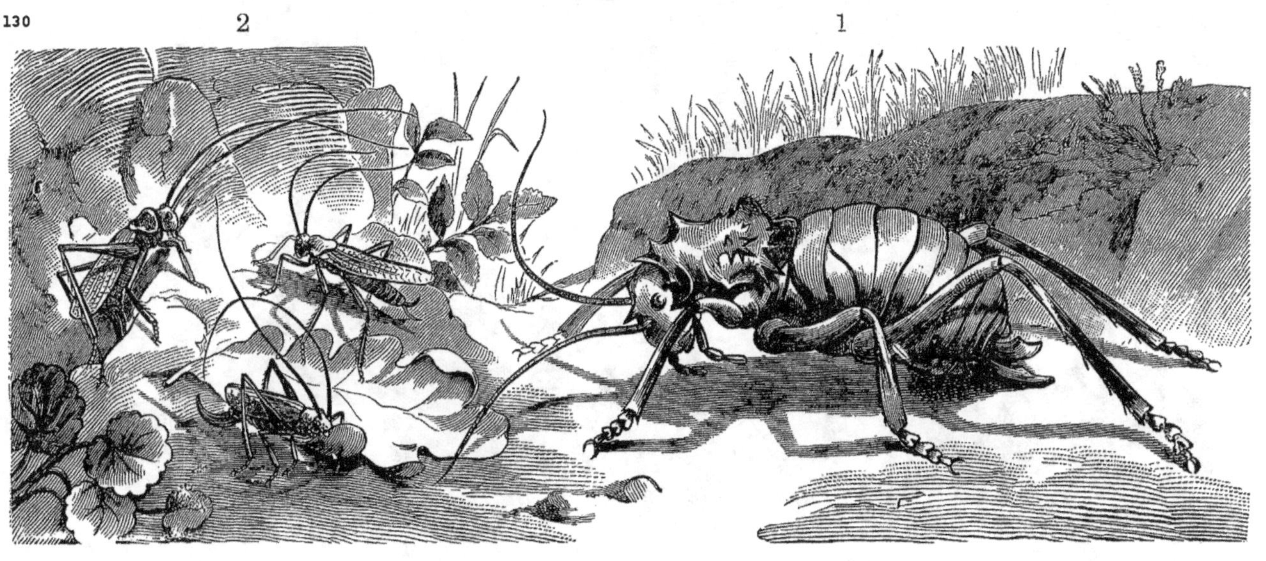

131

132

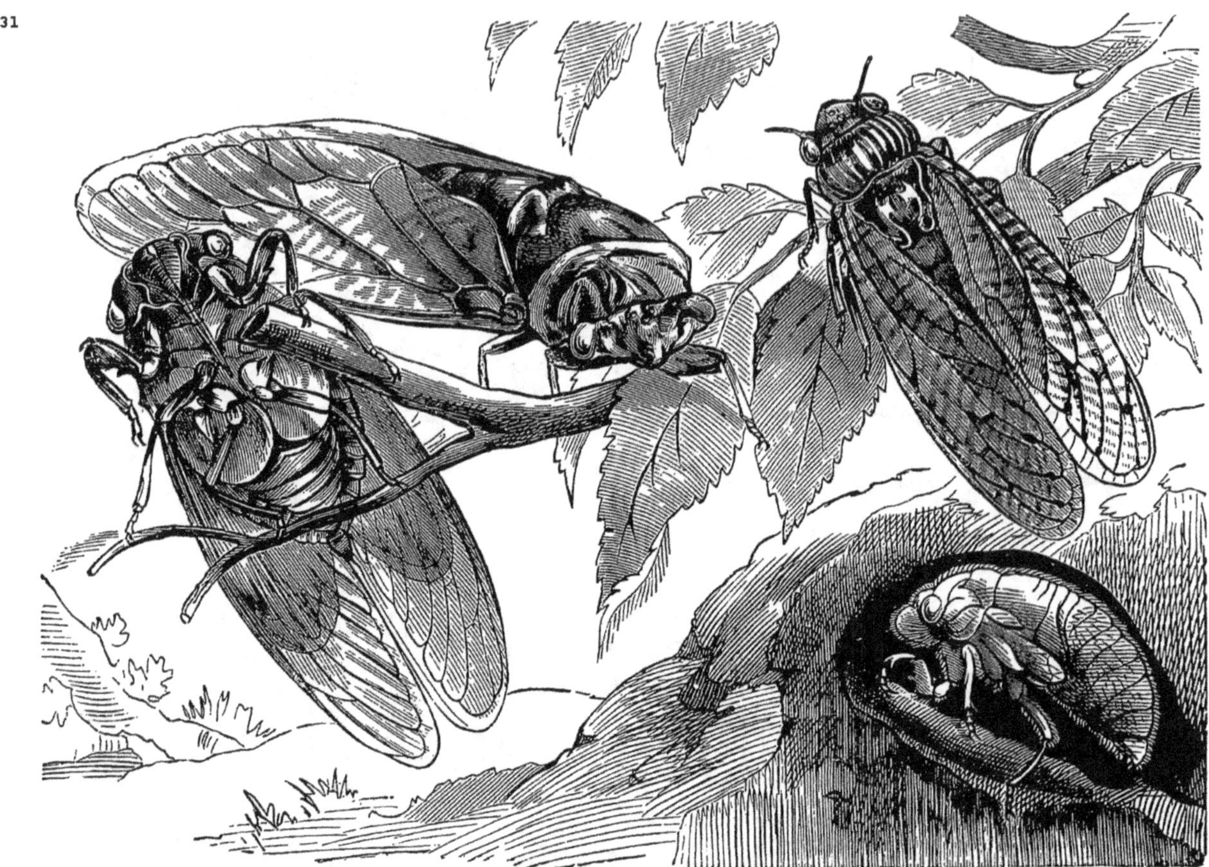

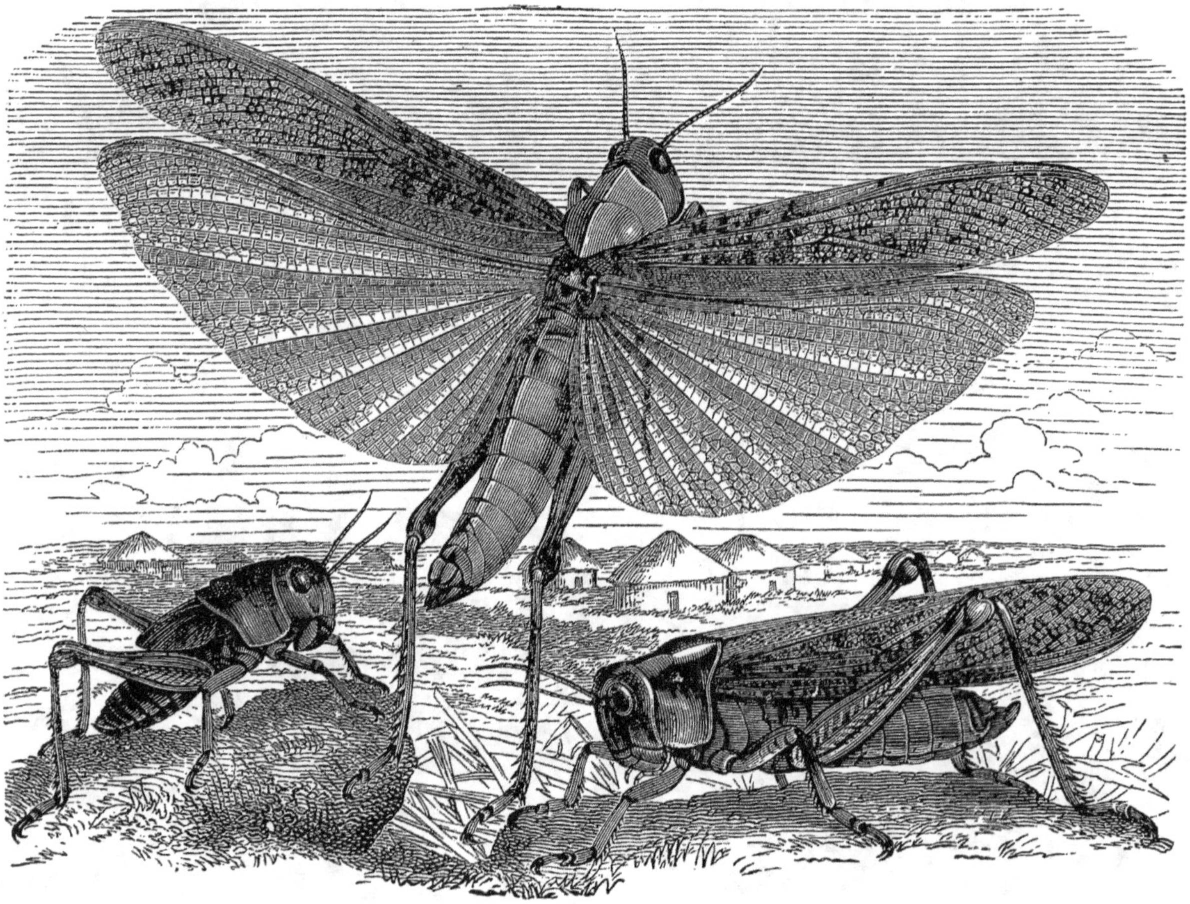

LOCUSTS, CRICKETS & GRASSHOPPERS

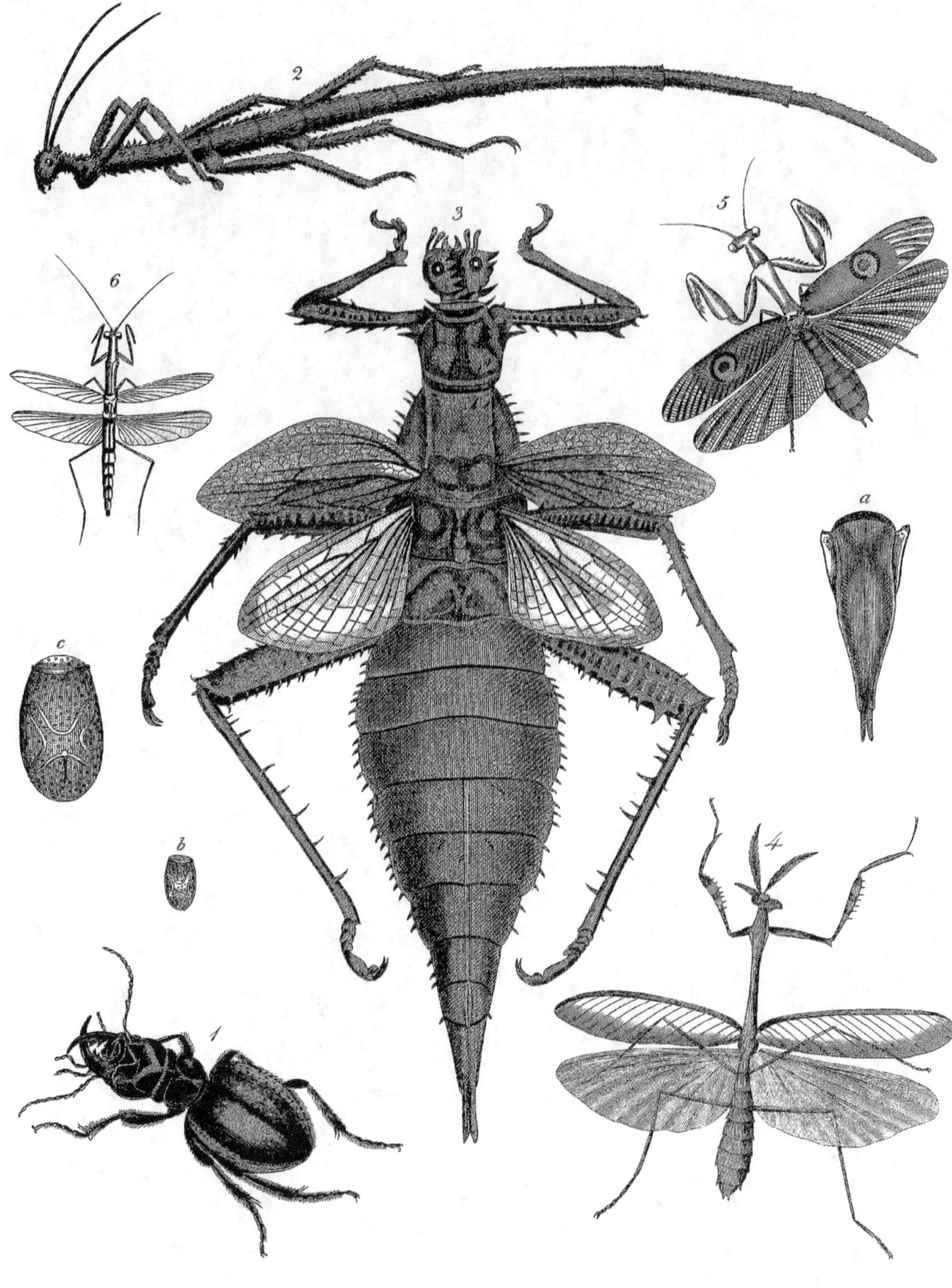

134

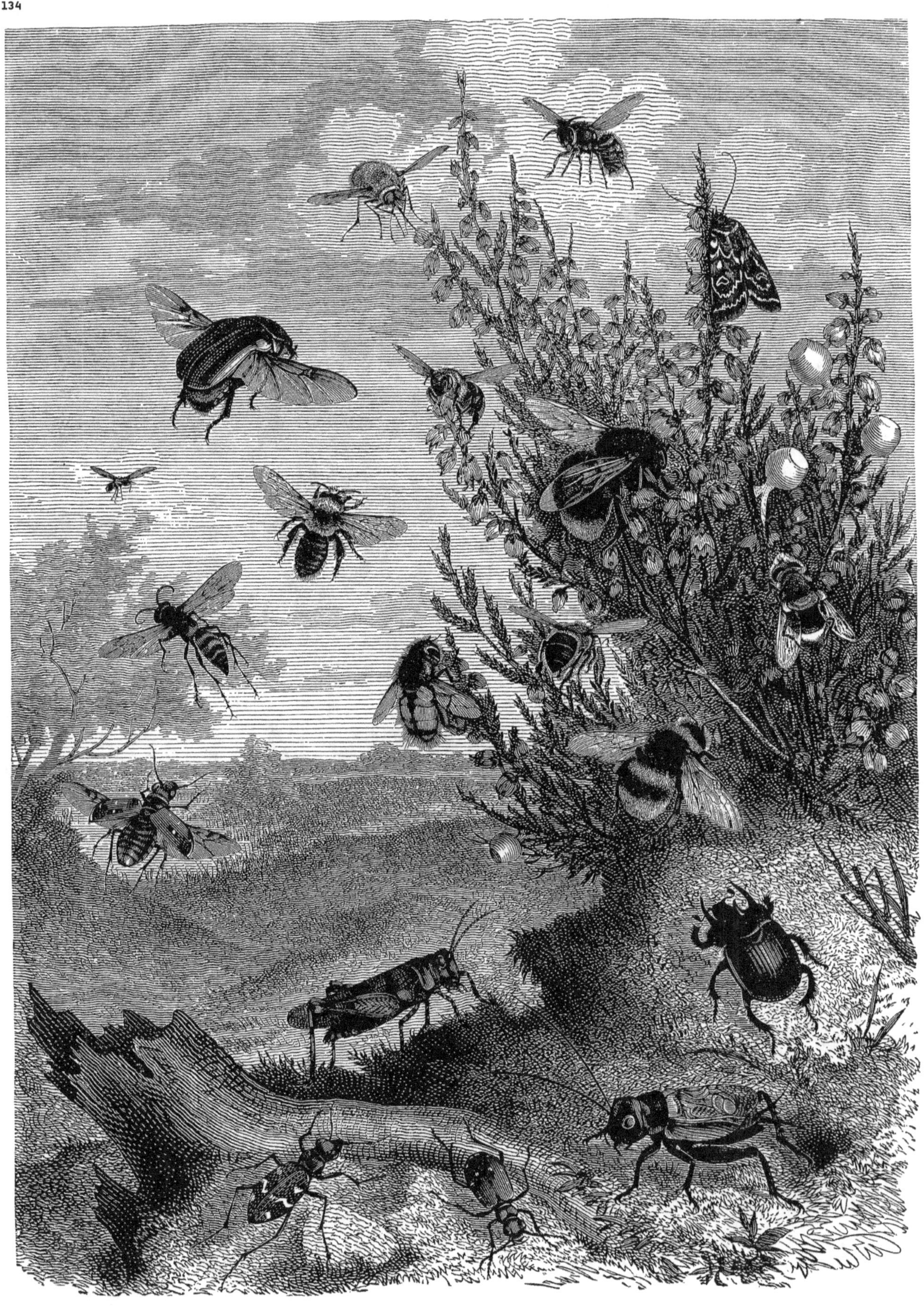

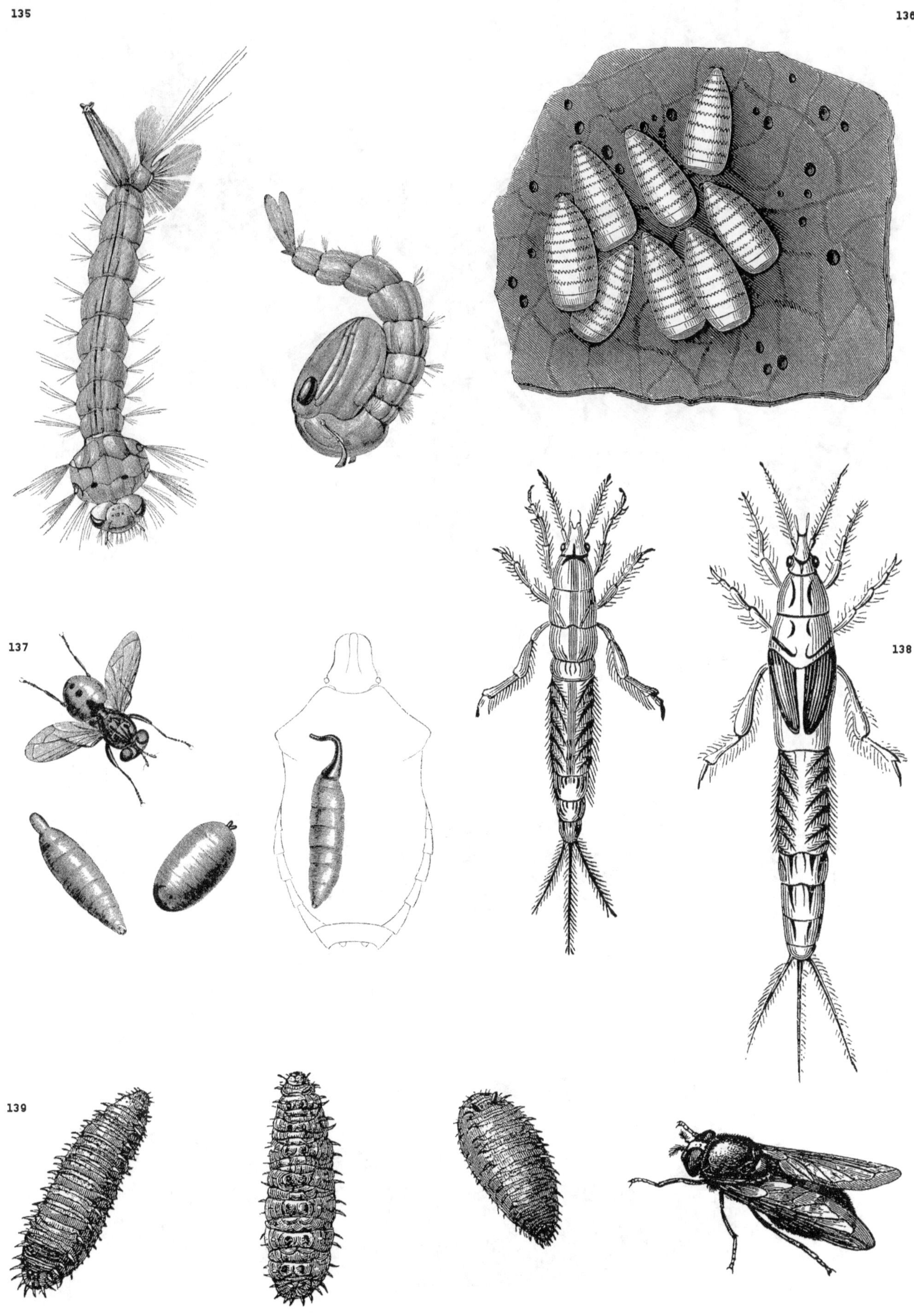

137

138

139

INSECTS

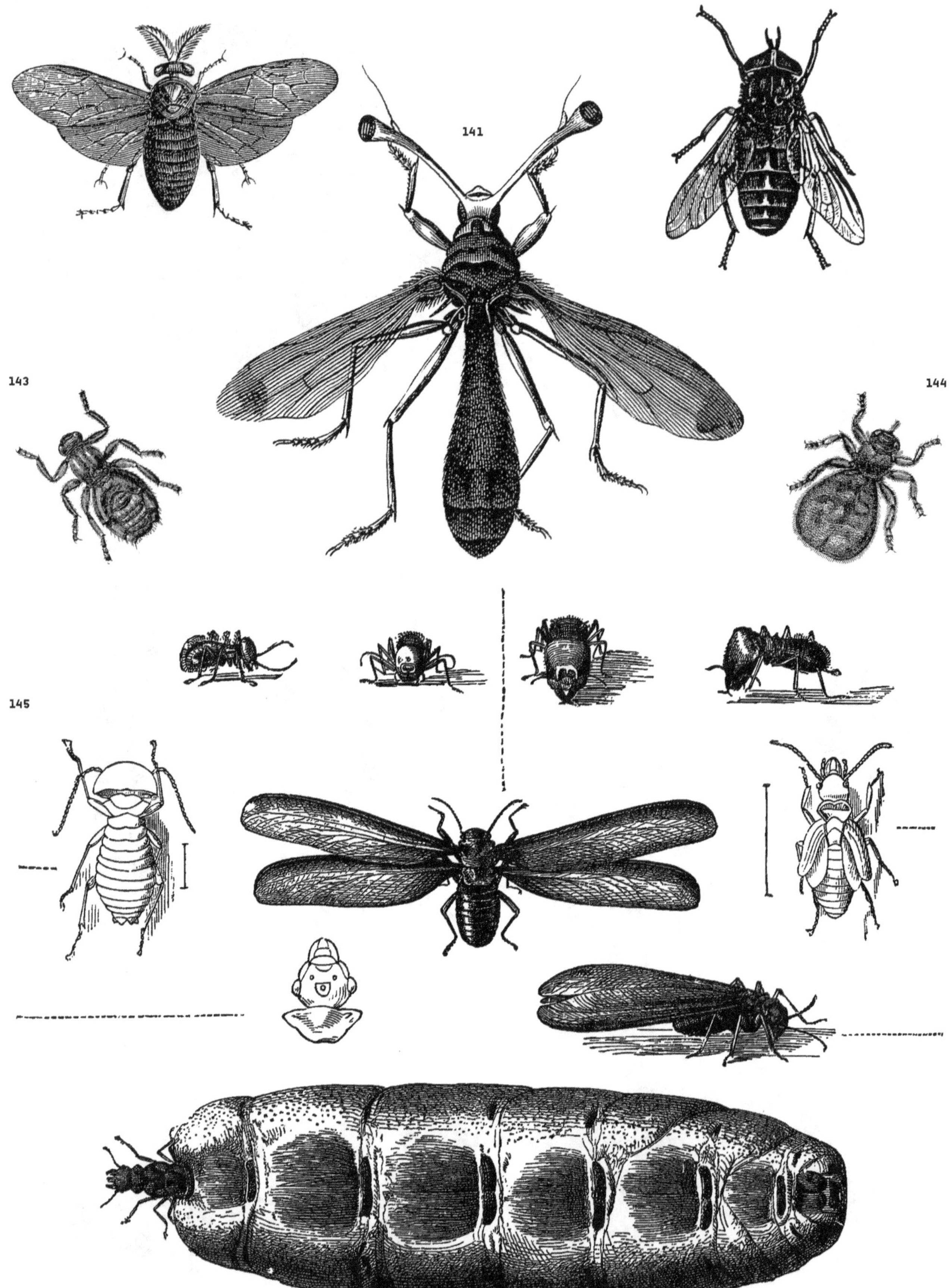

146

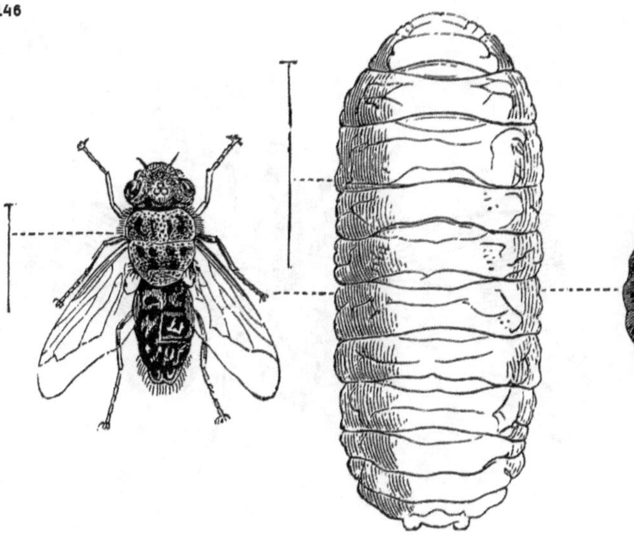

147

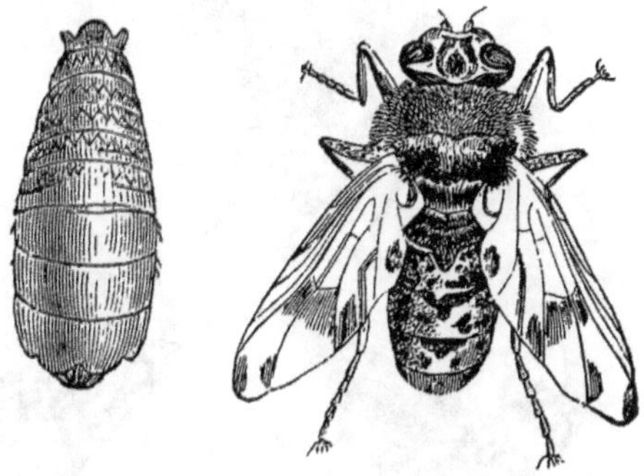

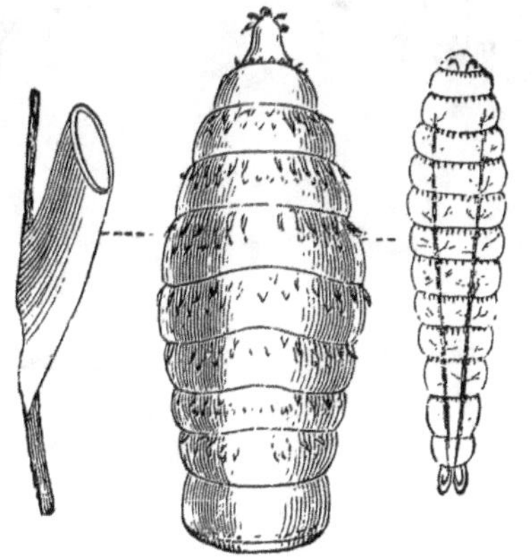

148

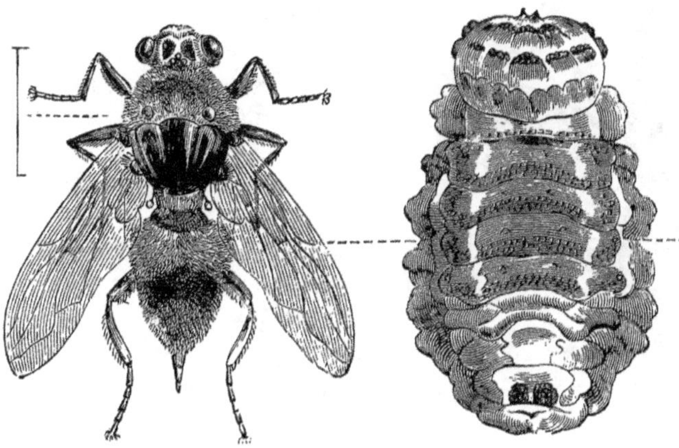

149

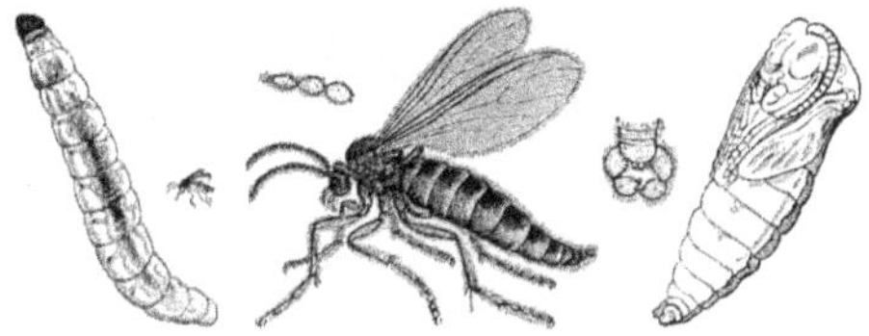

150

INSECTS

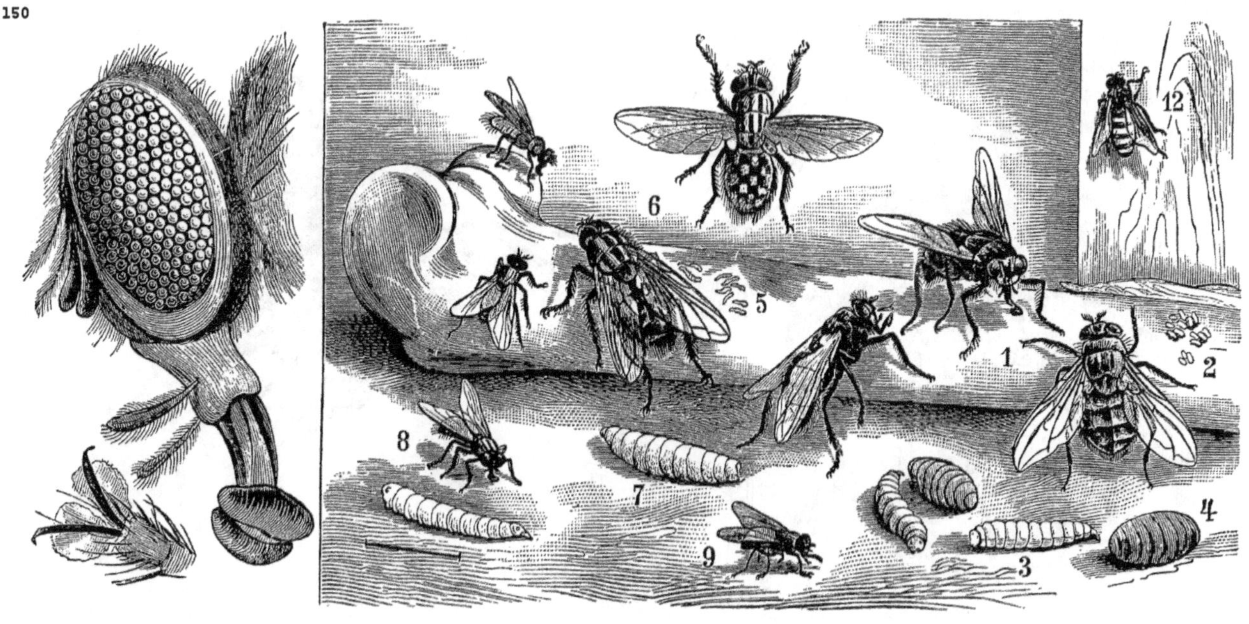

INSECTS

151

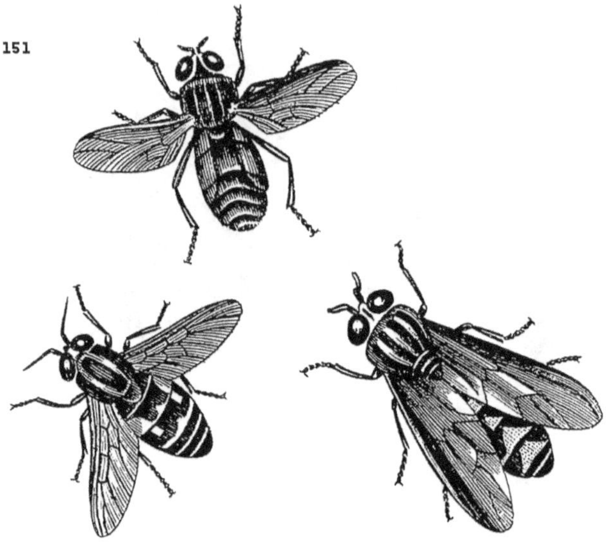

152

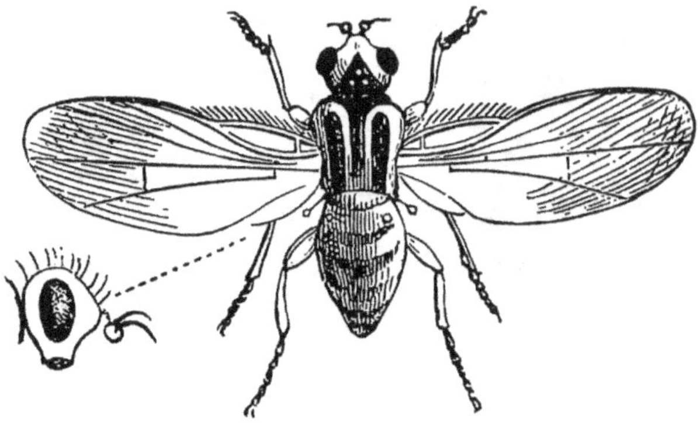

153

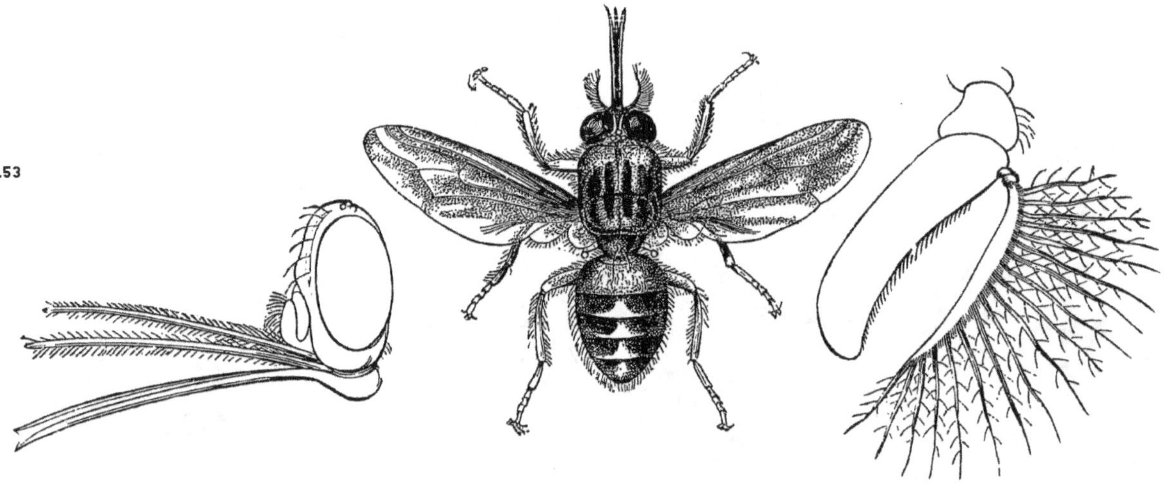

154

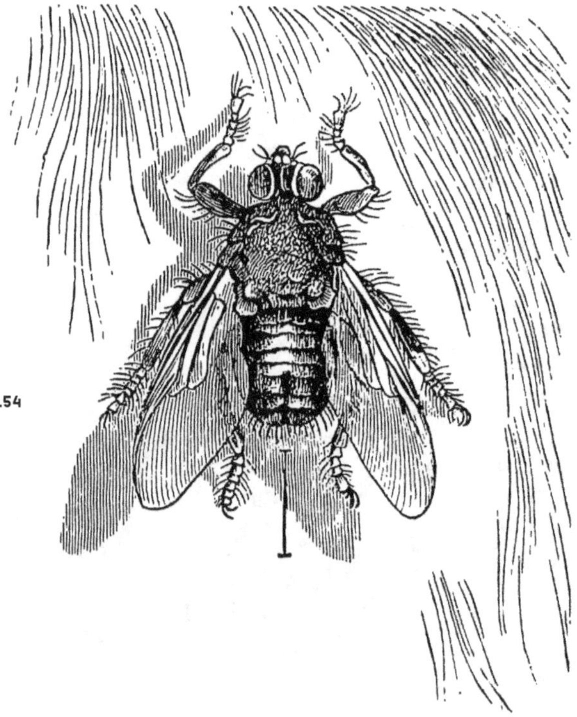

155

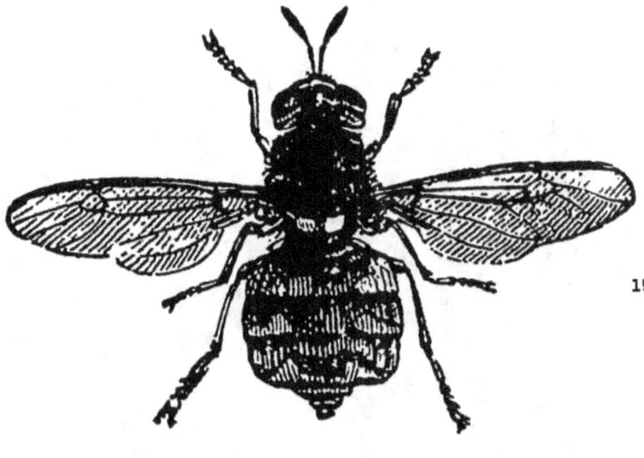

156

157

158

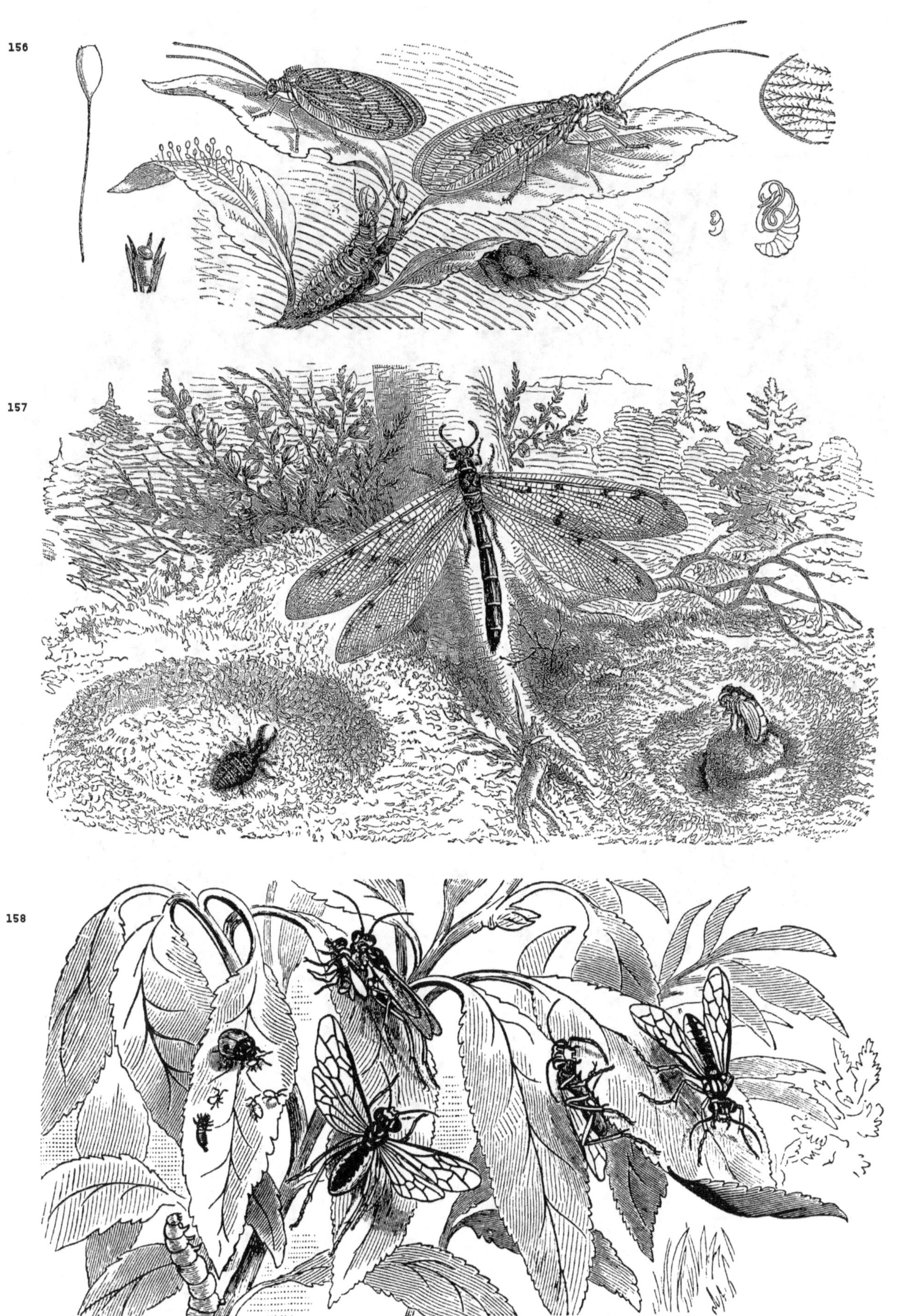

FLIES

FLIES

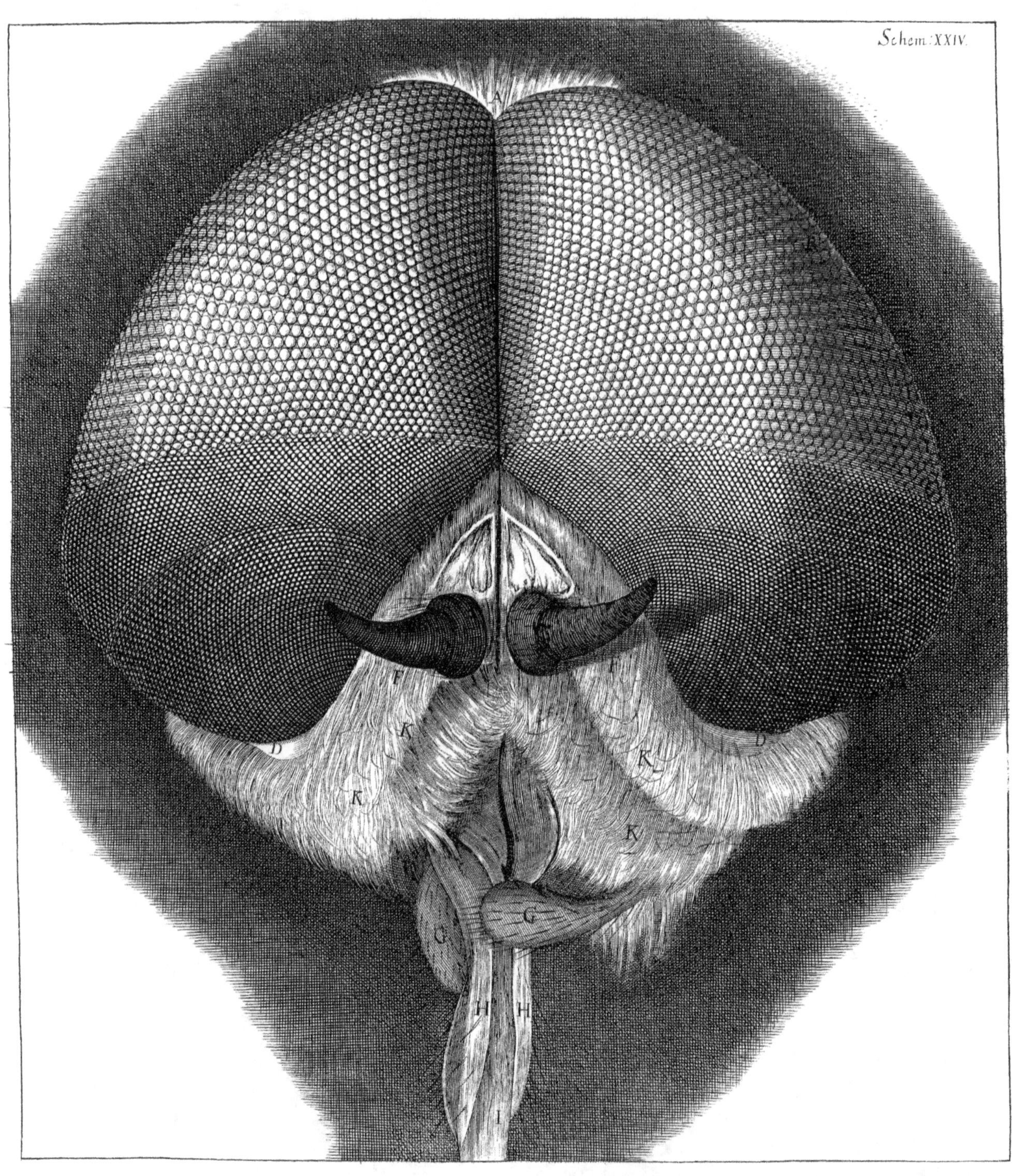

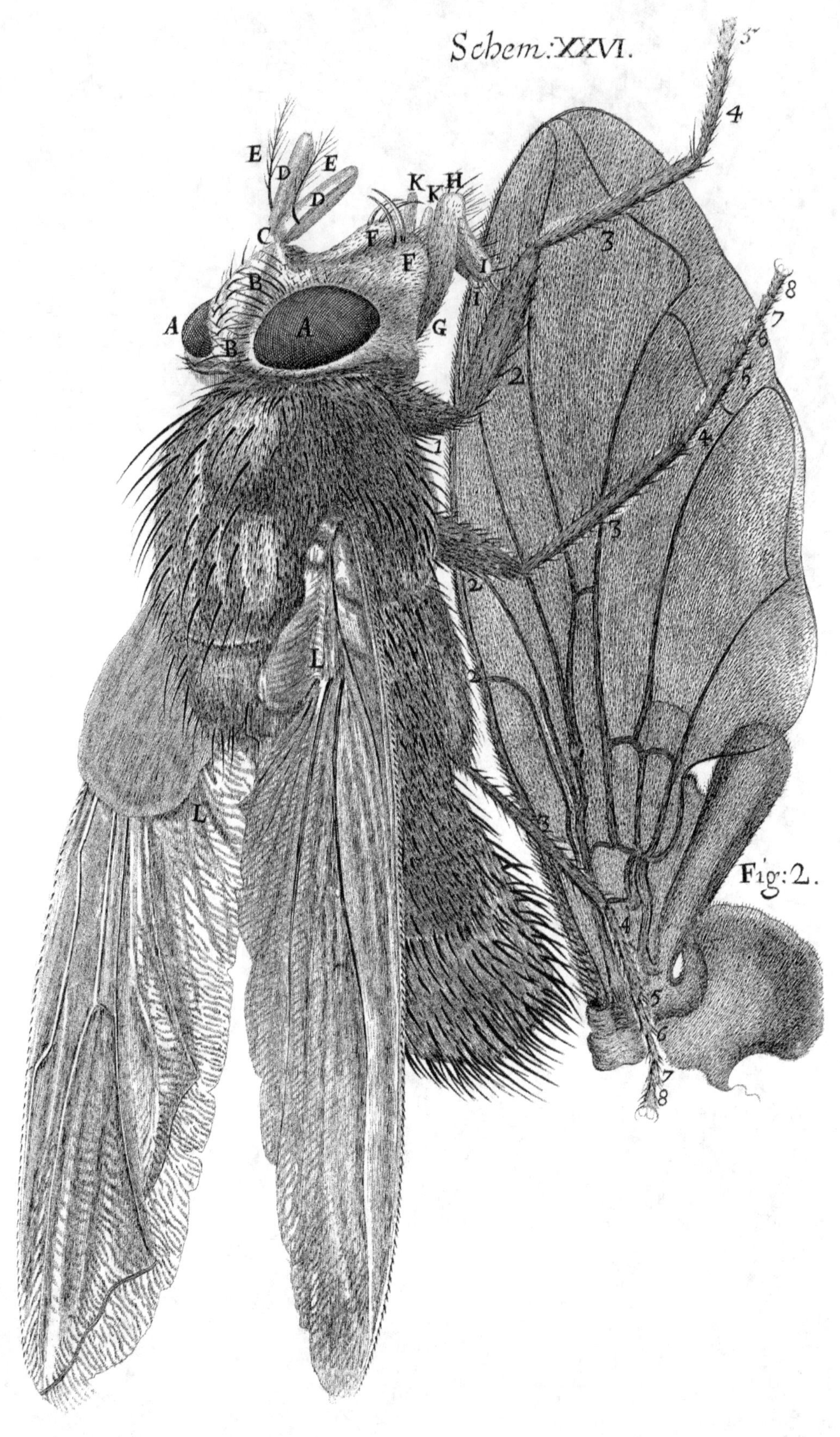
Schem:XXVI.
Fig:2.

161

INSECTS

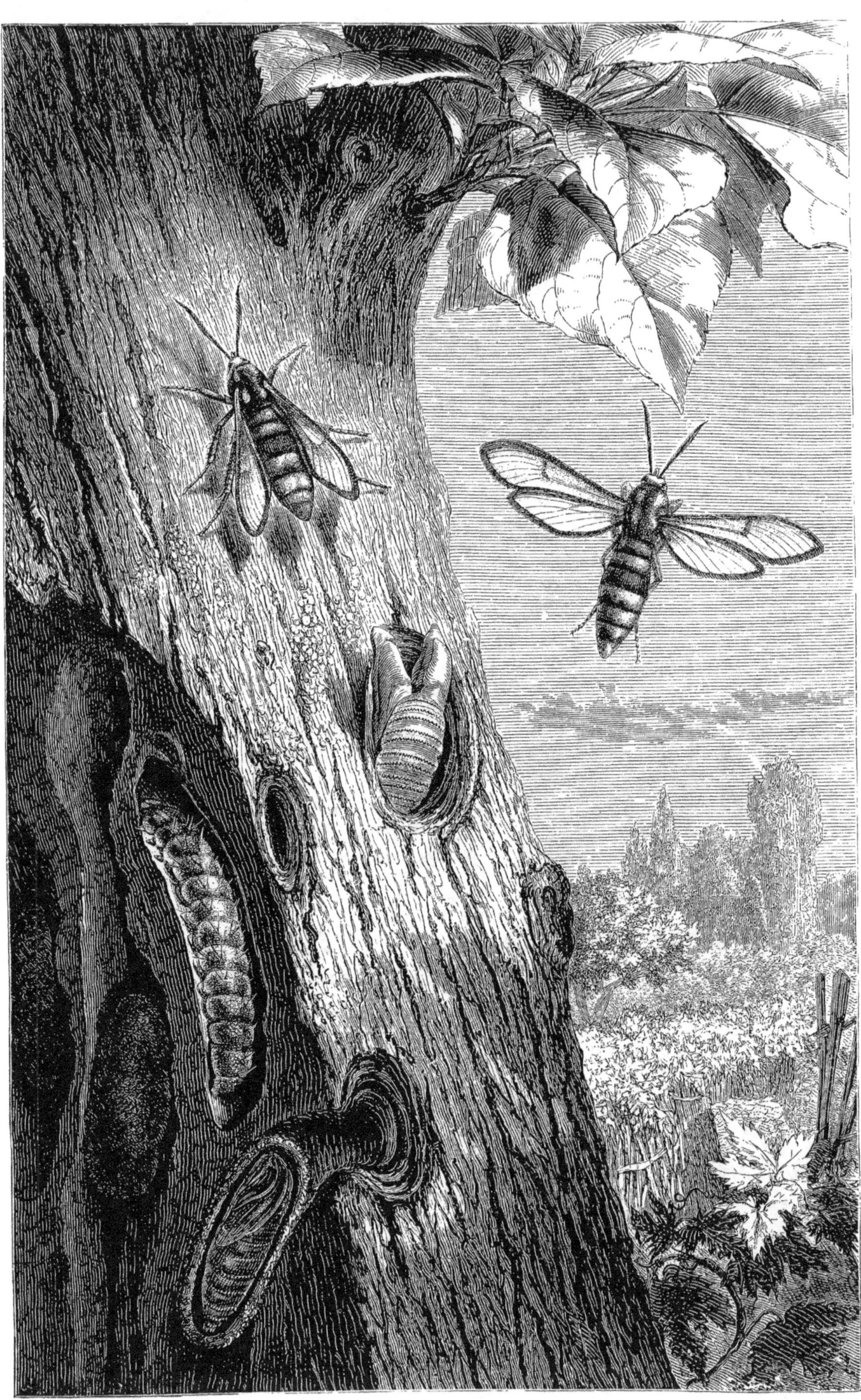

BEES, WASPS & HORNETS

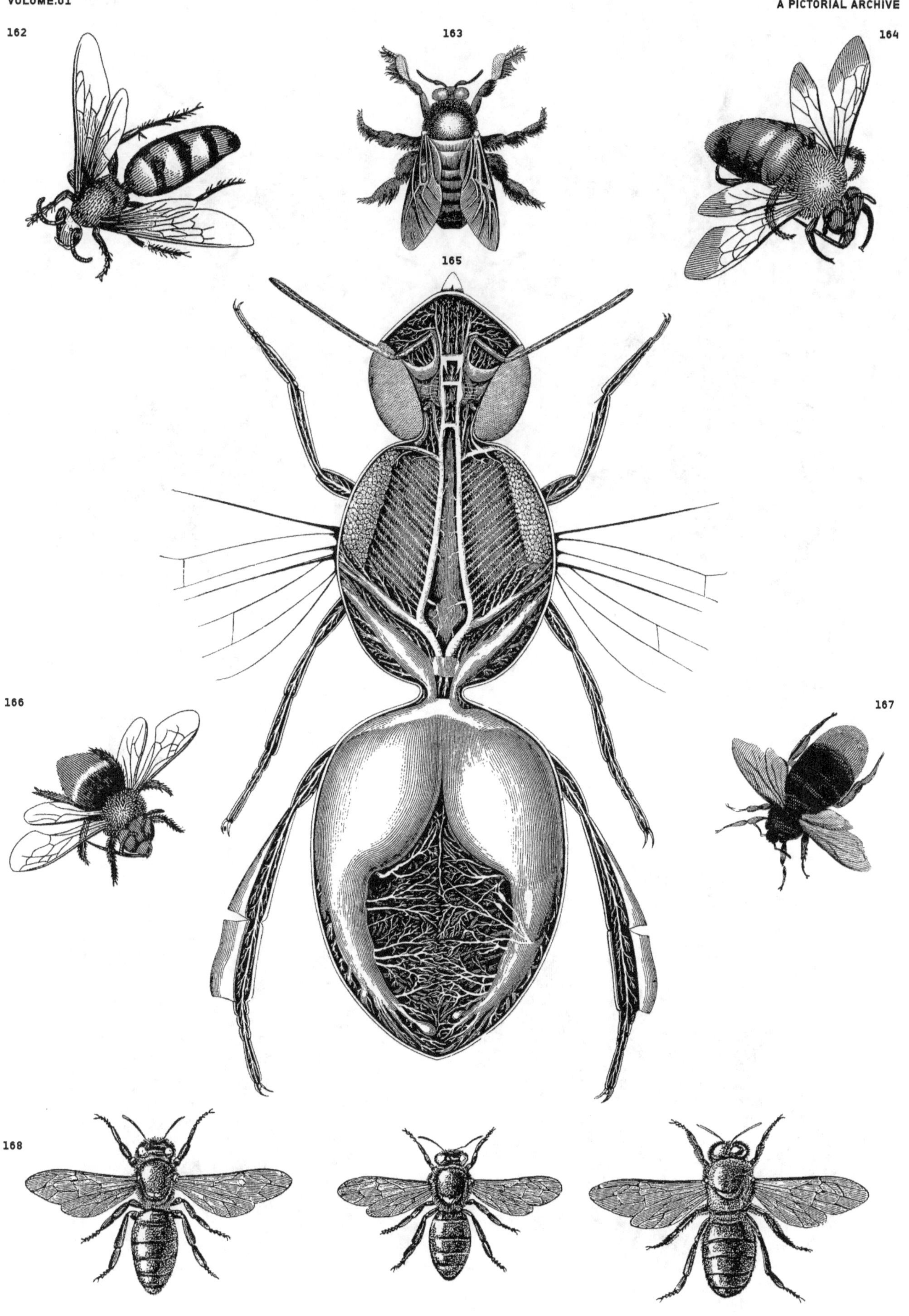

BEES, WASPS & HORNETS

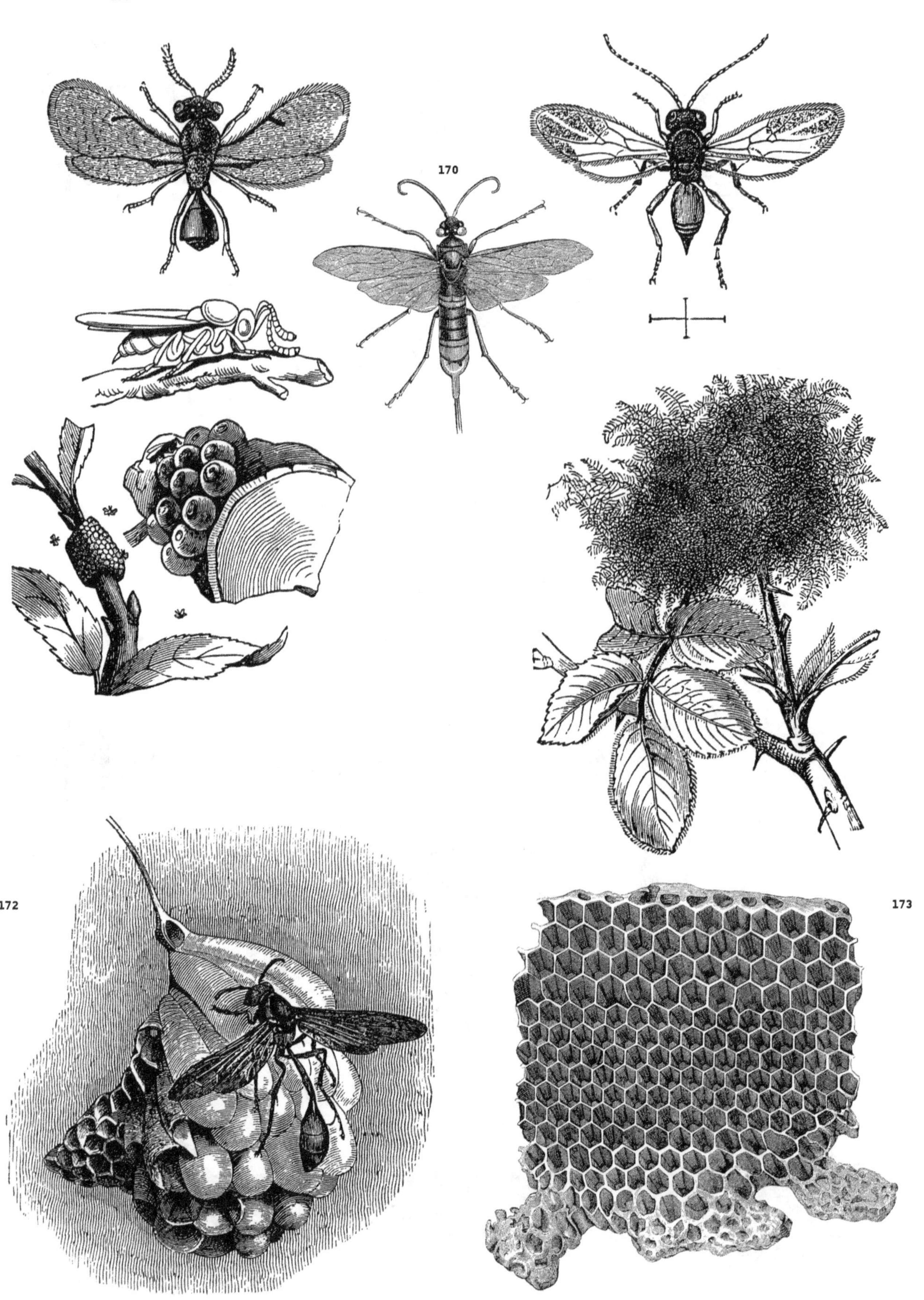

169

170

171

172

173

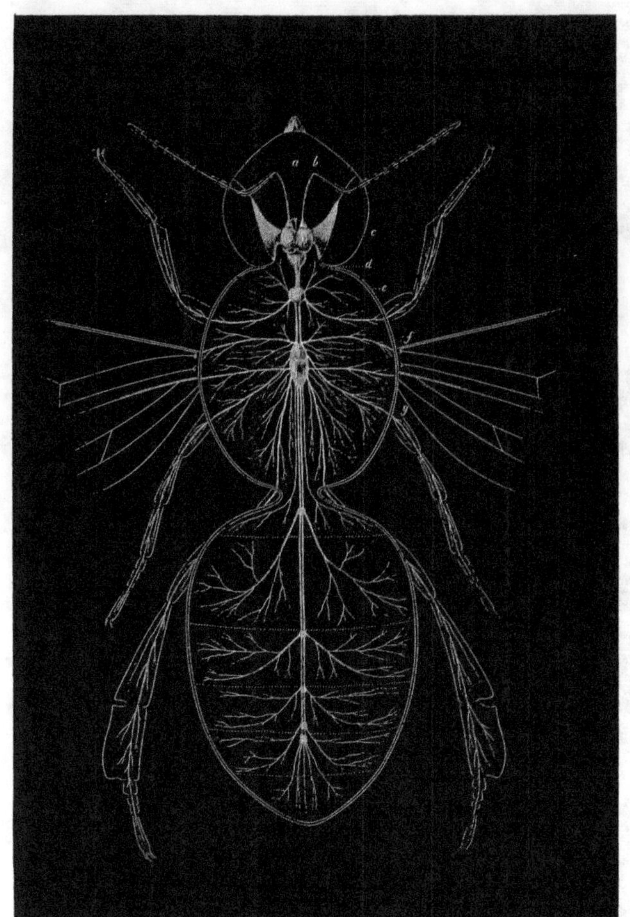

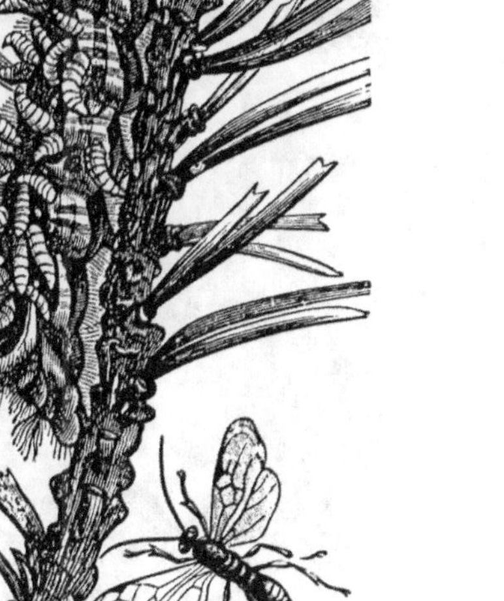

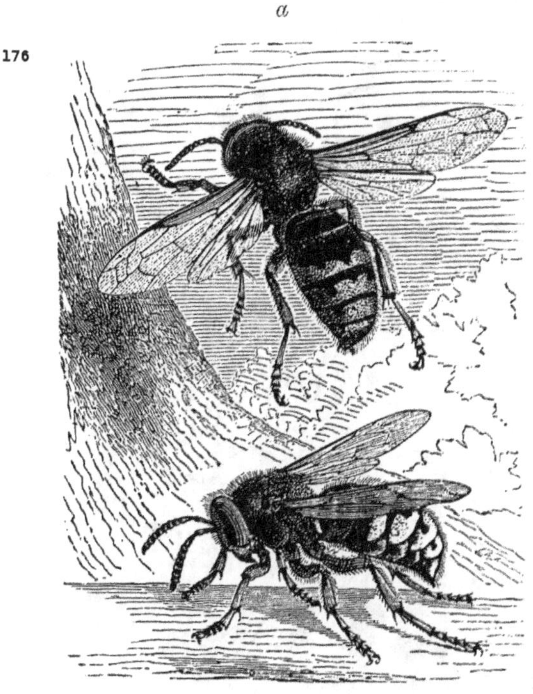

a

b

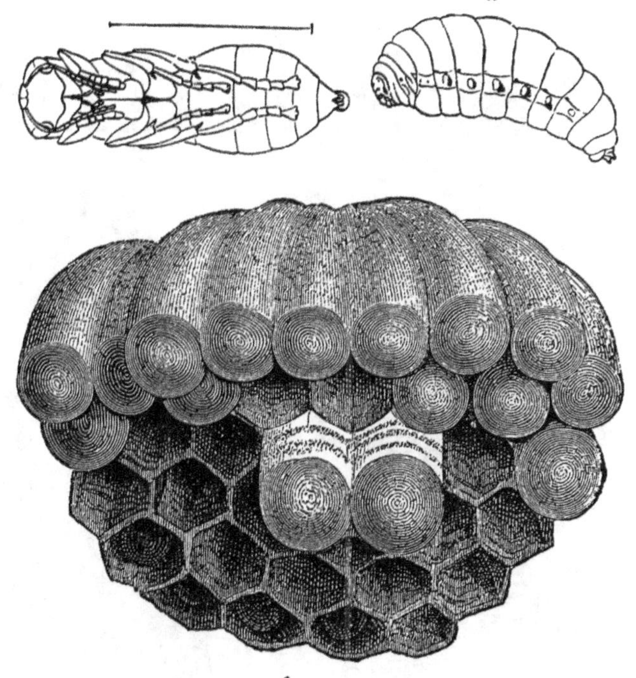

e

d

c

177

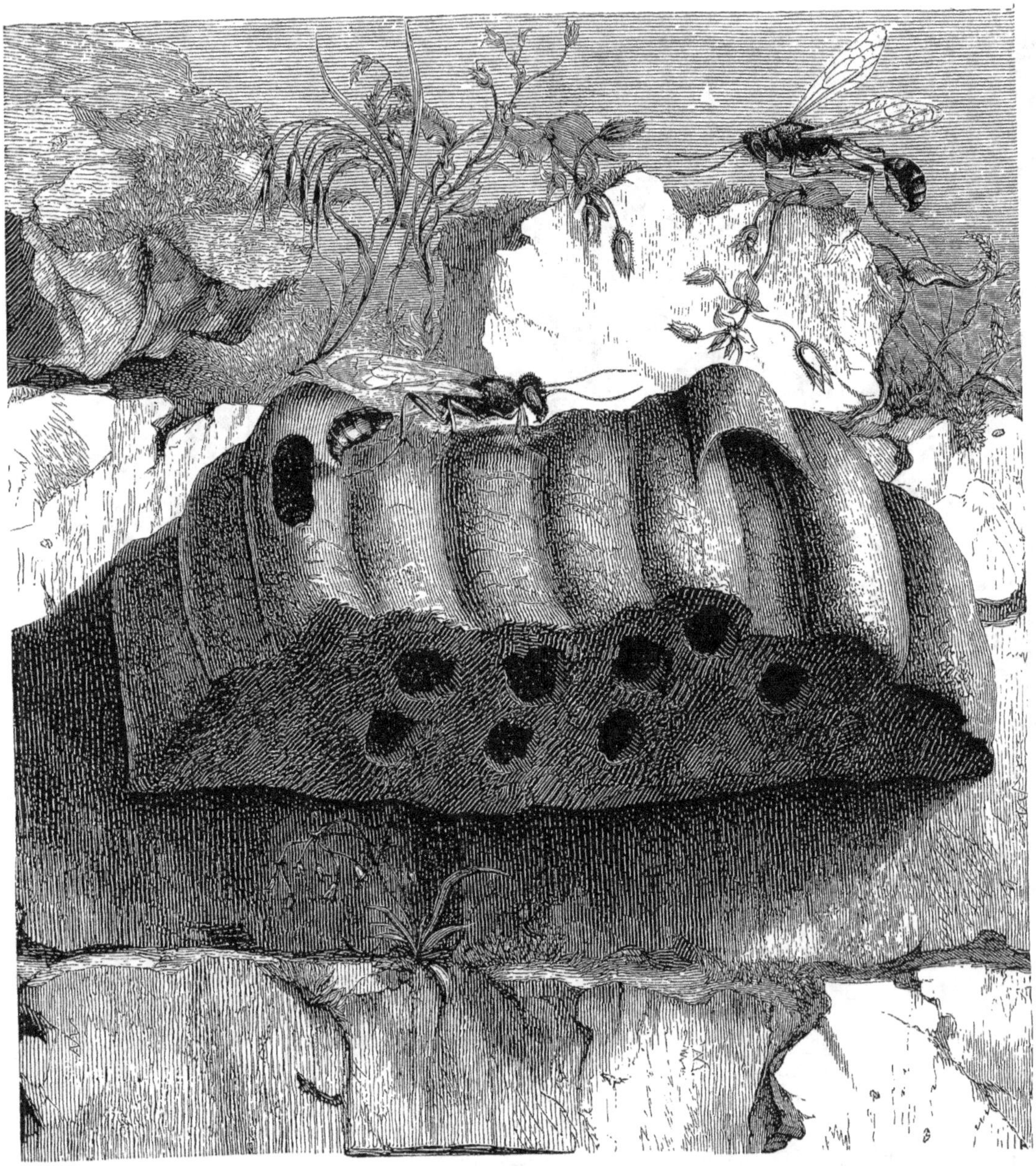

178

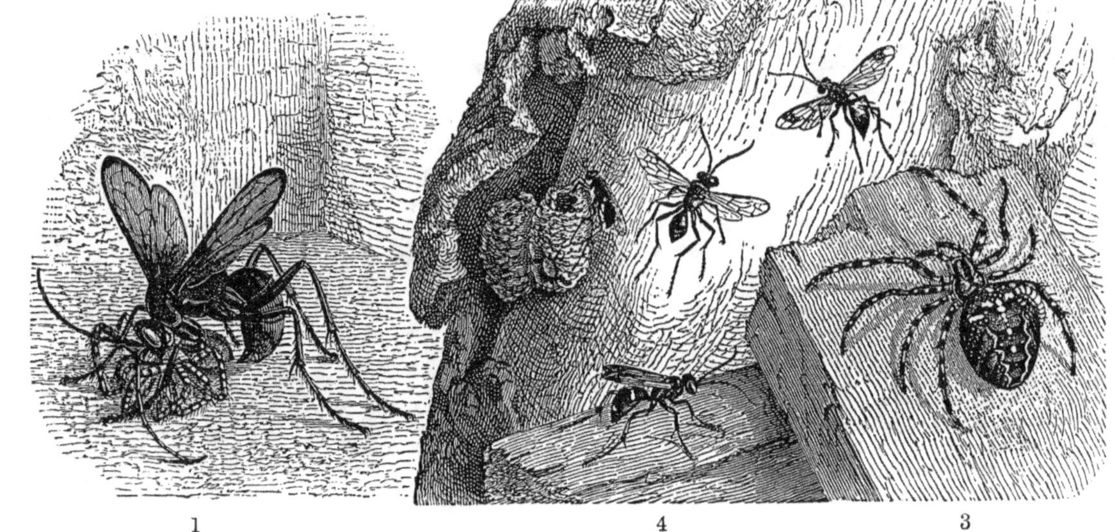

1   4   3

179

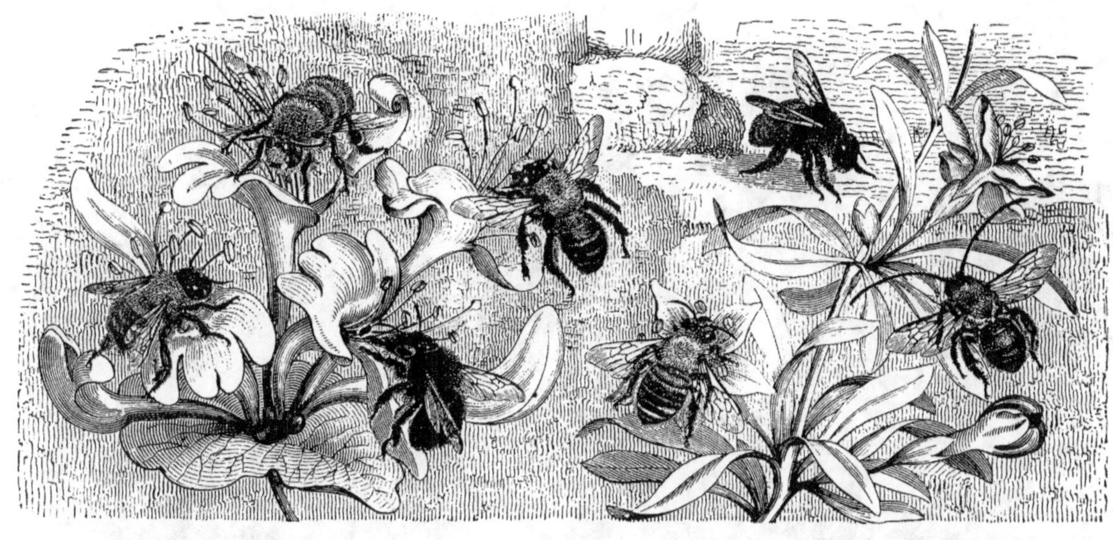

180

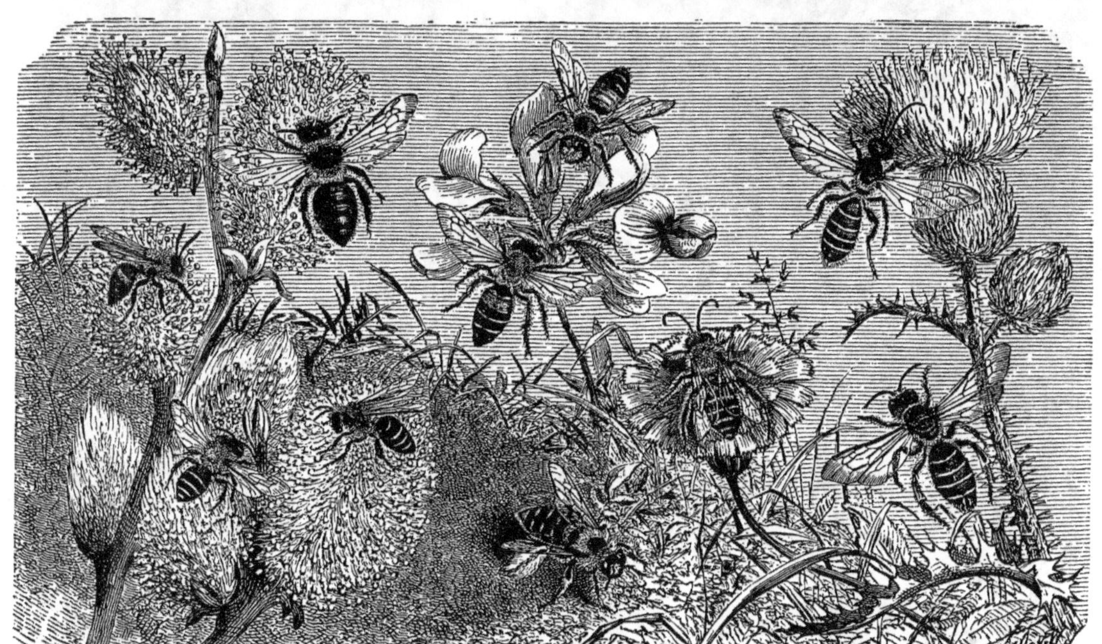

181

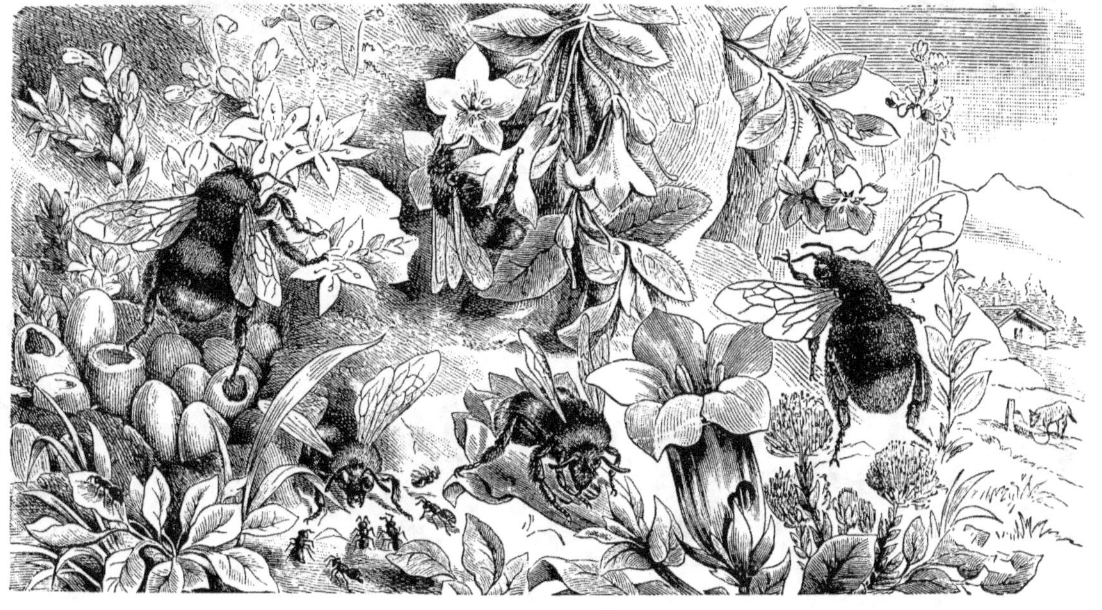

182

INSECTS

183

184

185

186

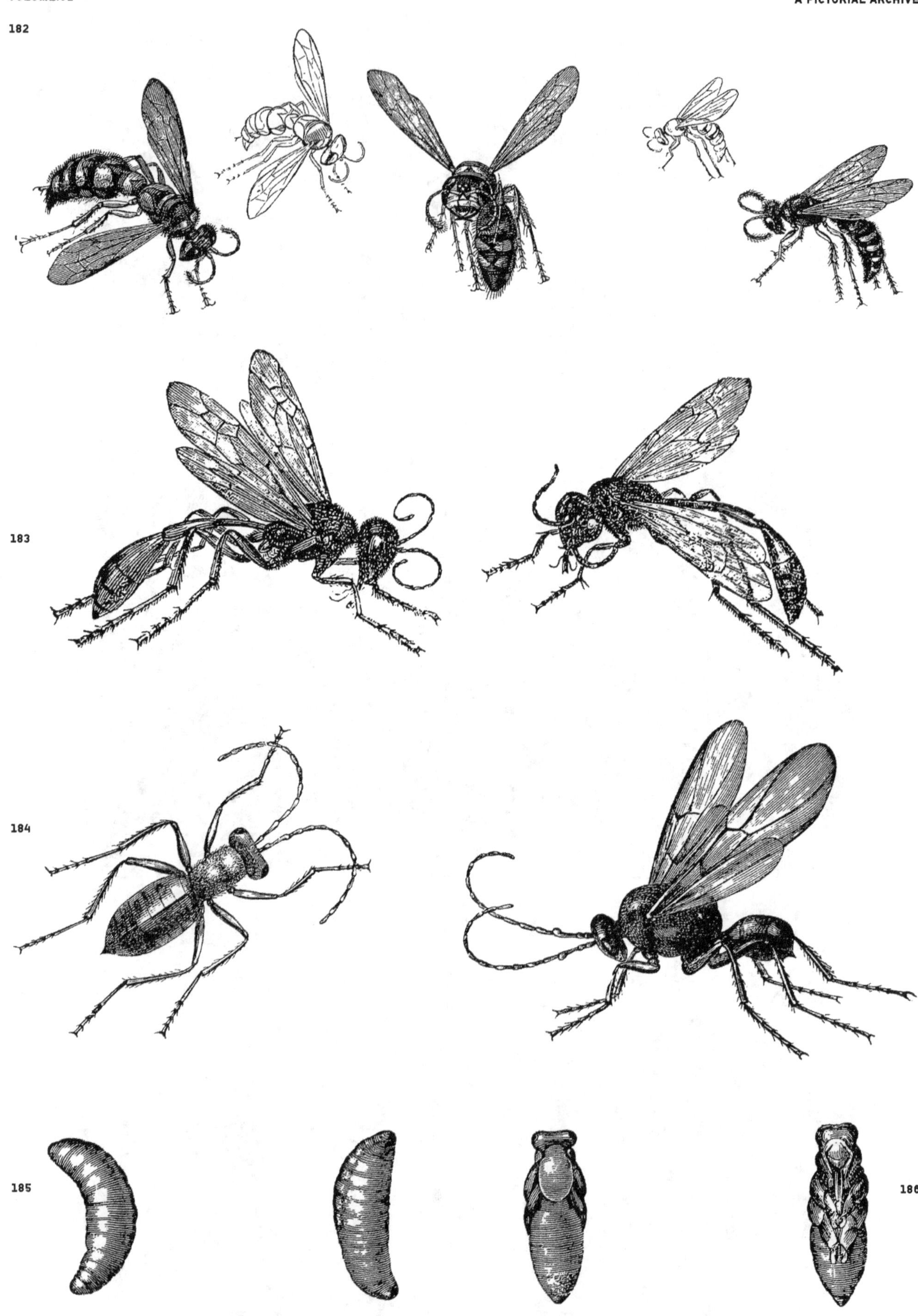

BEES, WASPS & HORNETS

187

188

189

190

191

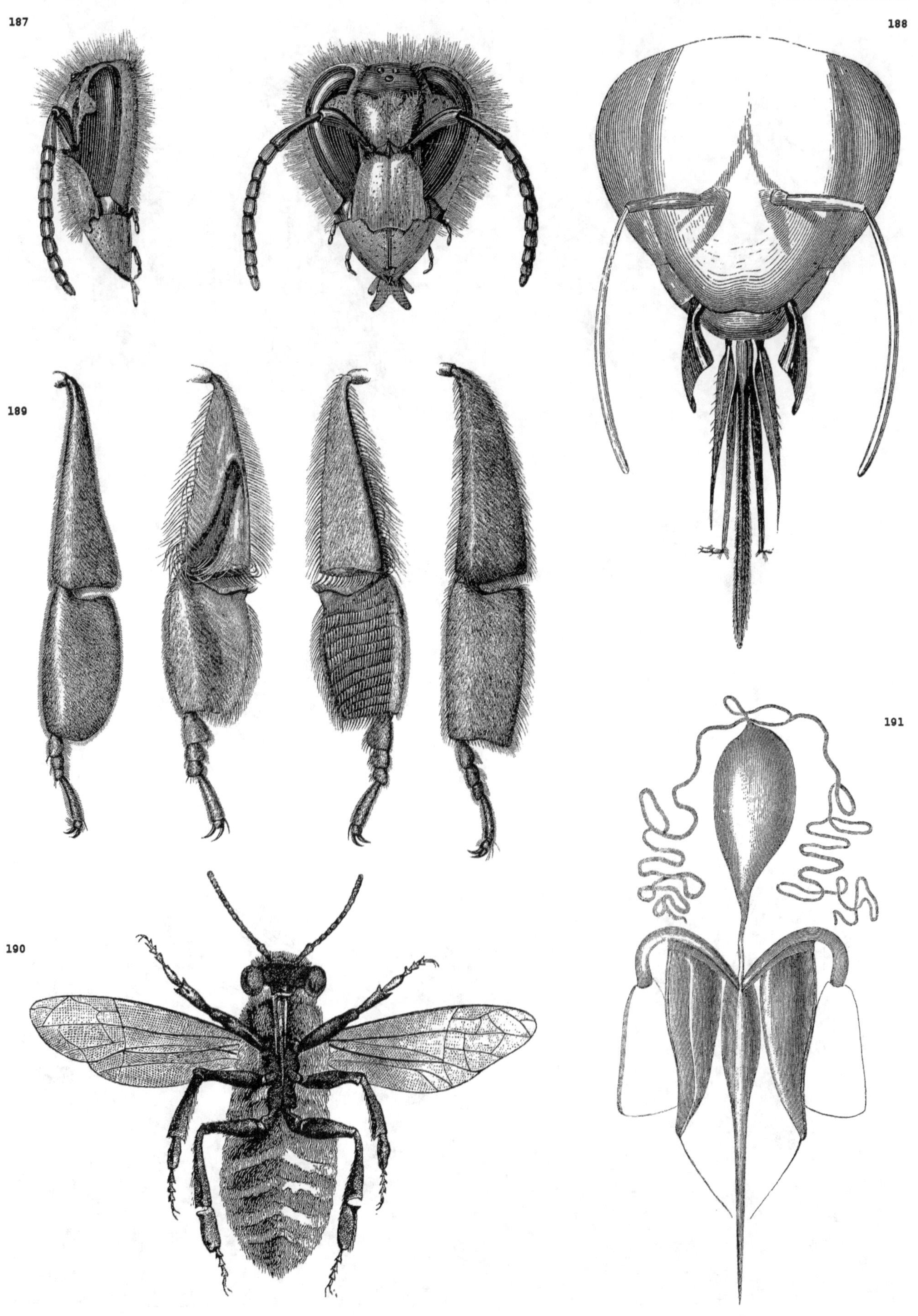

BEES, WASPS & HORNETS

192

193

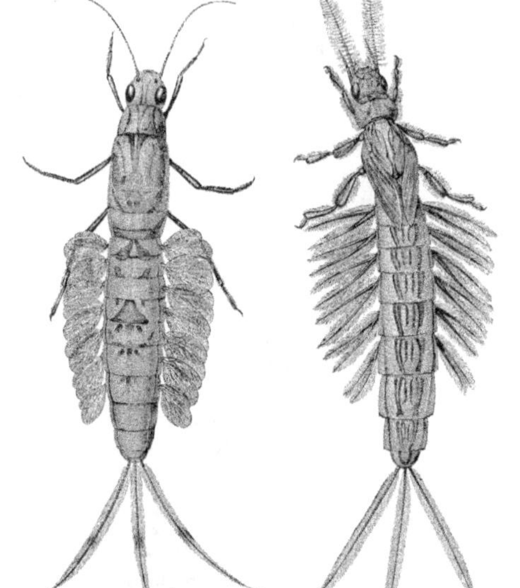

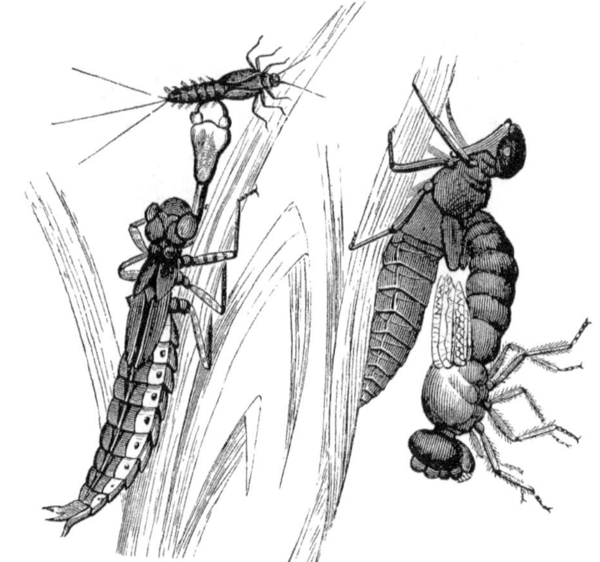

194

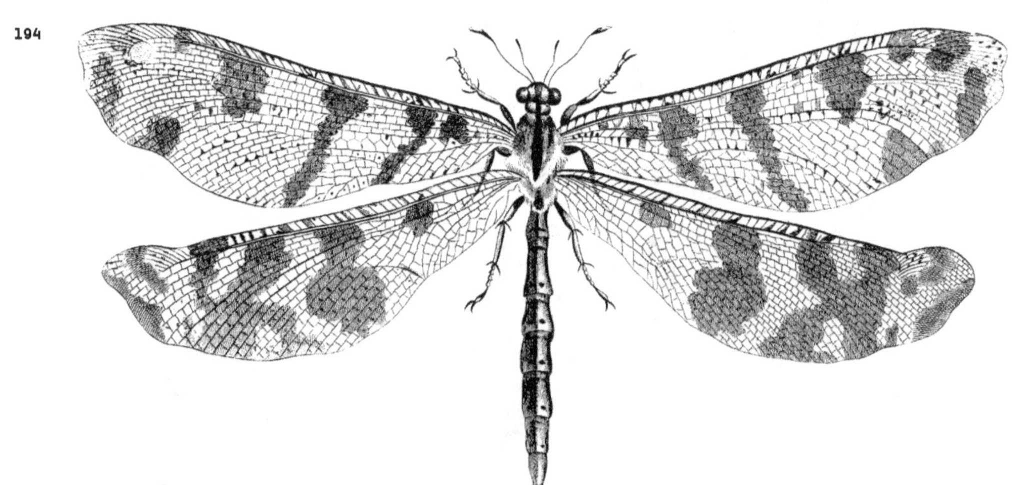

INSECTS

195

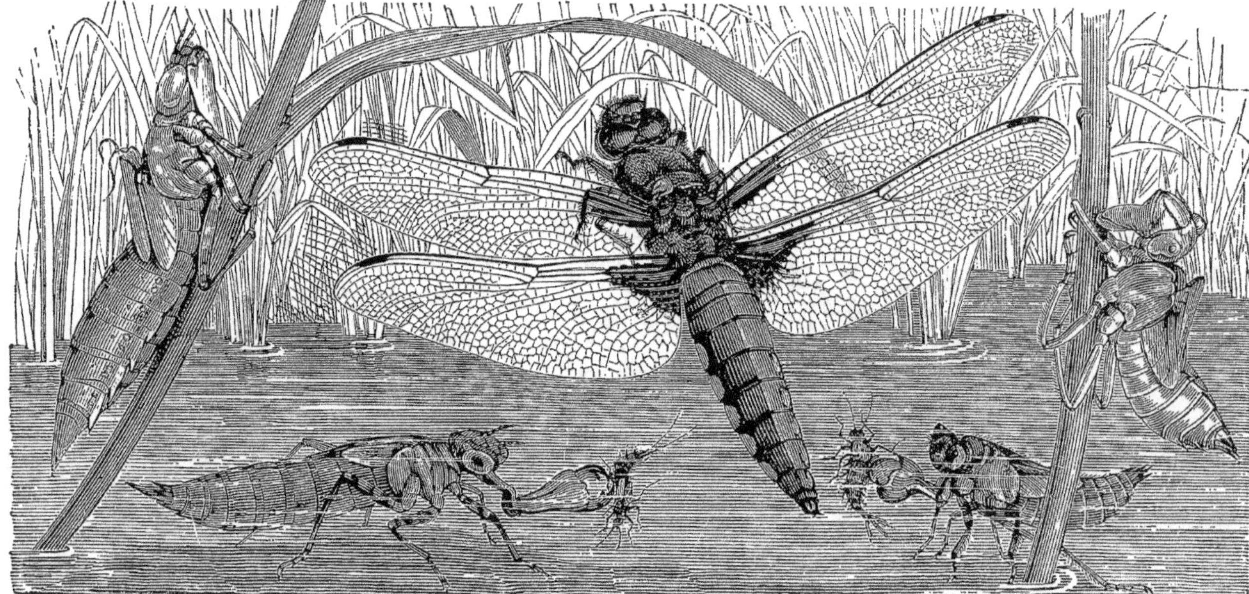

196

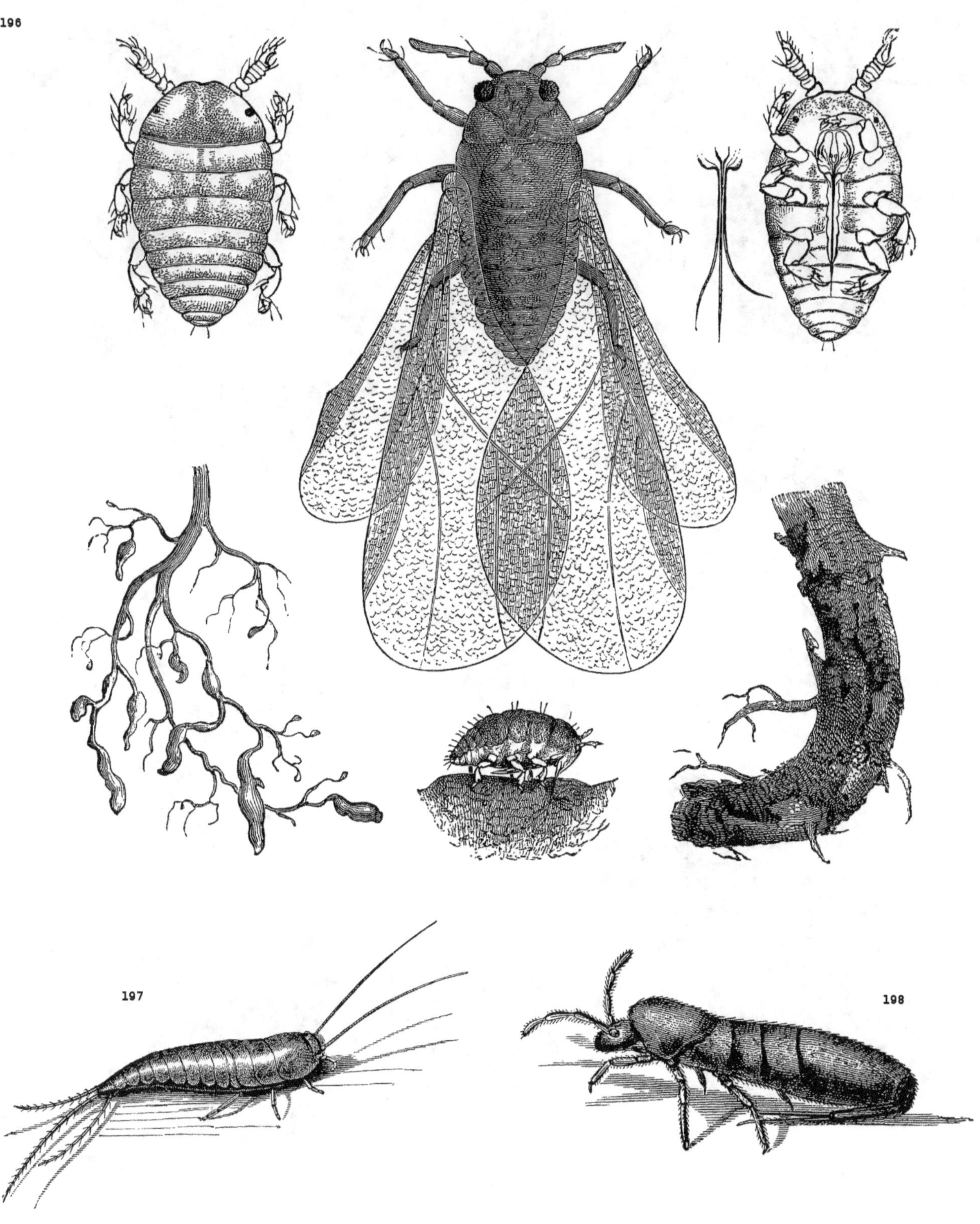

197

198

INSECTS

INSECTS

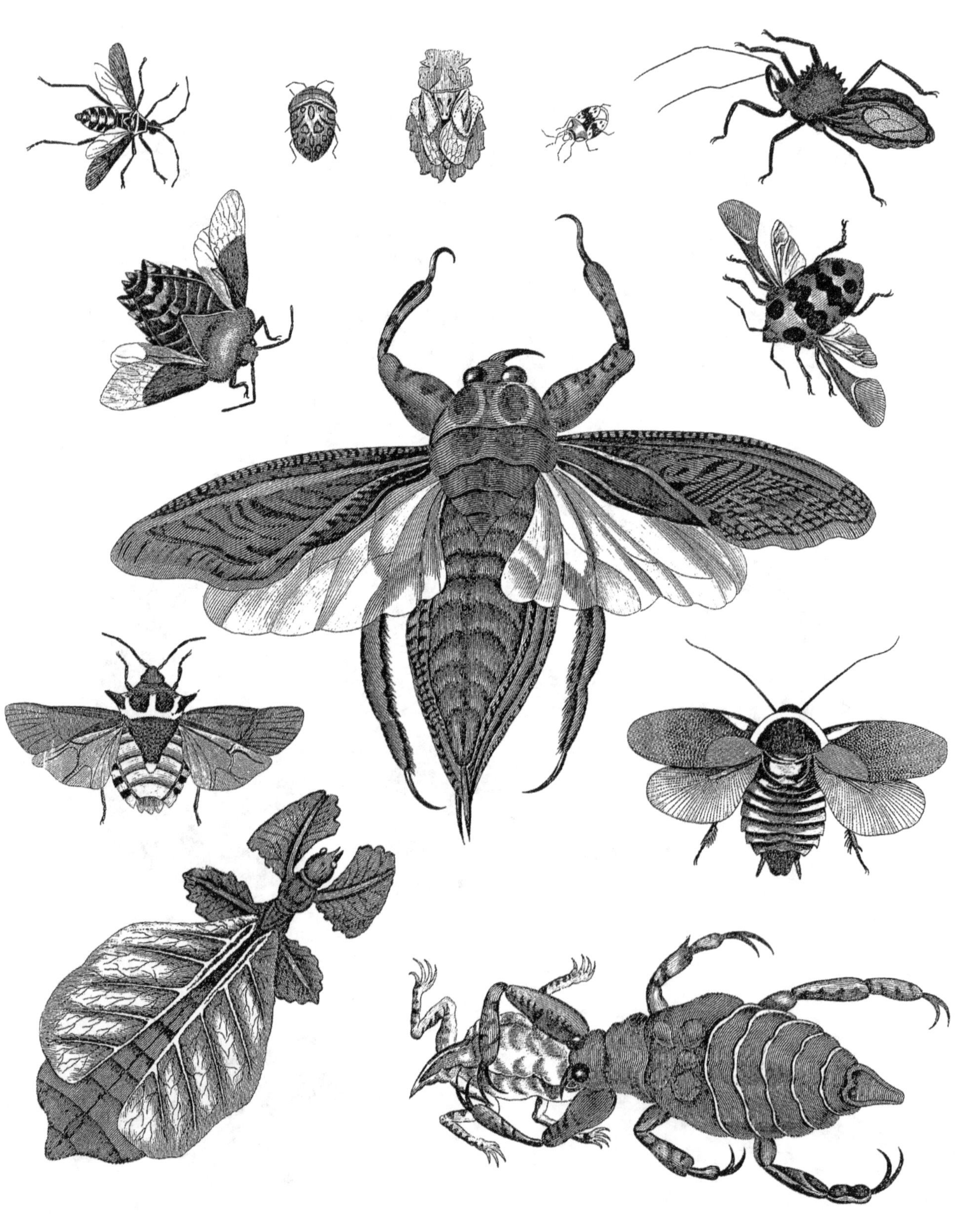

200

201

202

203

204

205

206

INSECTS

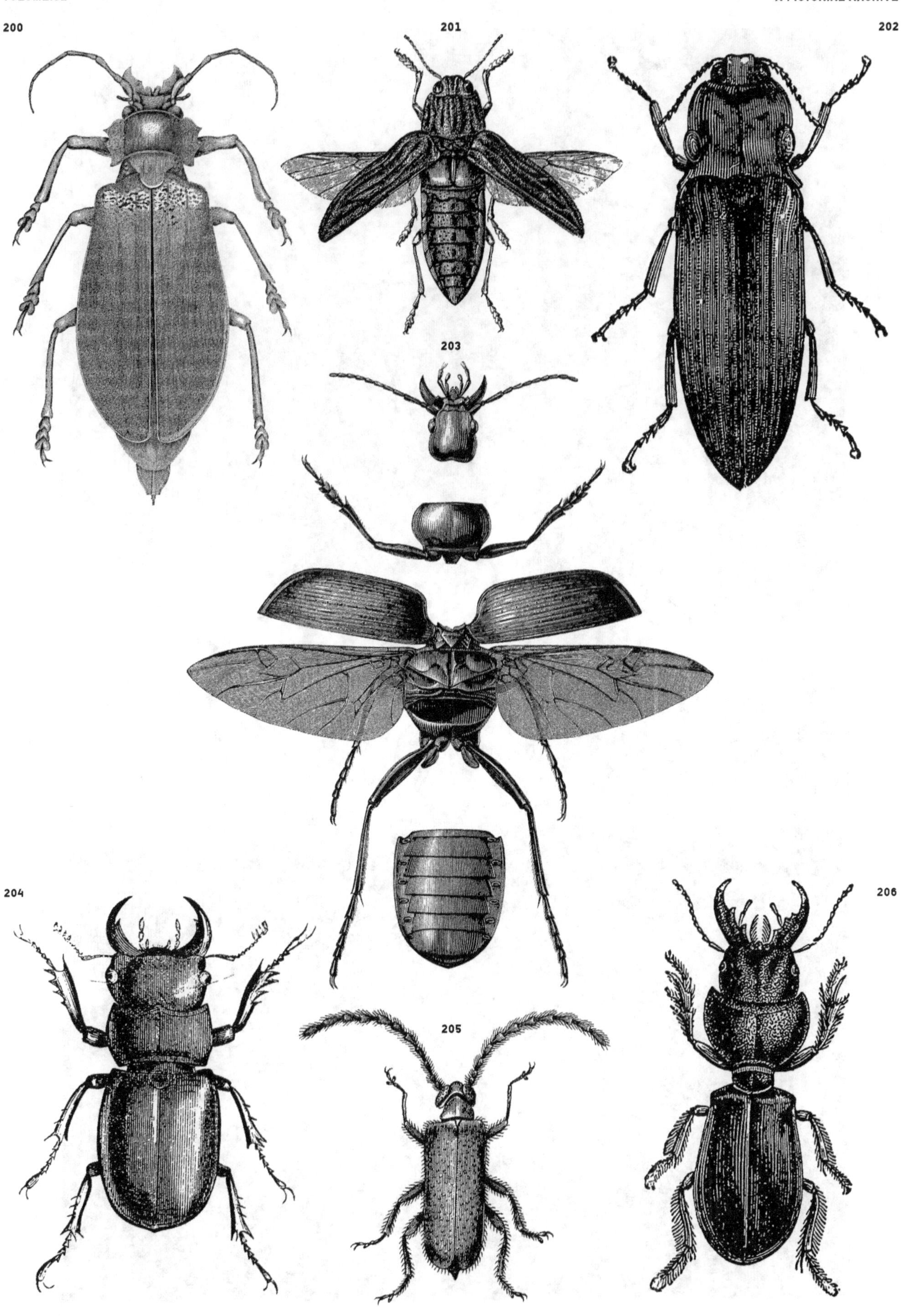

BEETLES

207

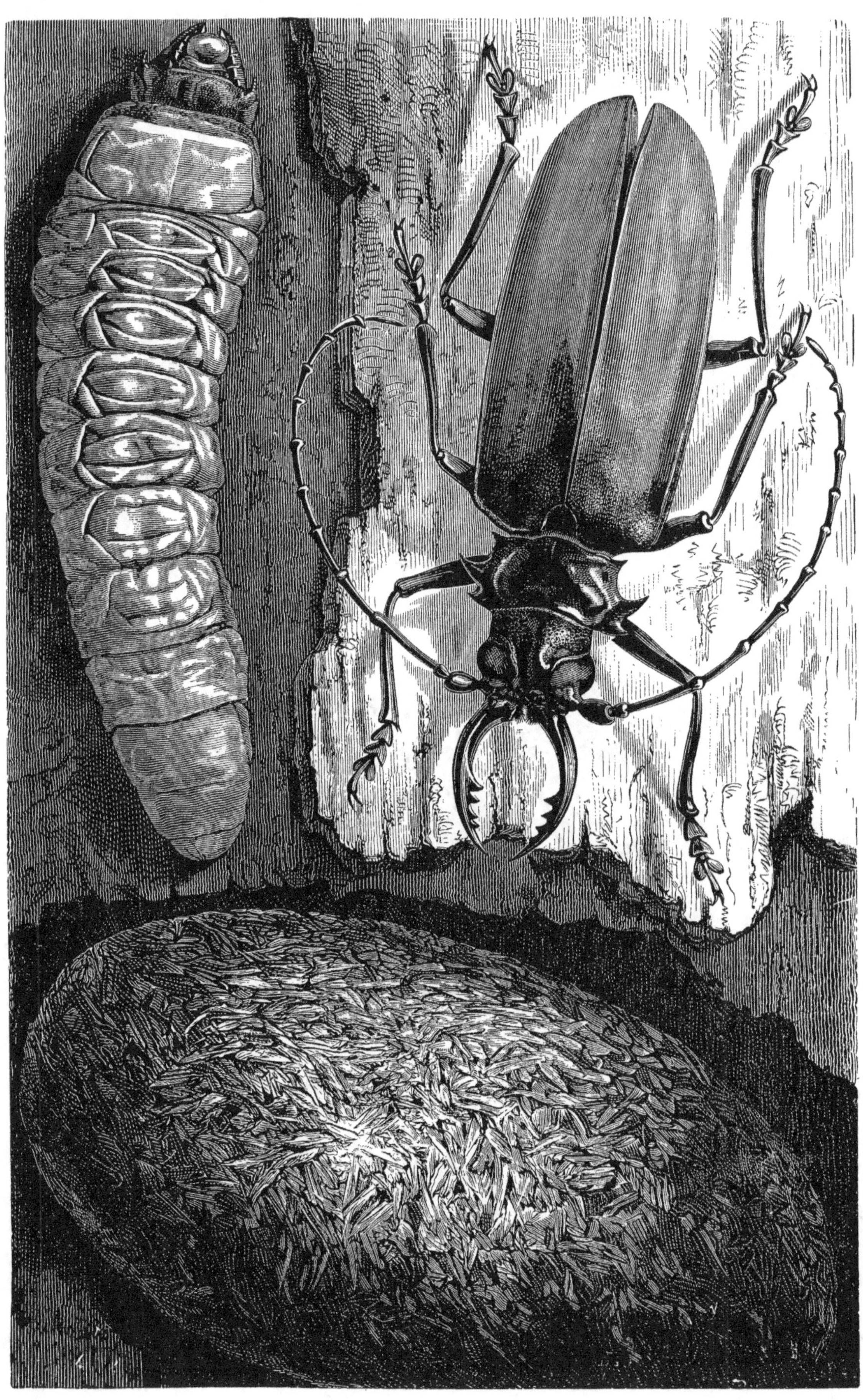

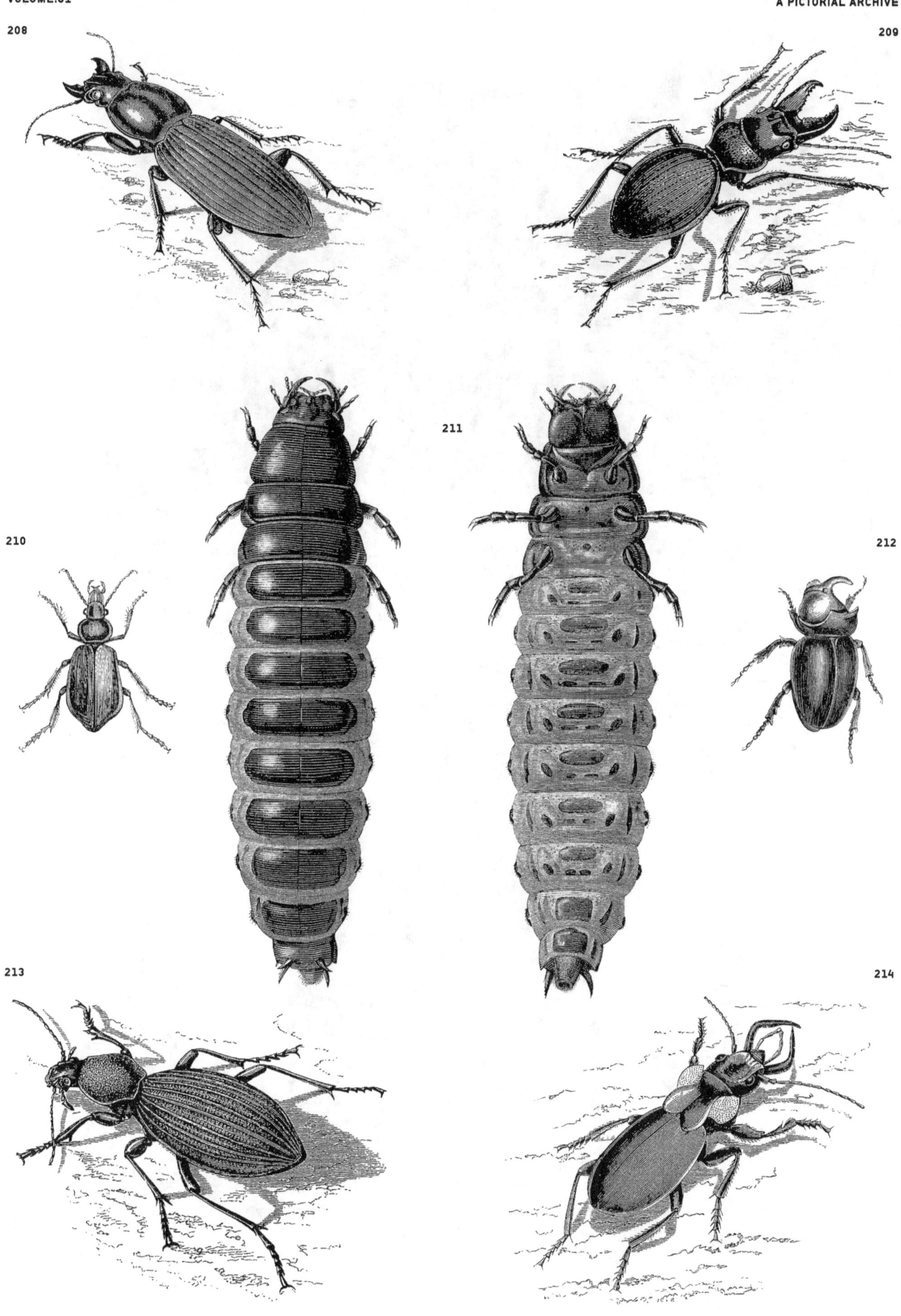

INSECTS

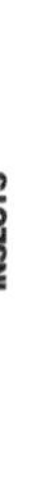

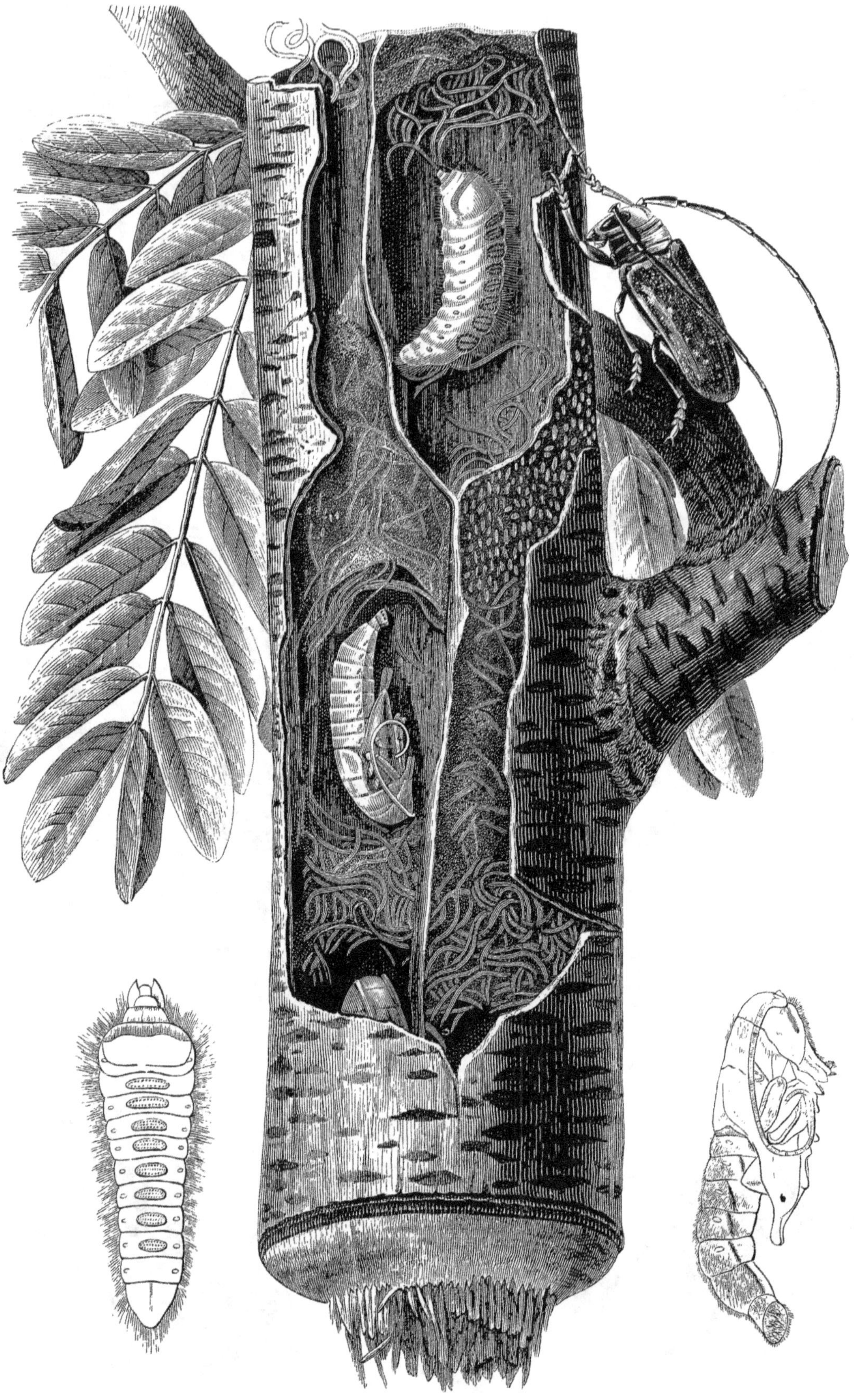

216

217

218

219

220

221

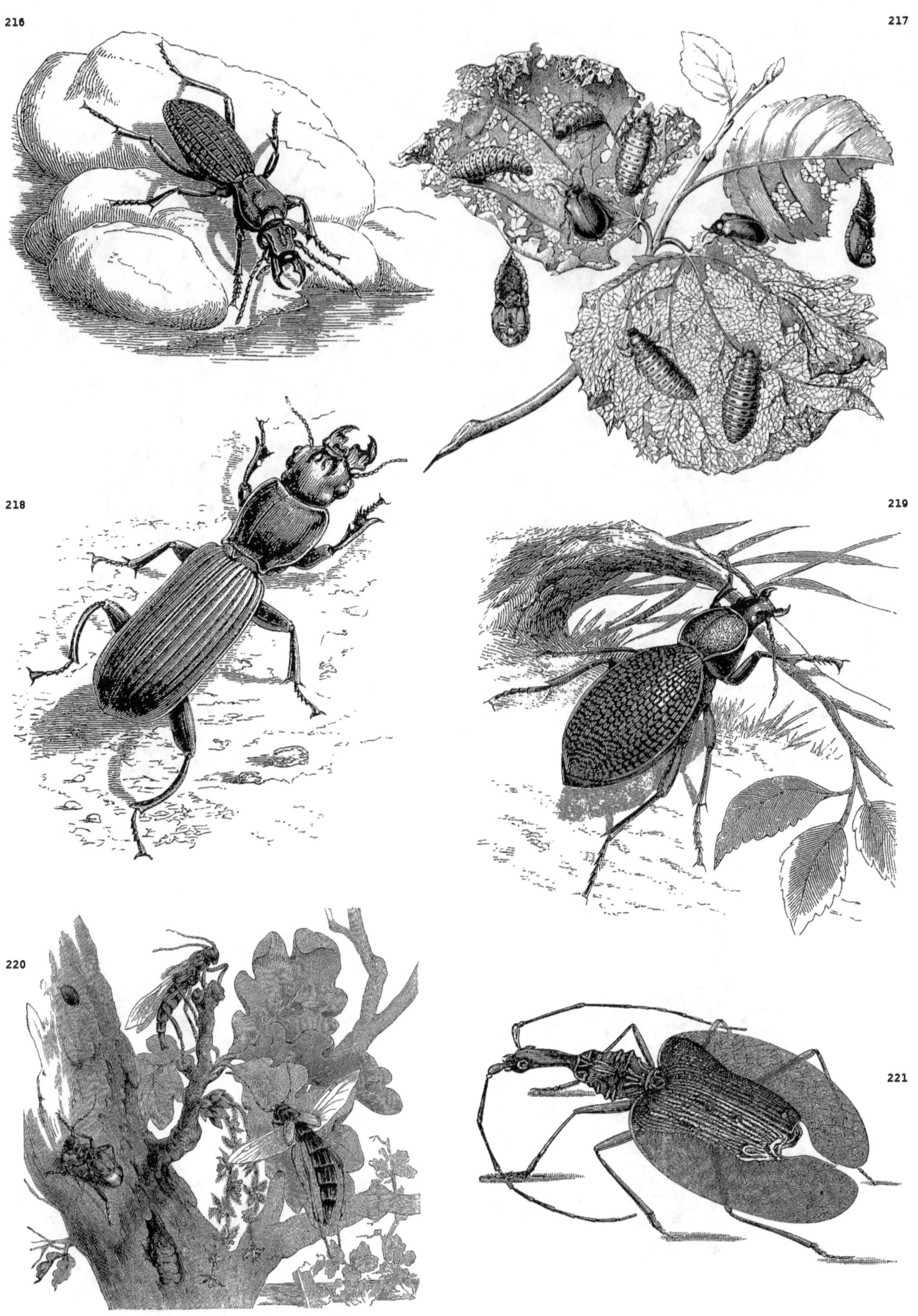

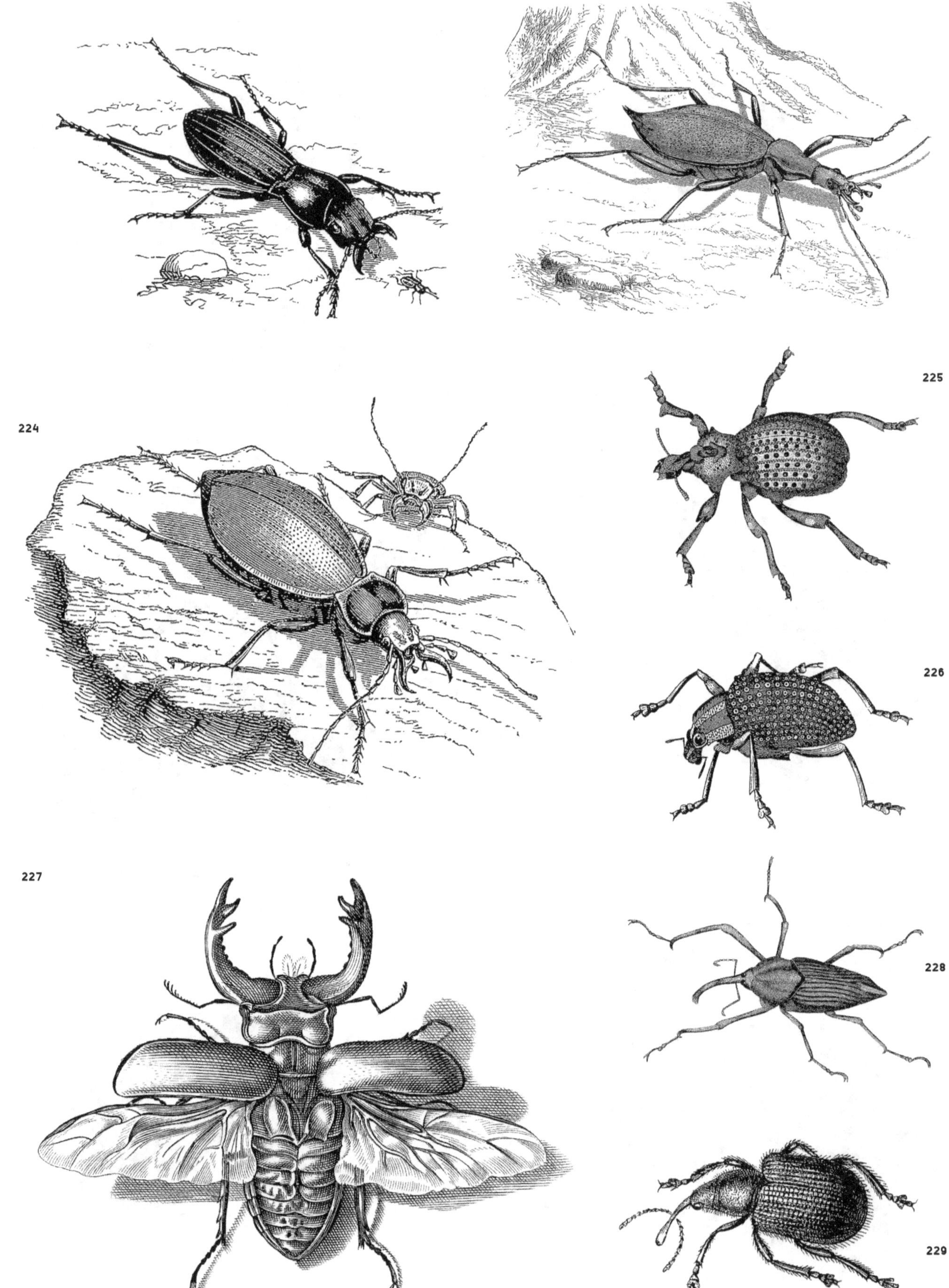

222

223

224

225

226

227

228

229

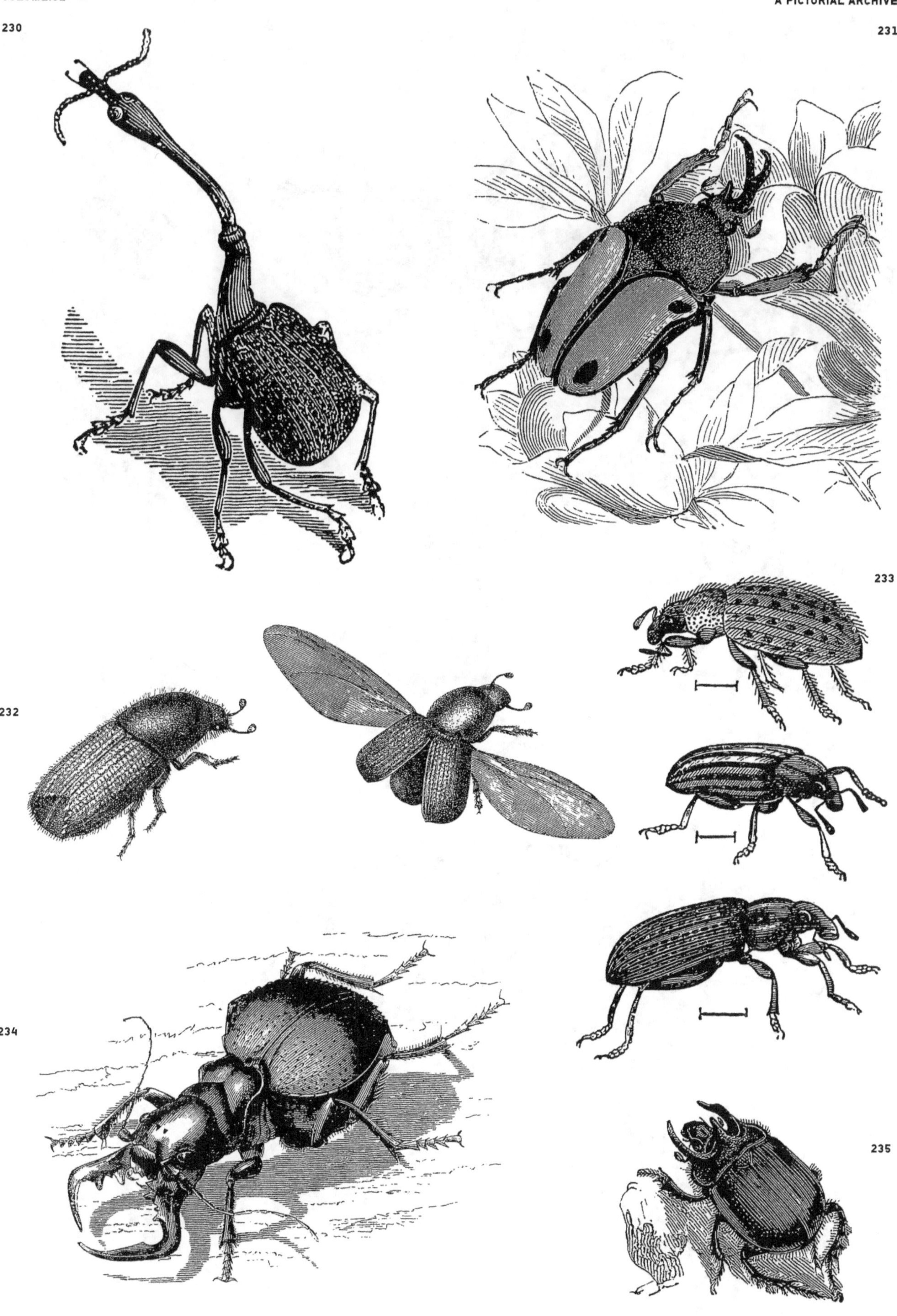

230
231
232
233
234
235
INSECTS

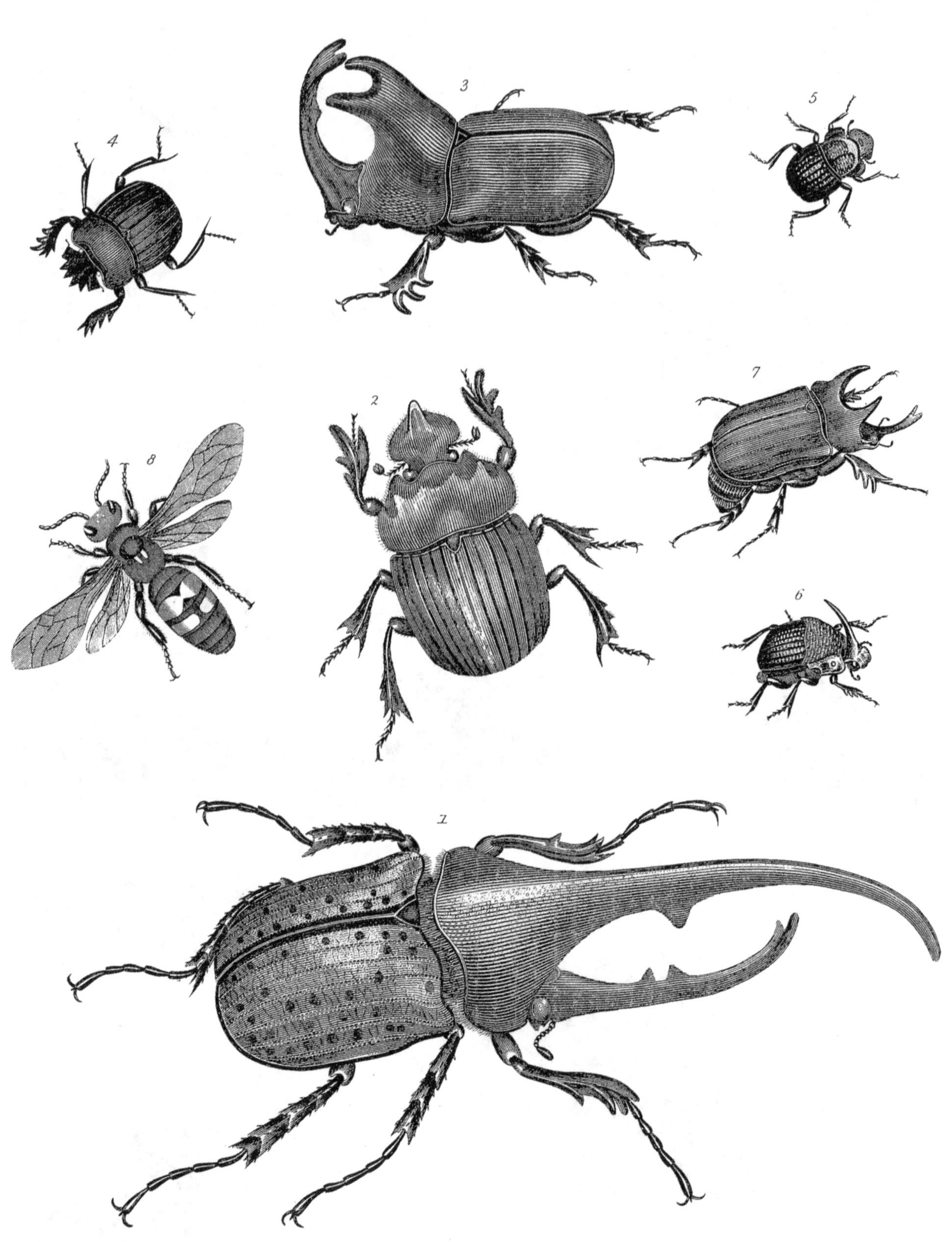

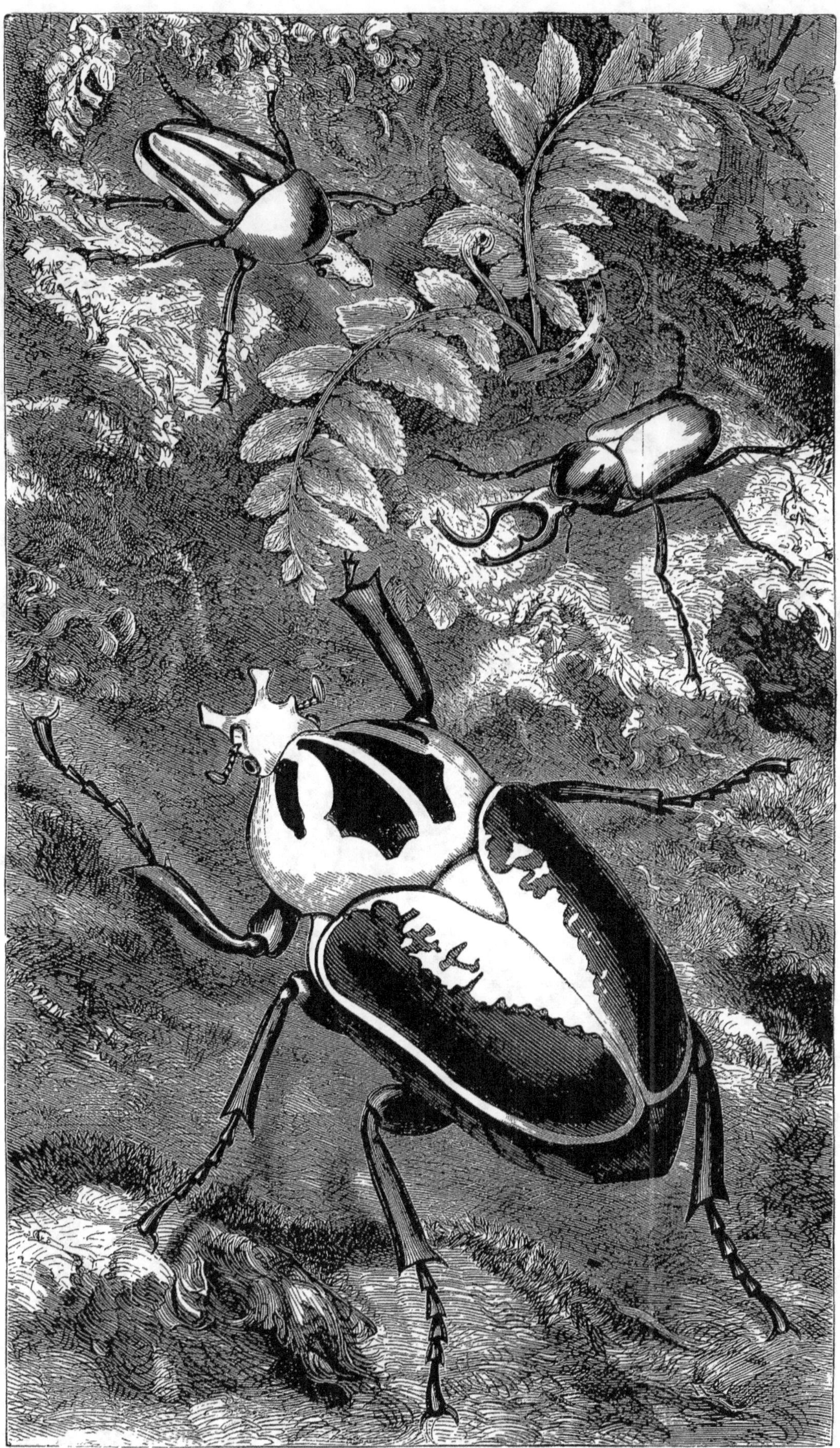

INSECTS

238

239

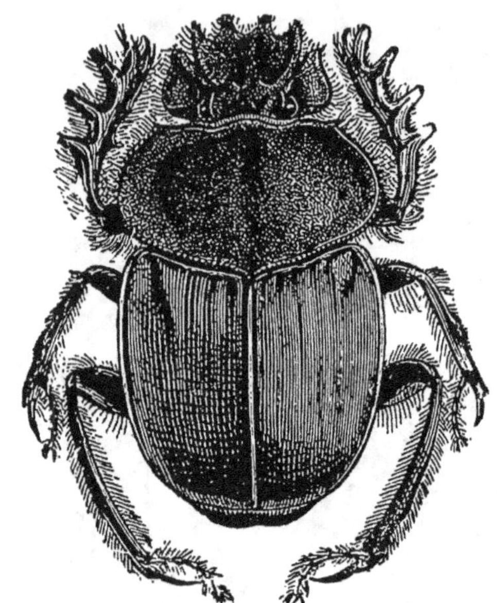

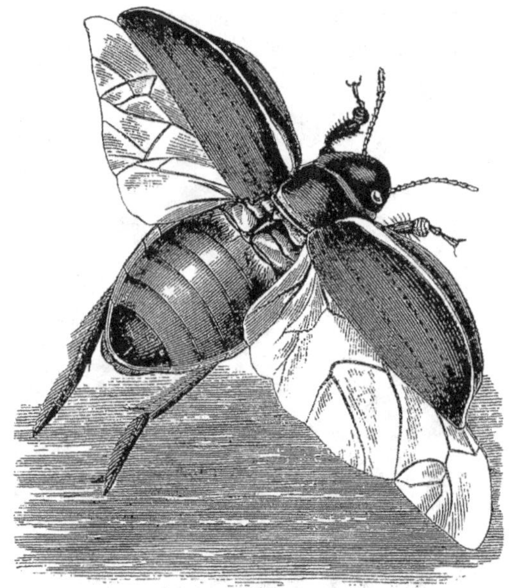

240

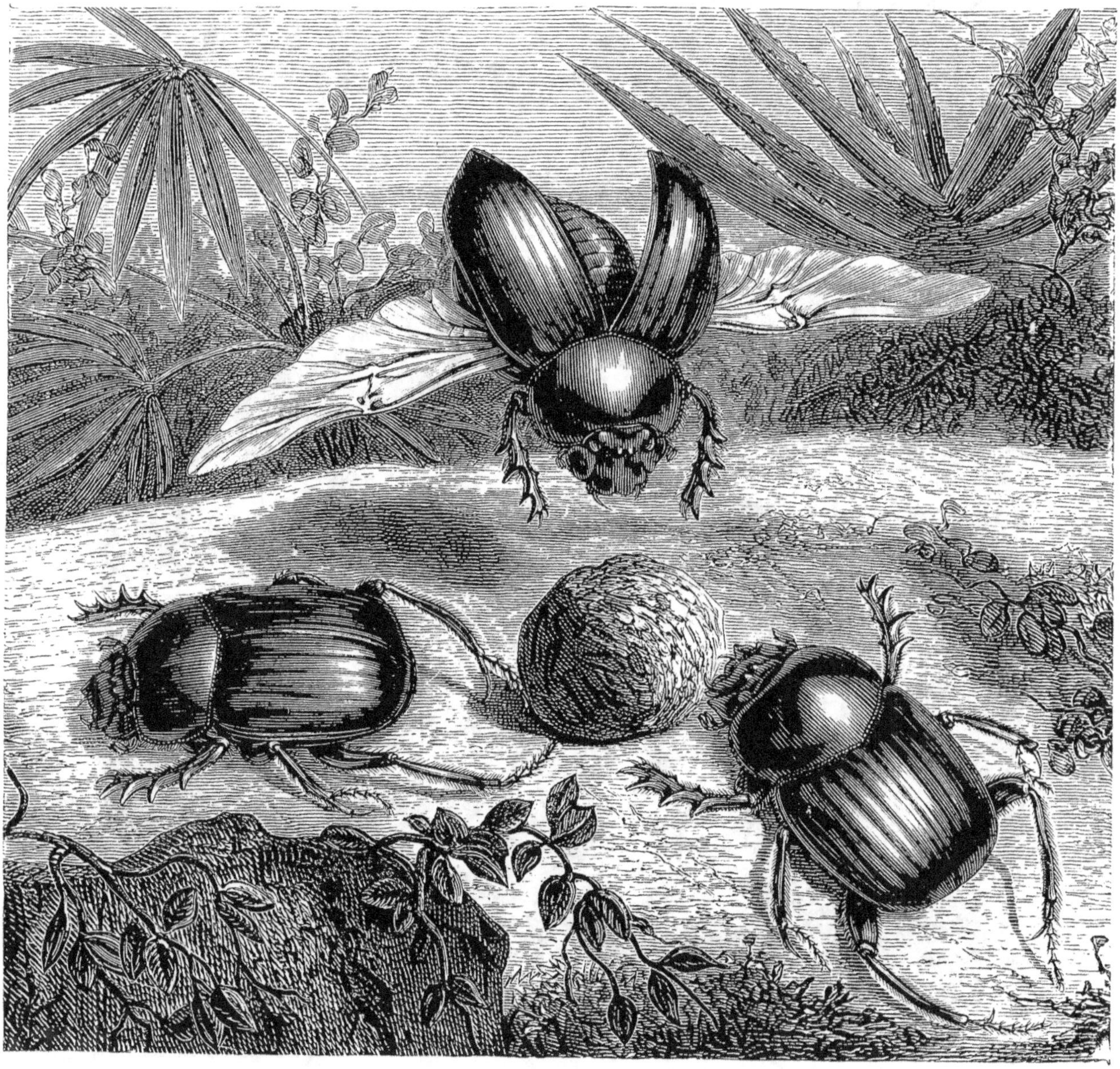

BEETLES

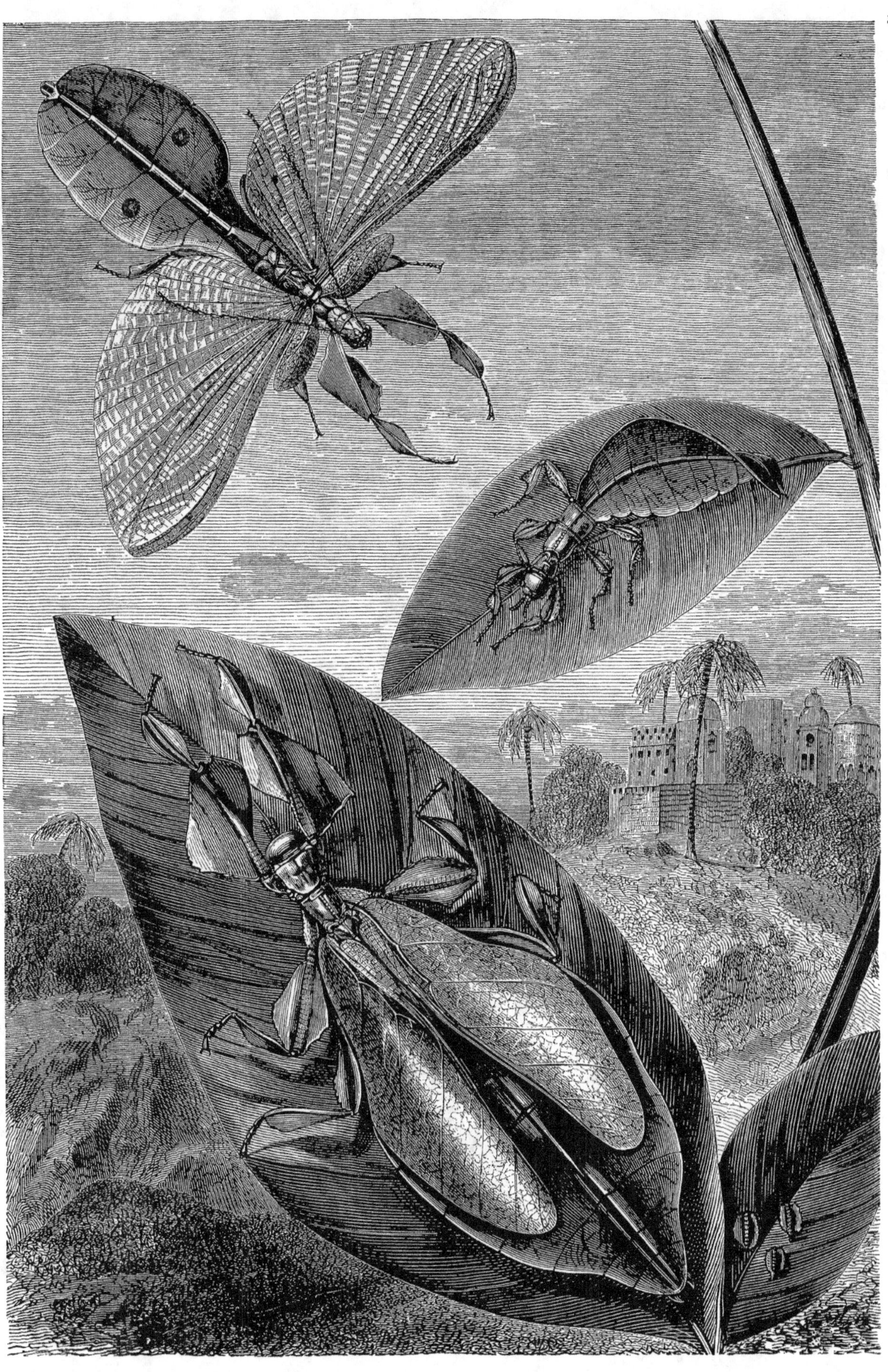

INSECTS

BEETLES

242

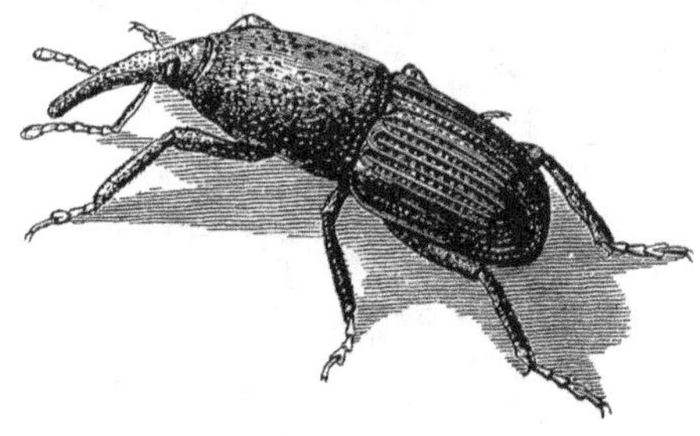

243 >

244

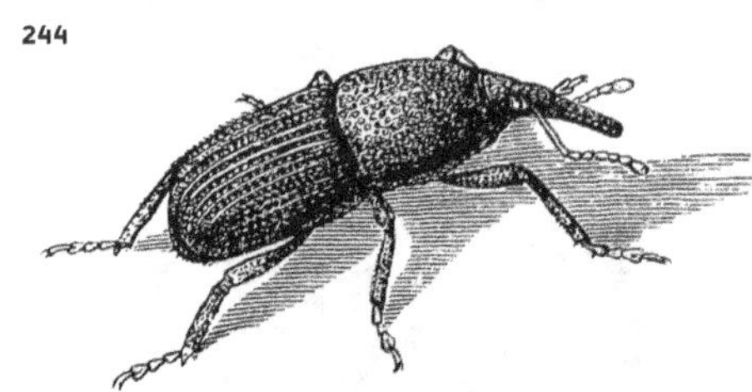

245

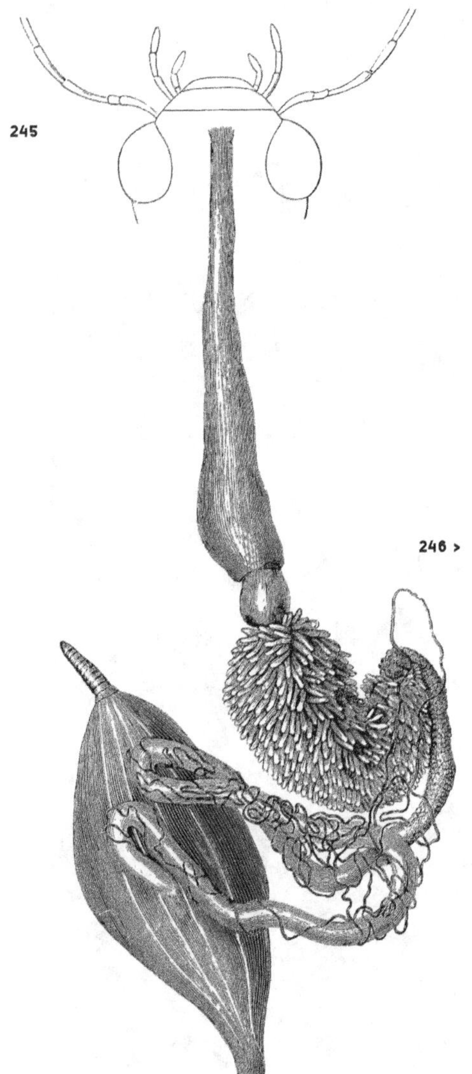

246 >

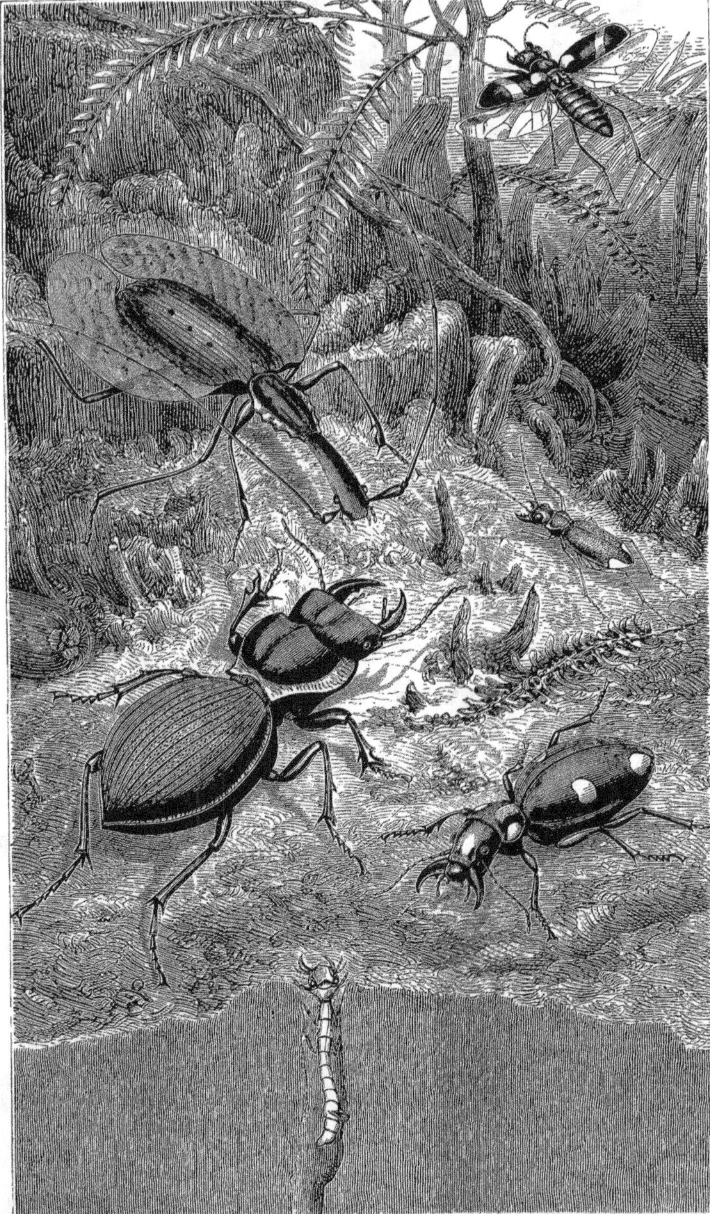

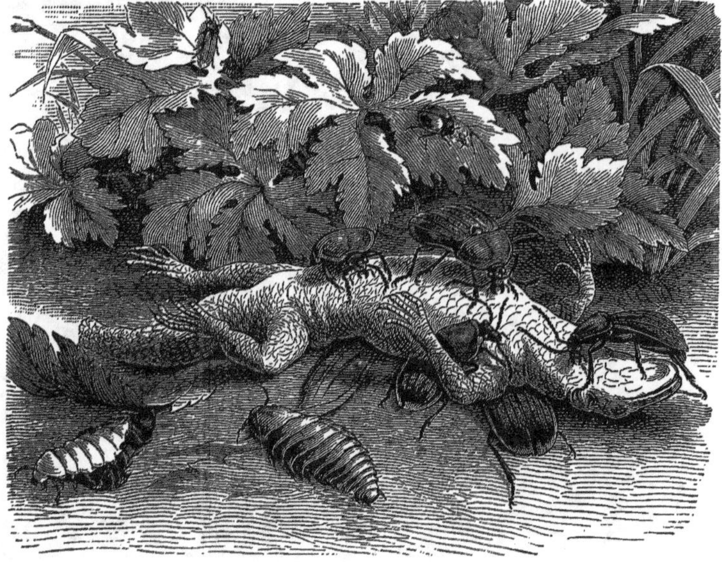

INSECTS

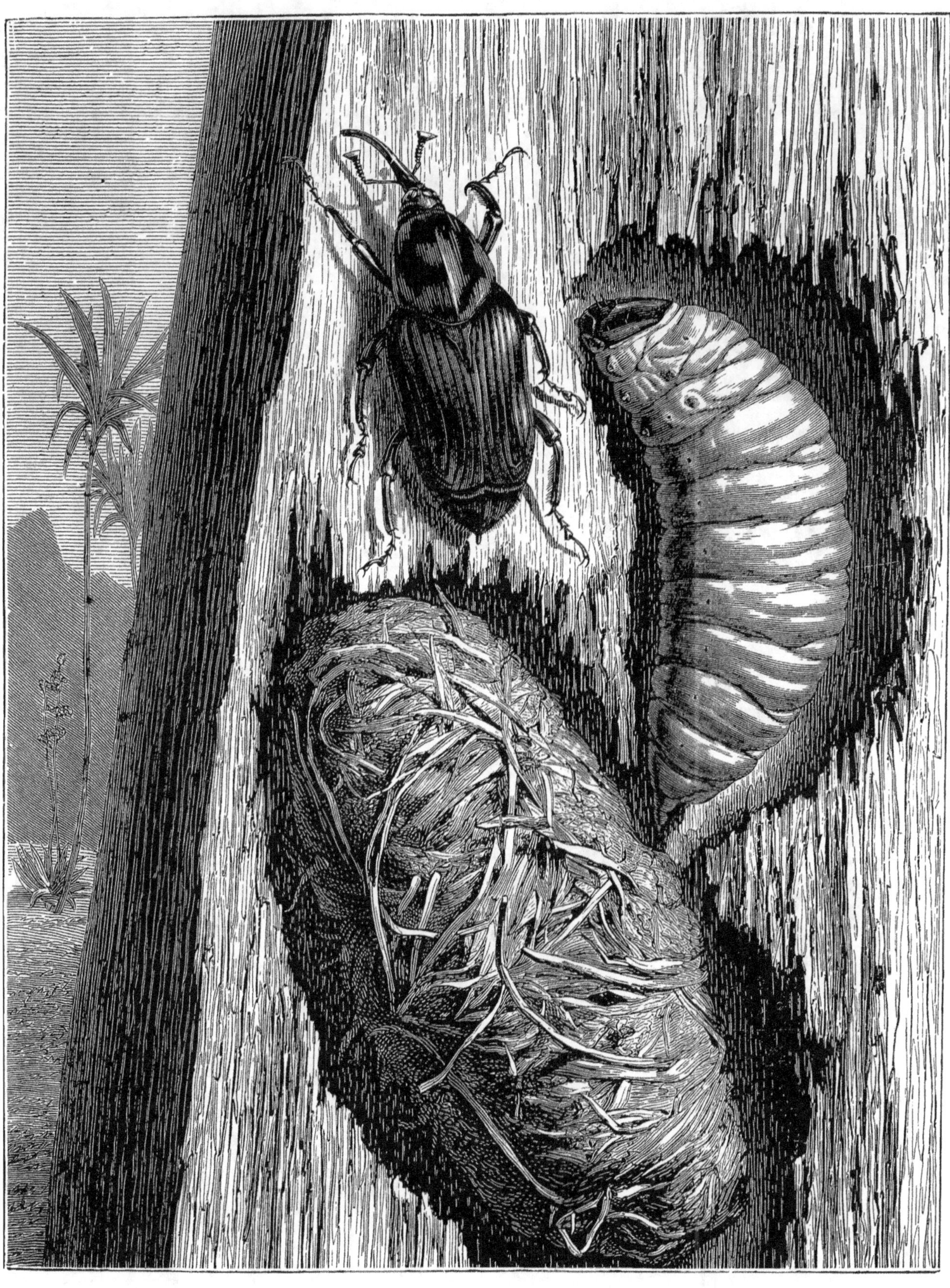

BEETLES

248
249
250
251
252
255
254
253
256
257
INSECTS

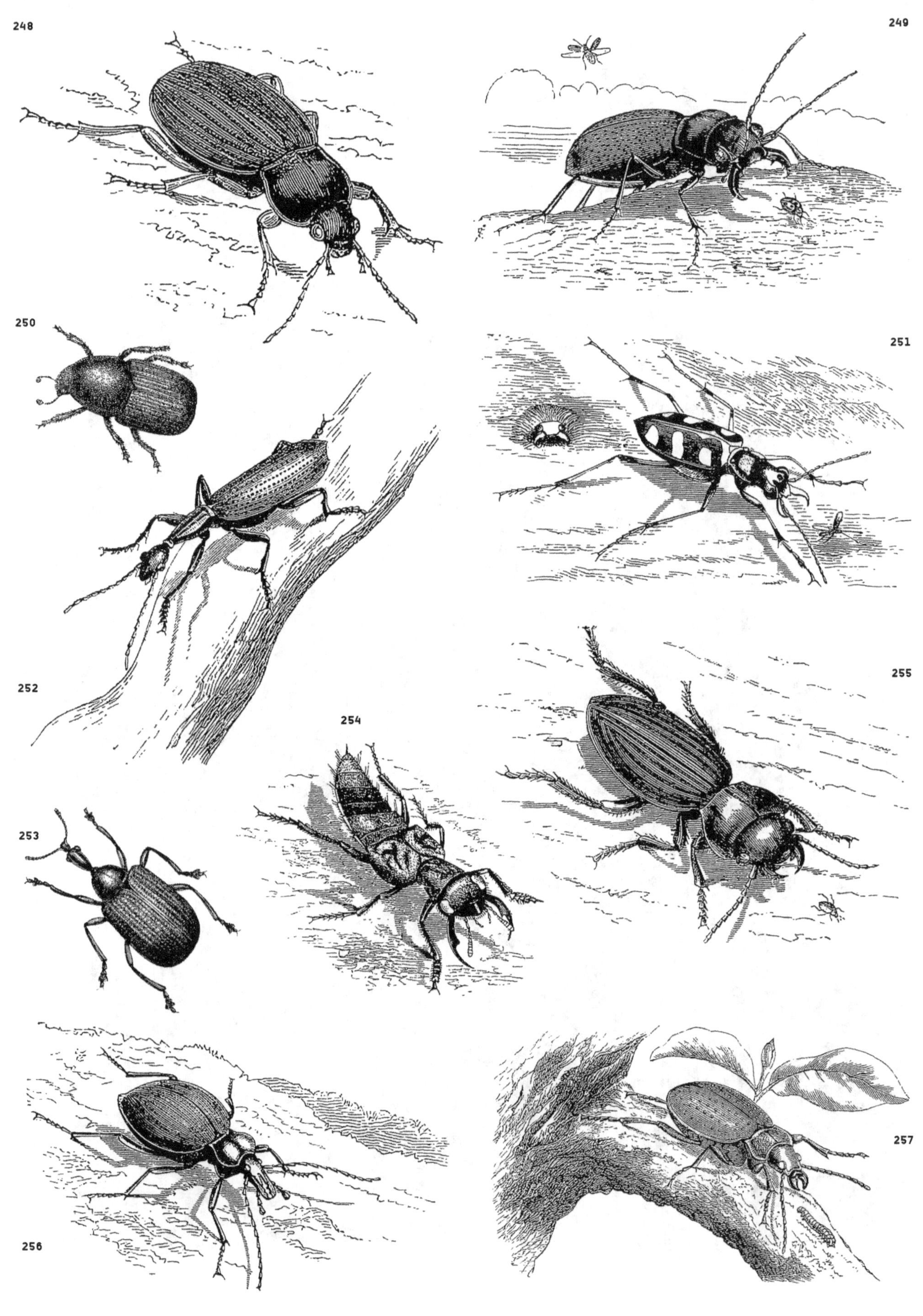

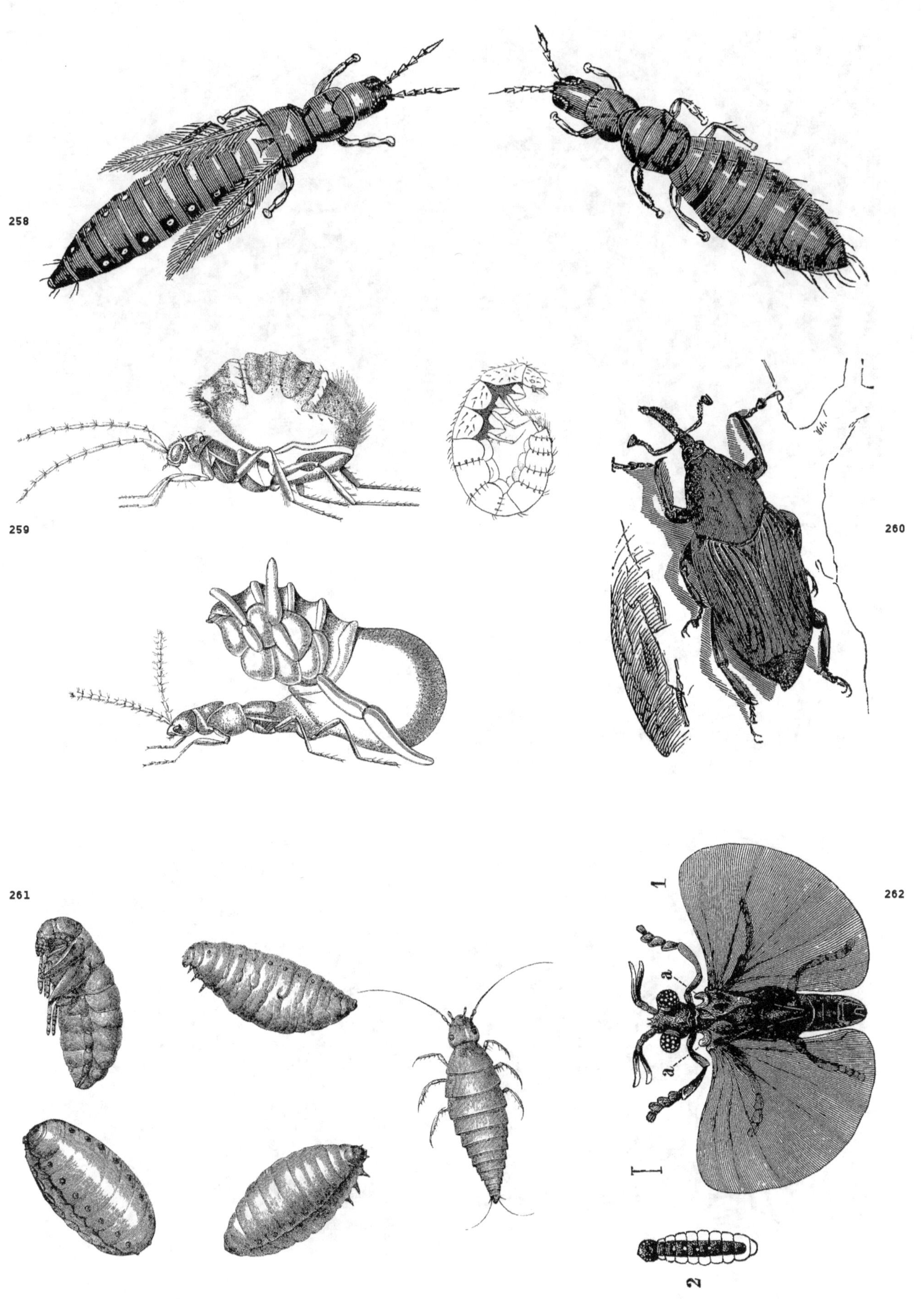

258

259

260

261

262

INSECTS

263

264

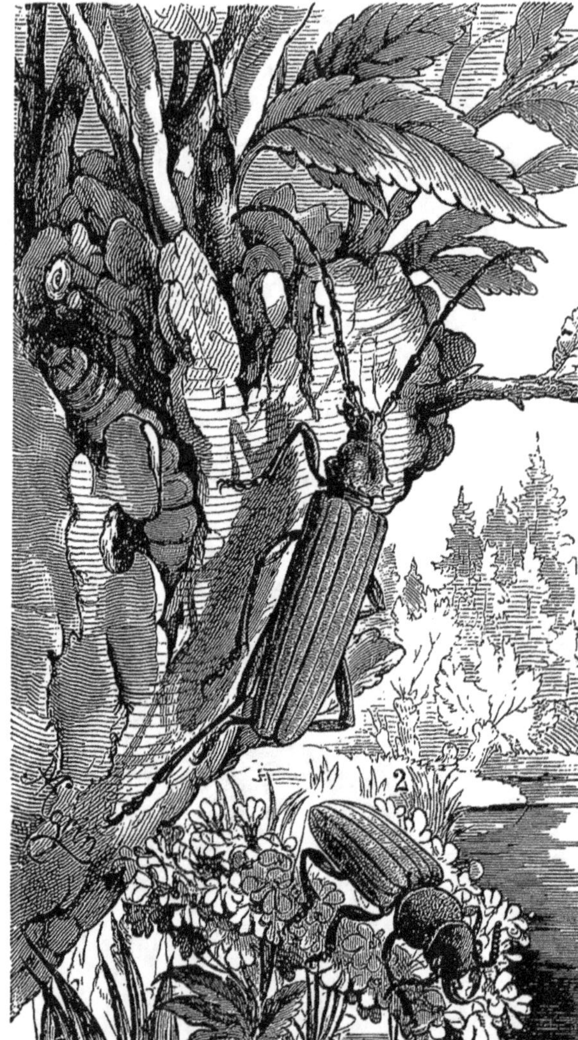

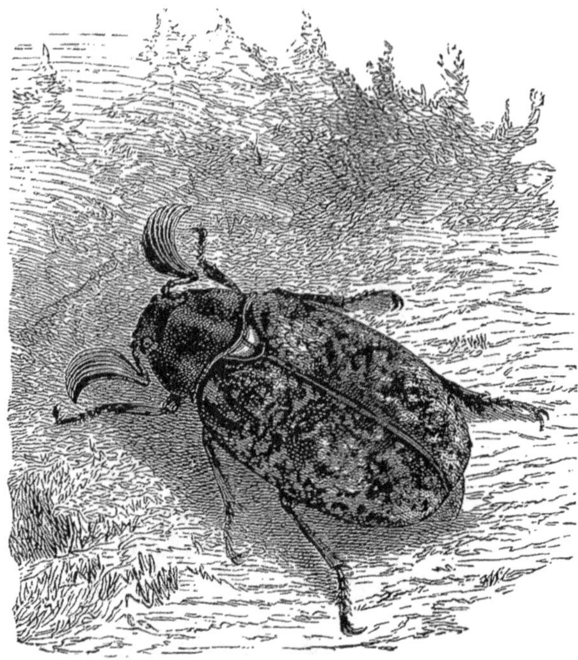

265

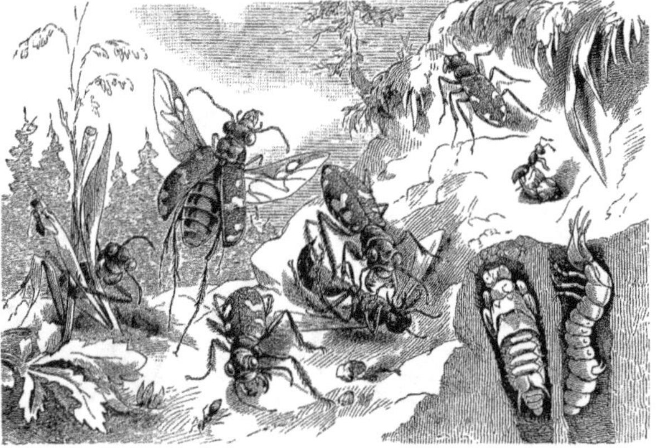

266

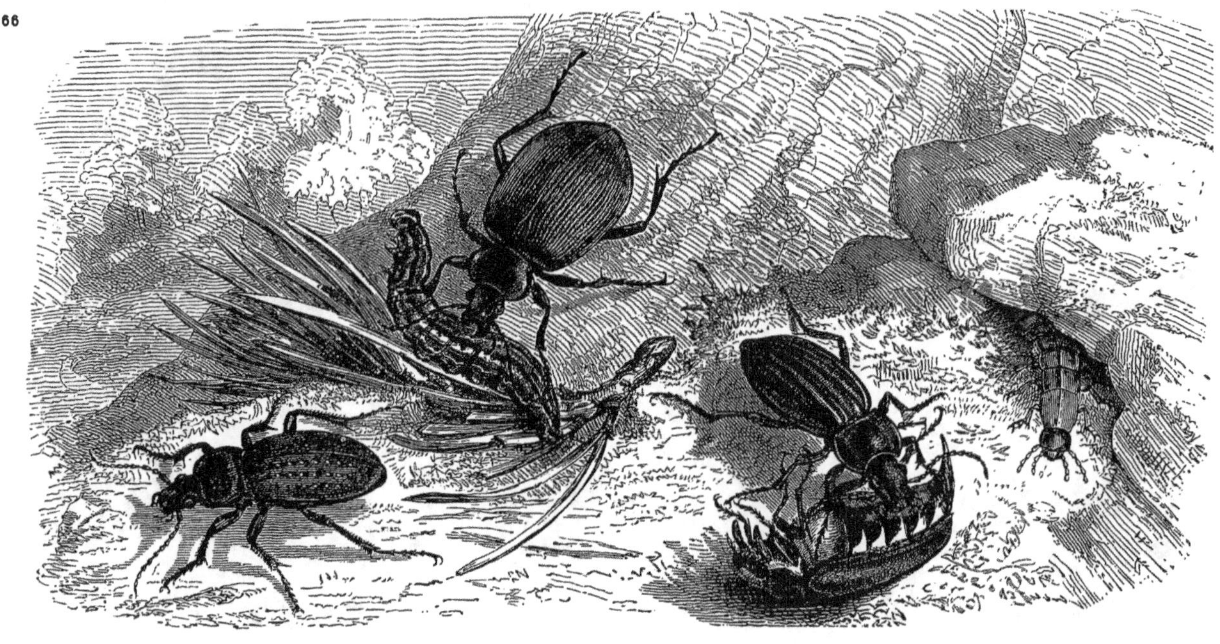

267

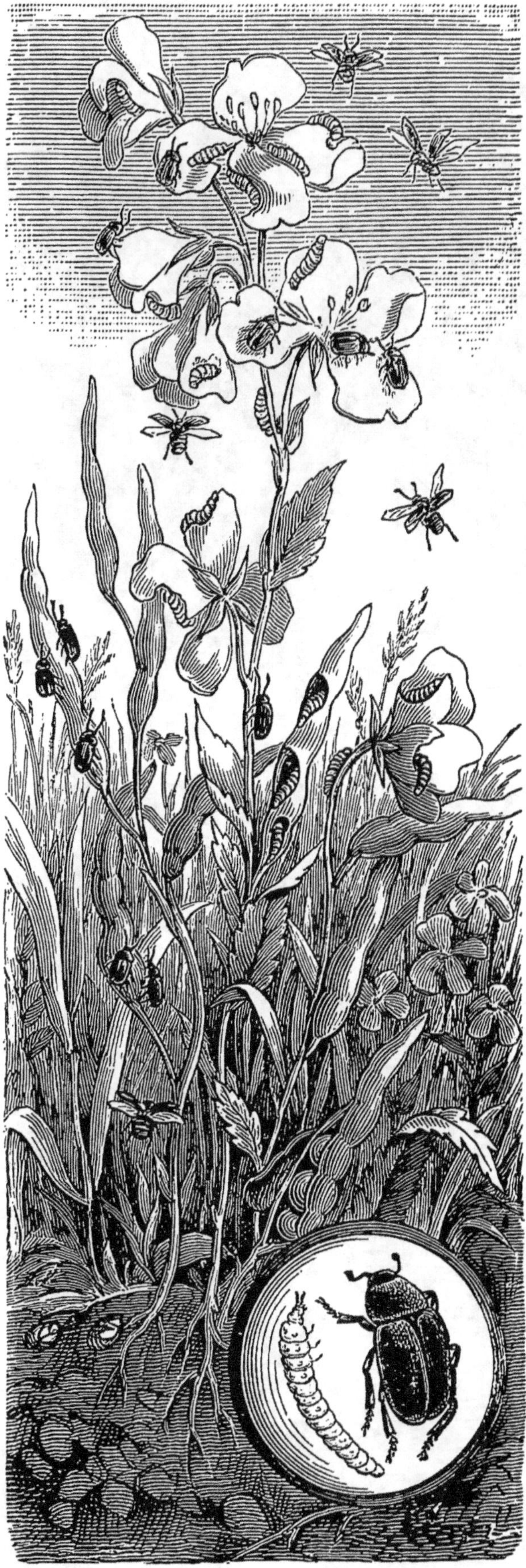

268

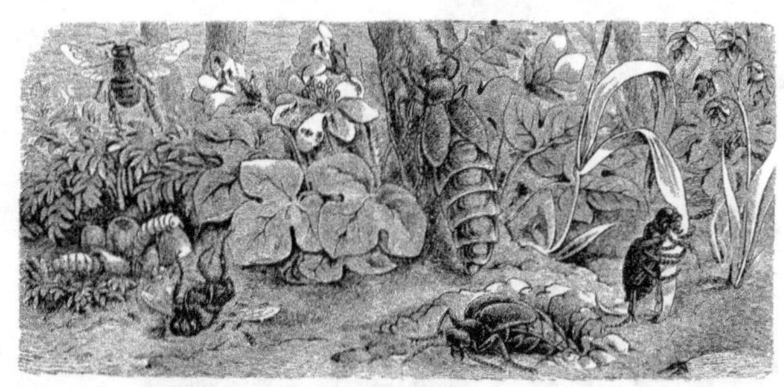

269

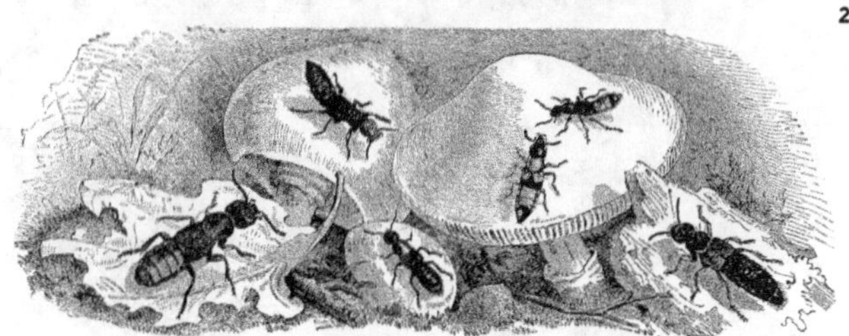

270

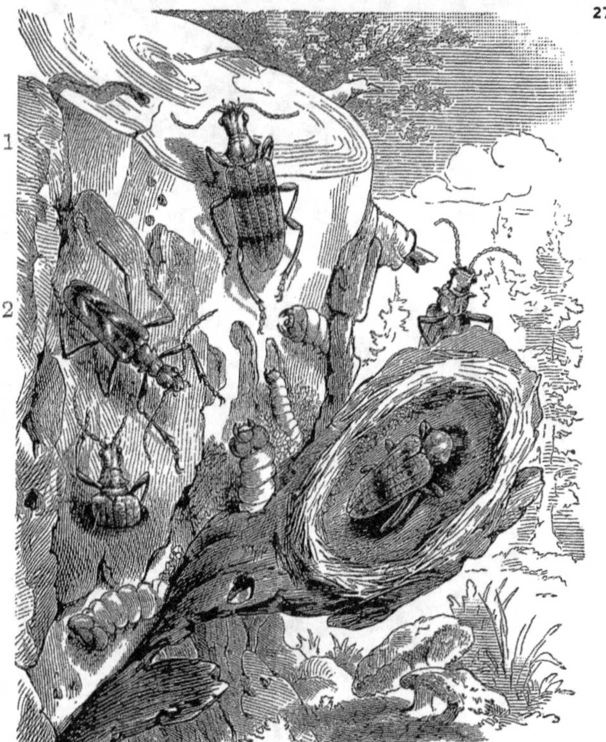

271

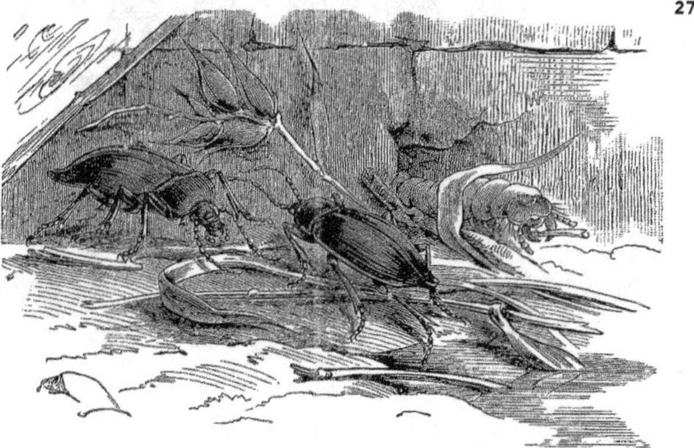

INSECTS

272

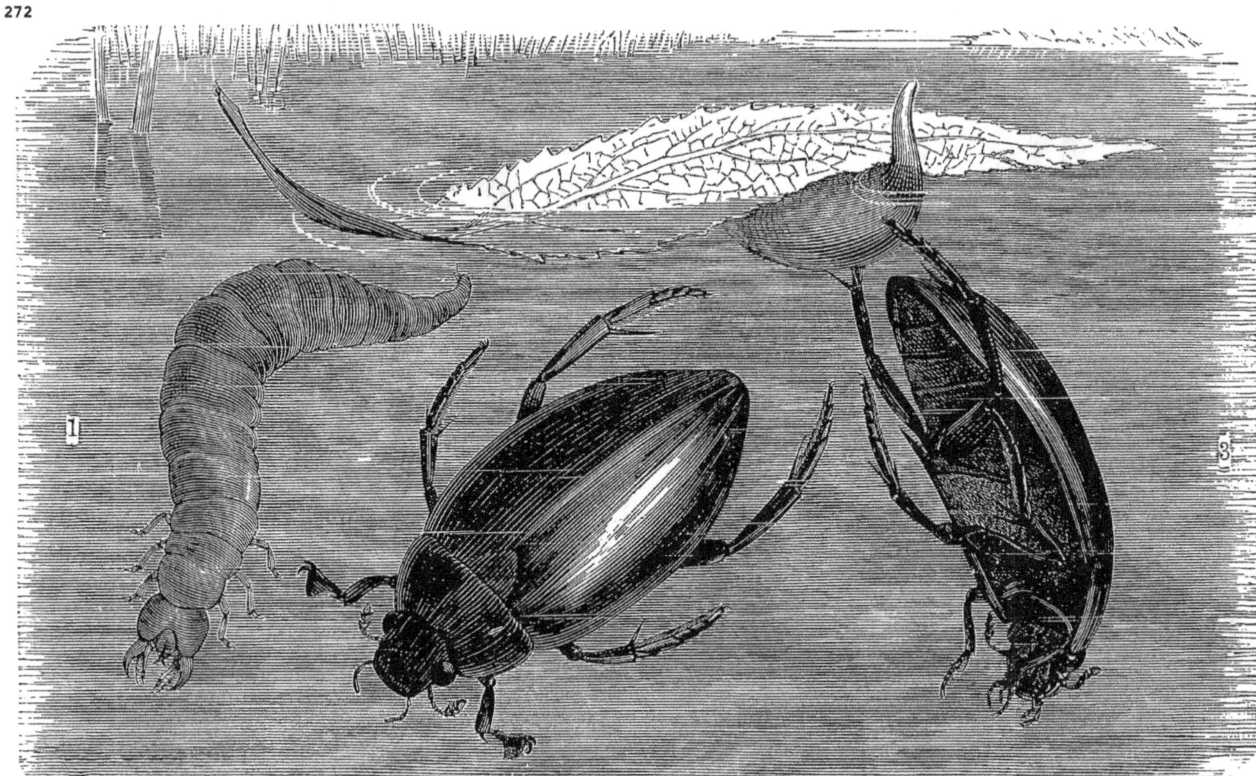

273

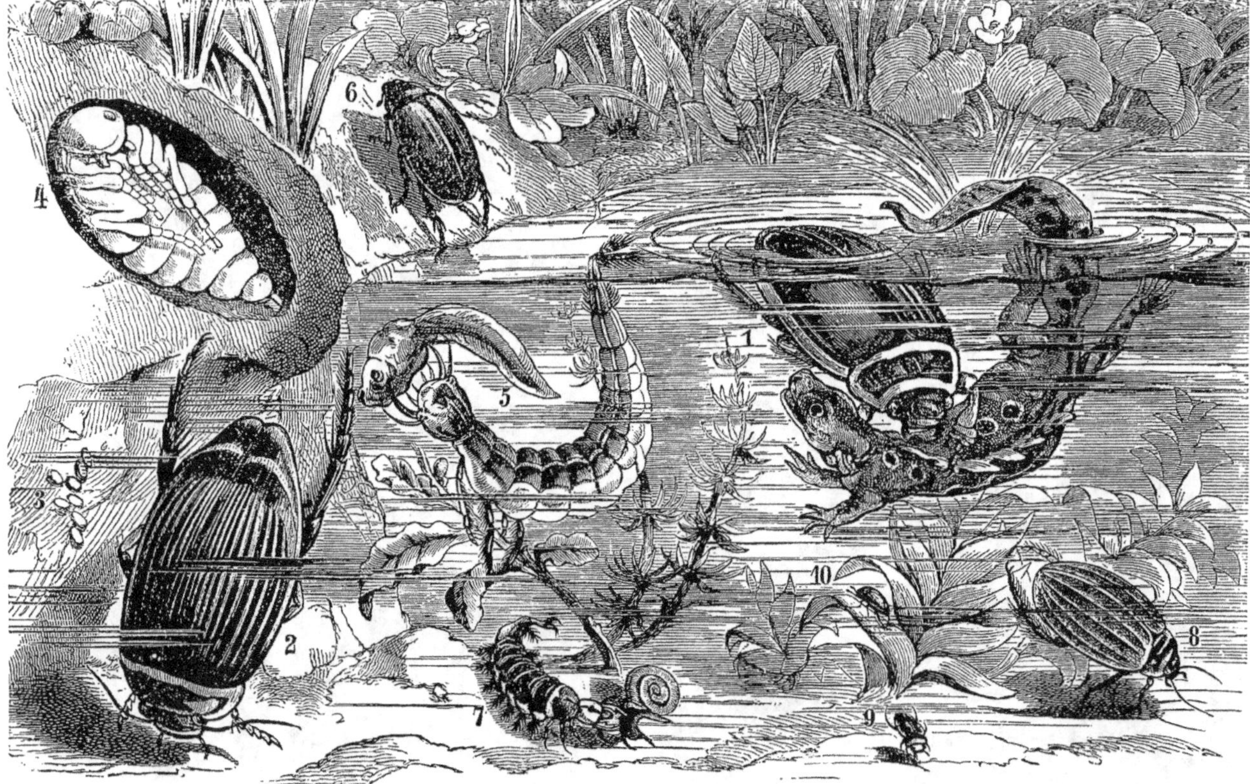

274

275

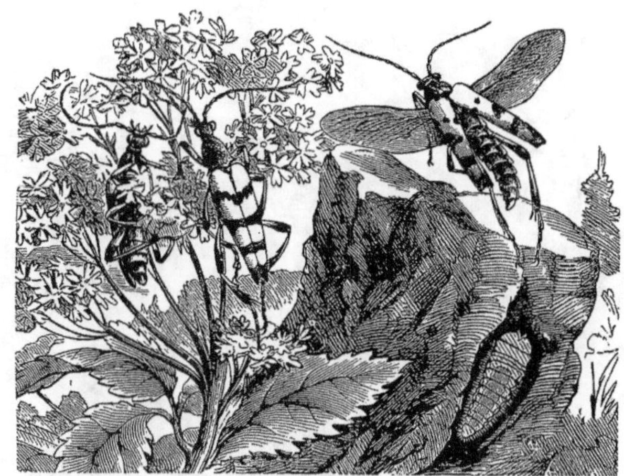

276

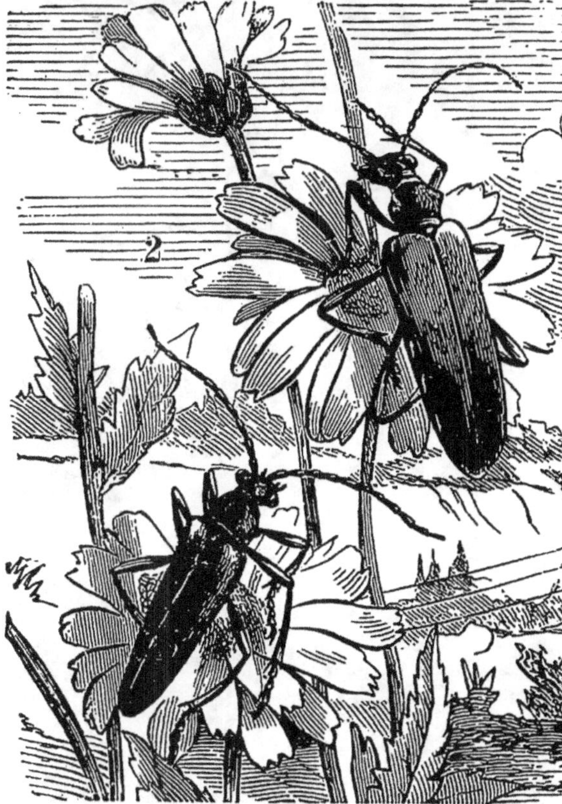

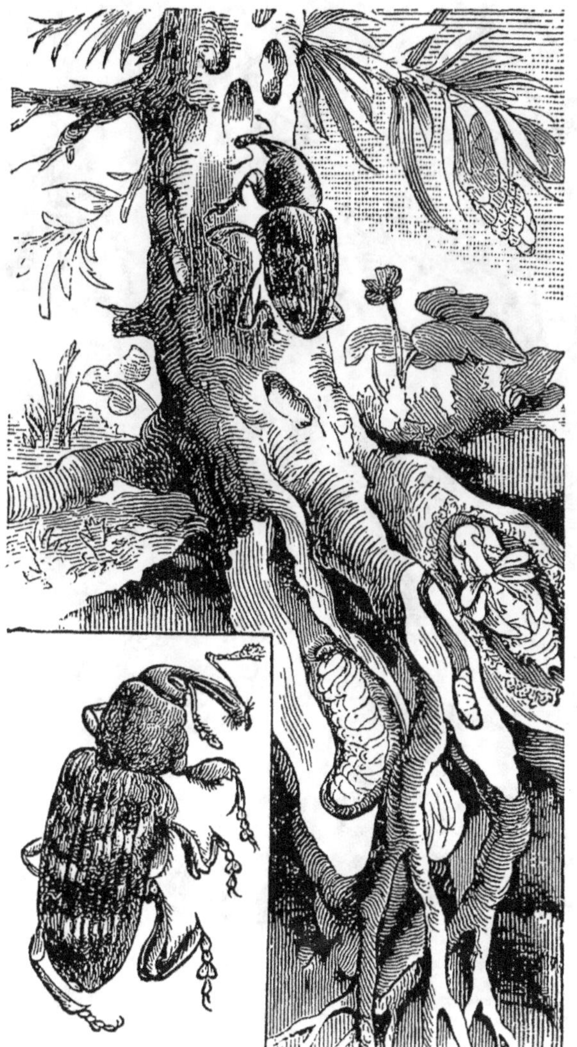

277

278

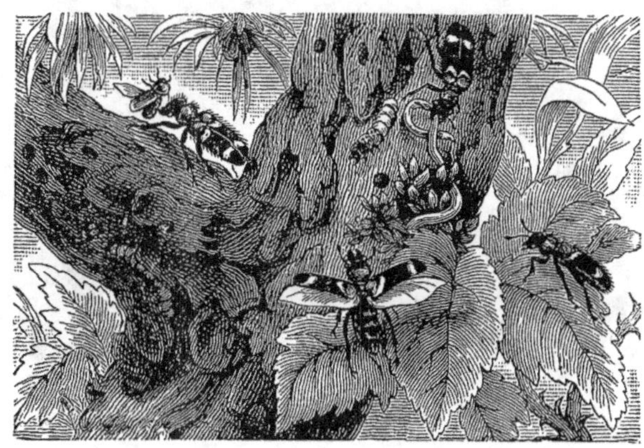

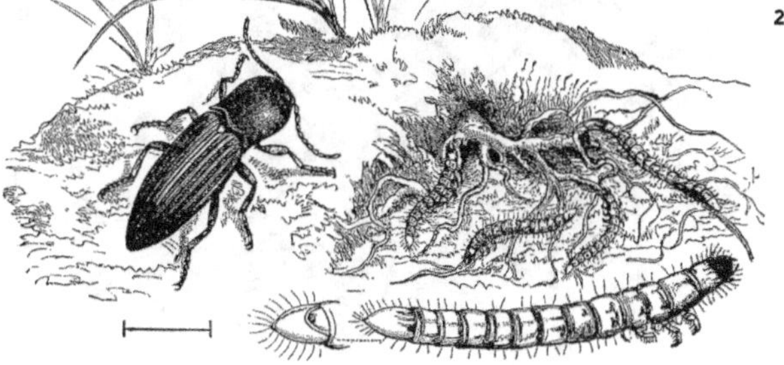

279

280

281

282

283

284

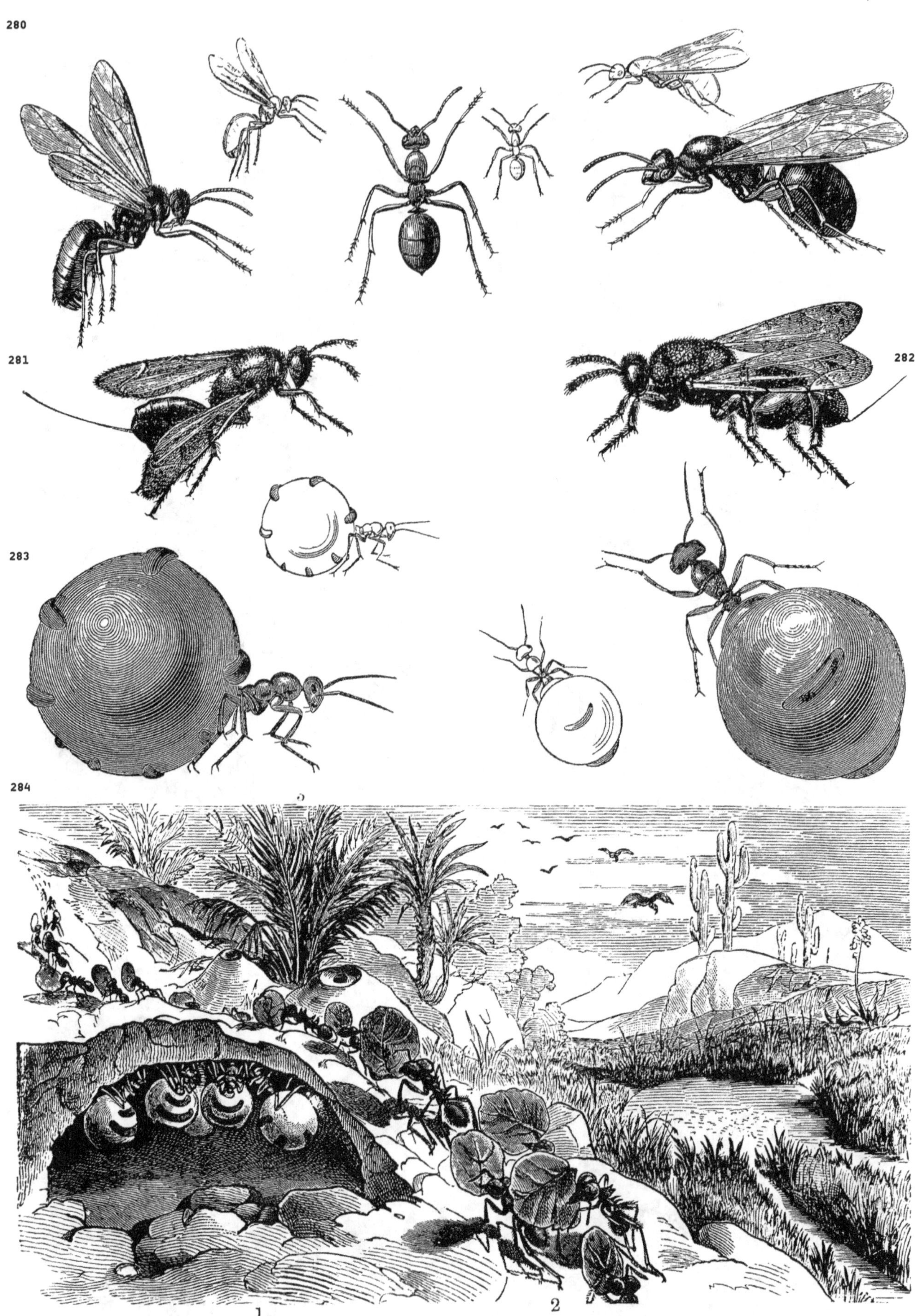

ANTS

285

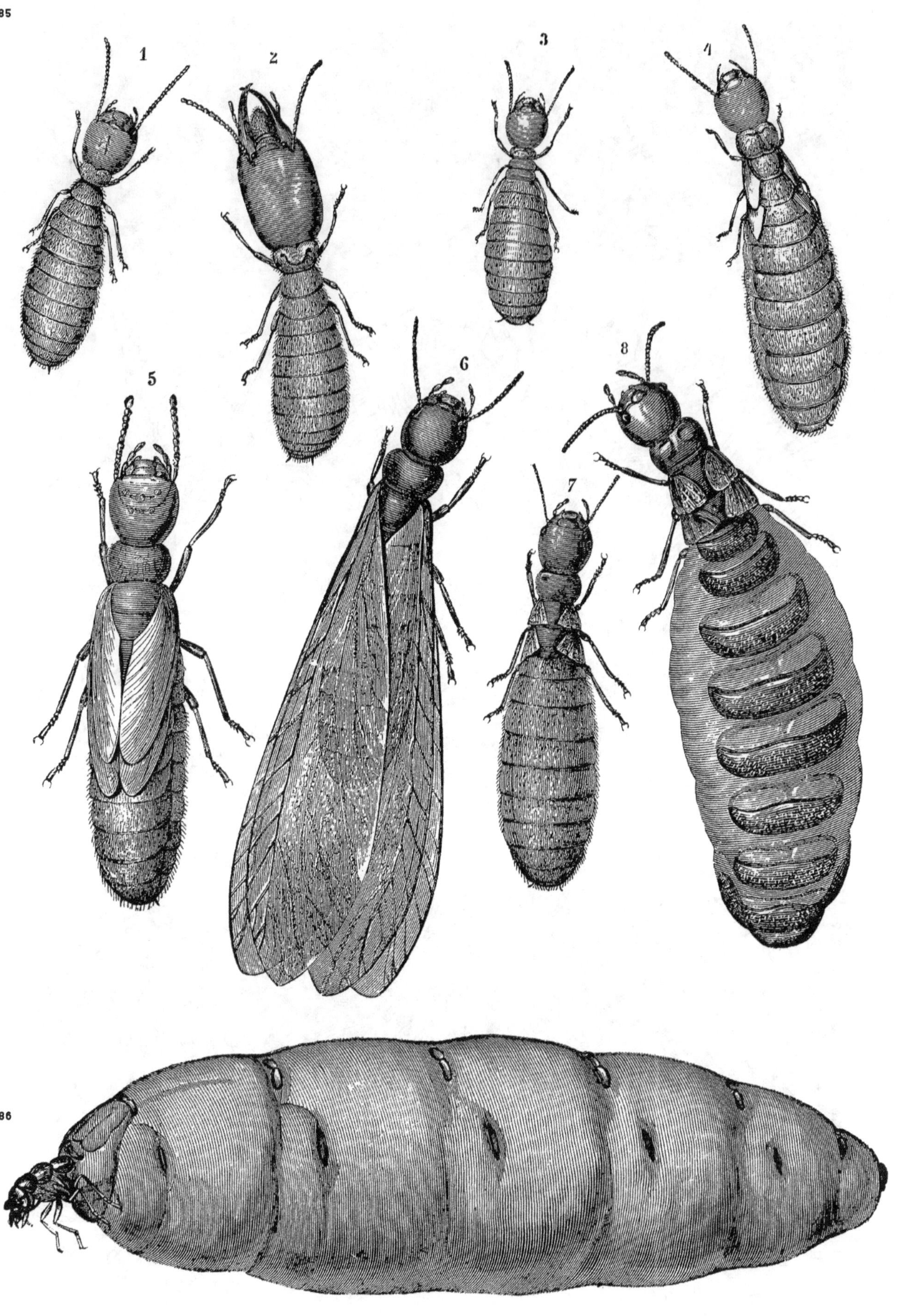

286

ANTS

287

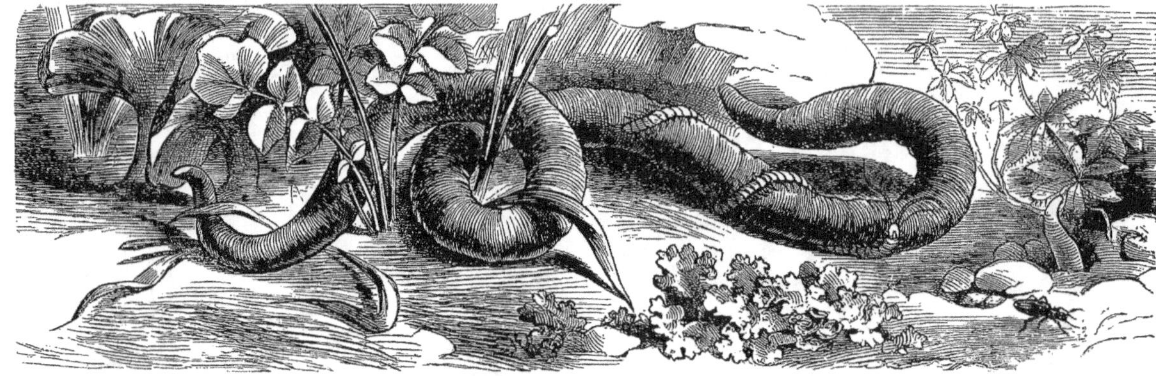

288

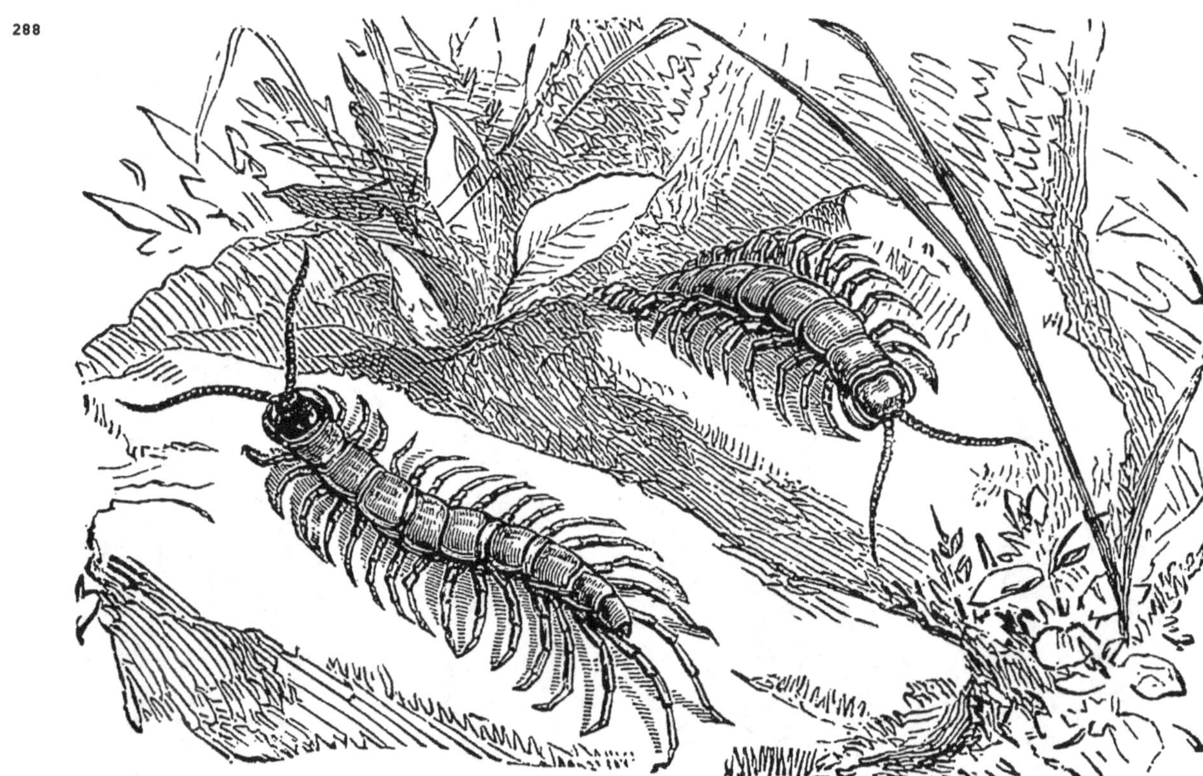

INSECTS

289

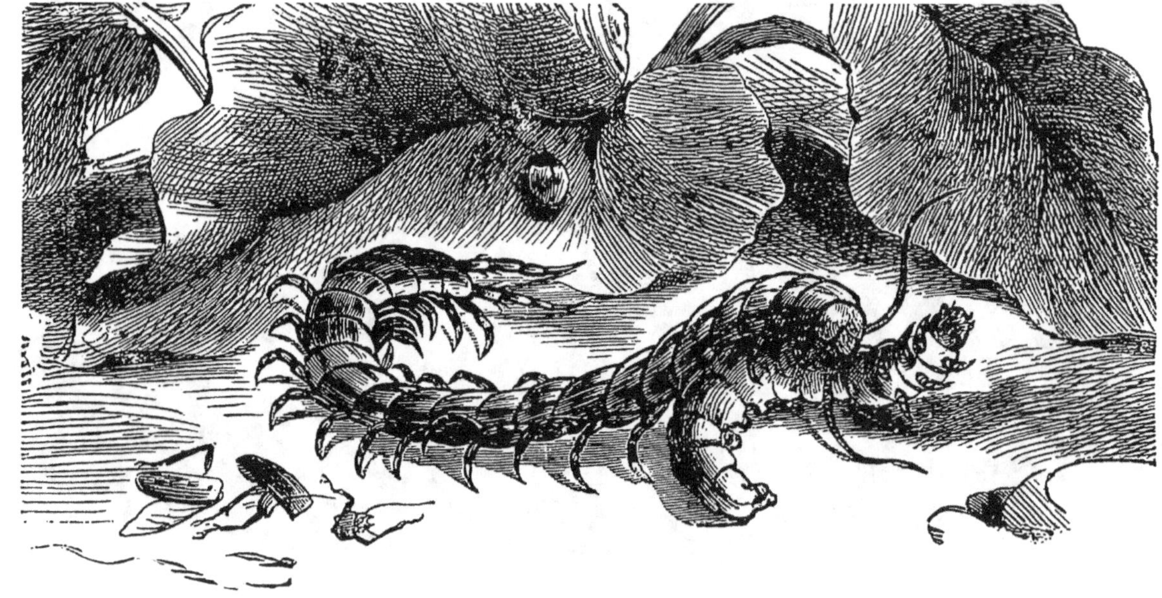

CENTIPEDES, SCORPIONS & SPIDERS

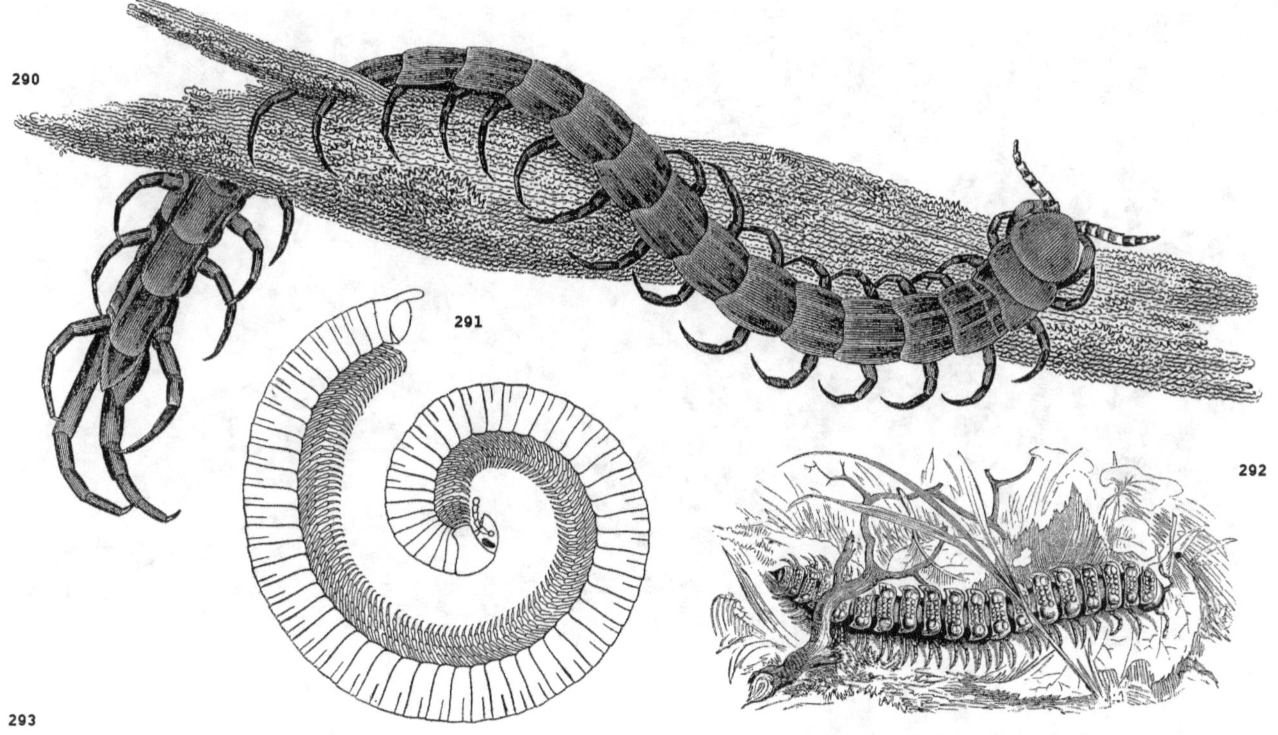

290

291

292

293

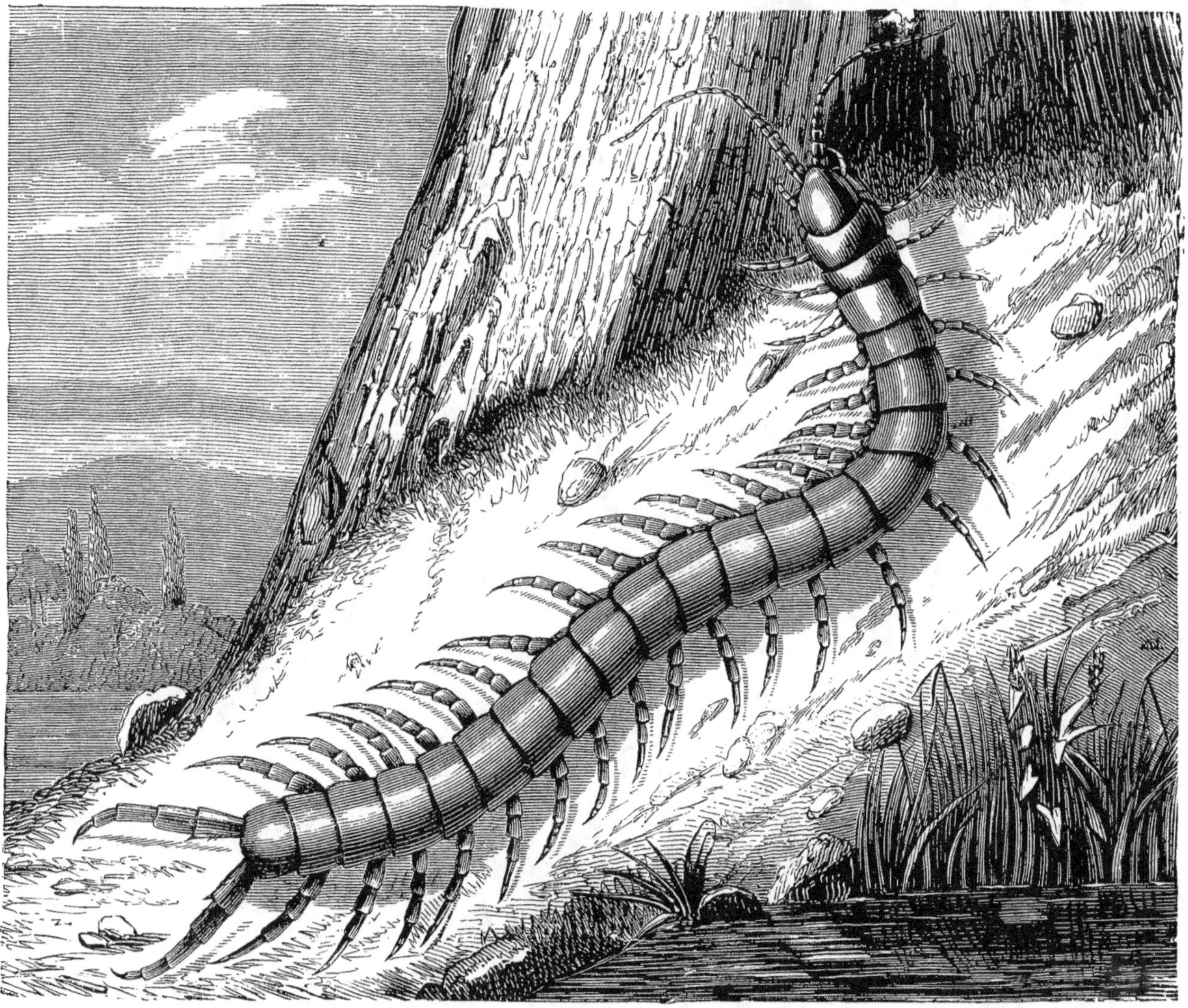

CENTIPEDES, SCORPIONS & SPIDERS

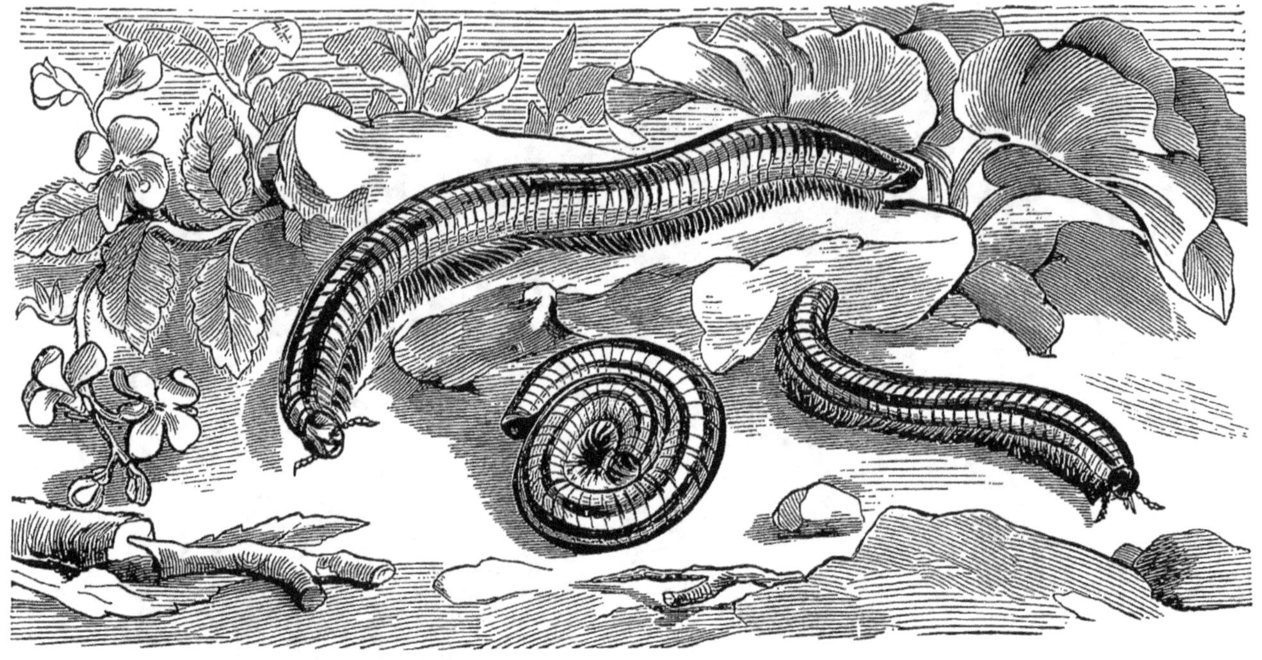

294

295

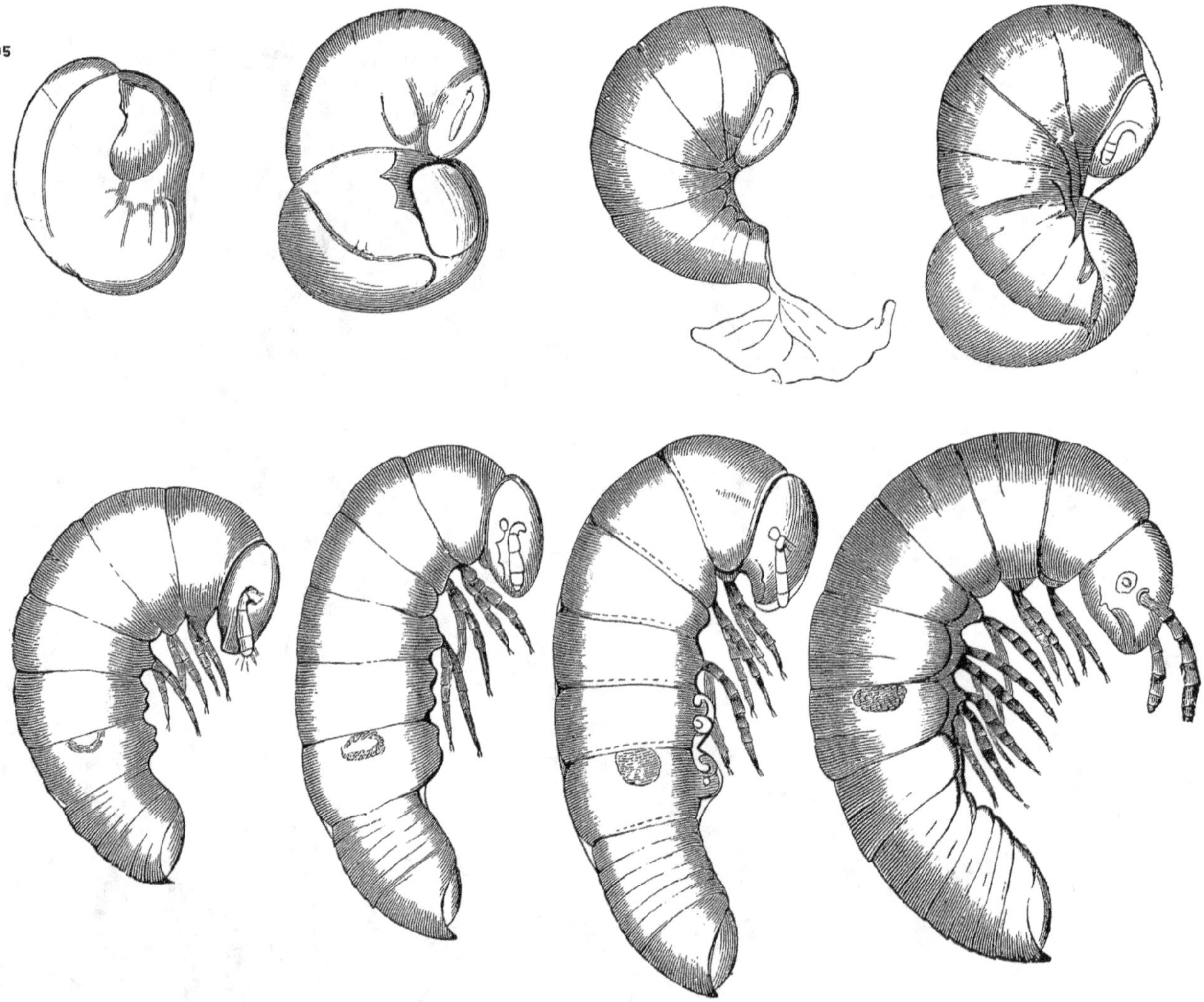

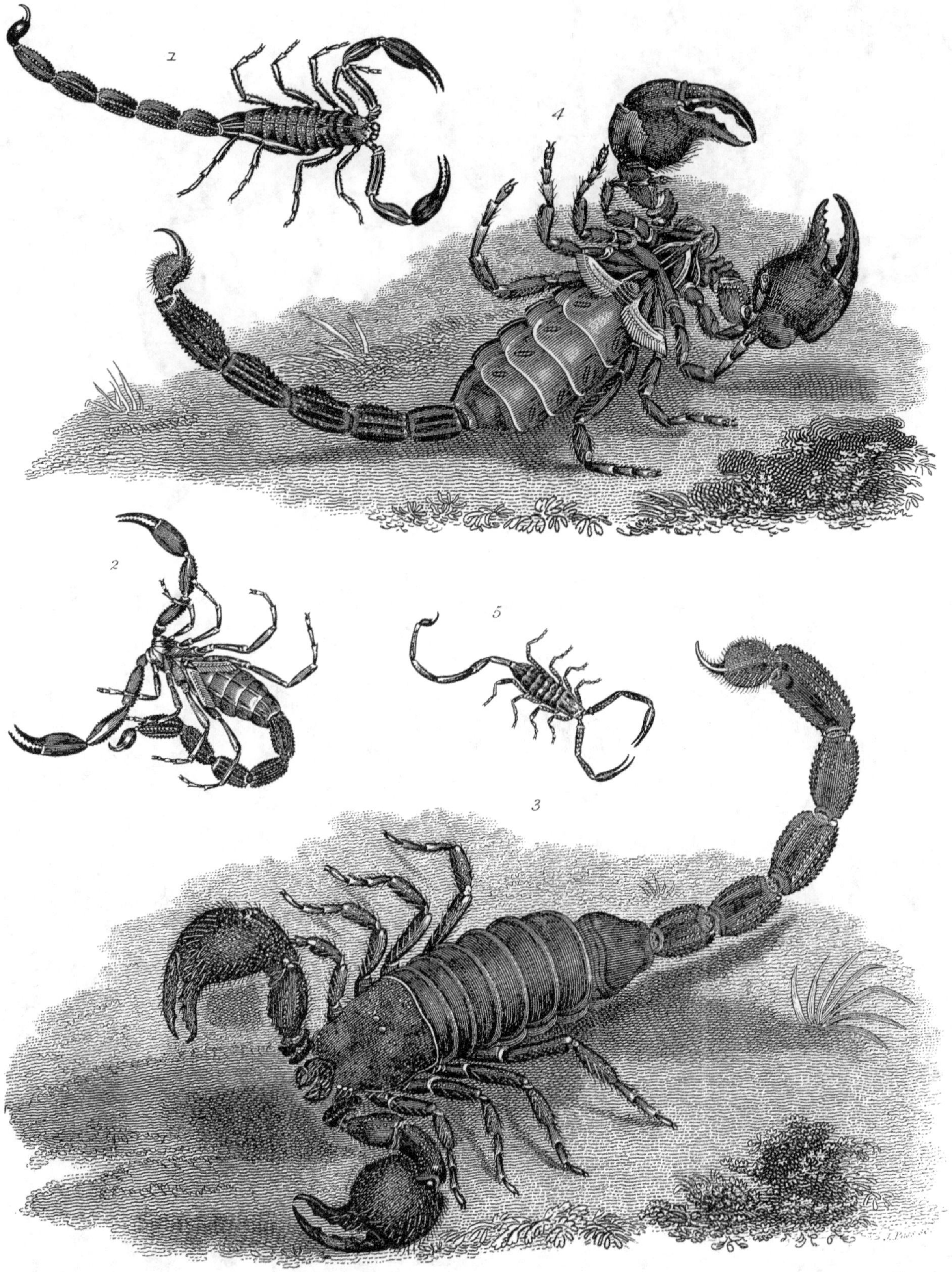

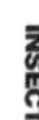

INSECTS

297

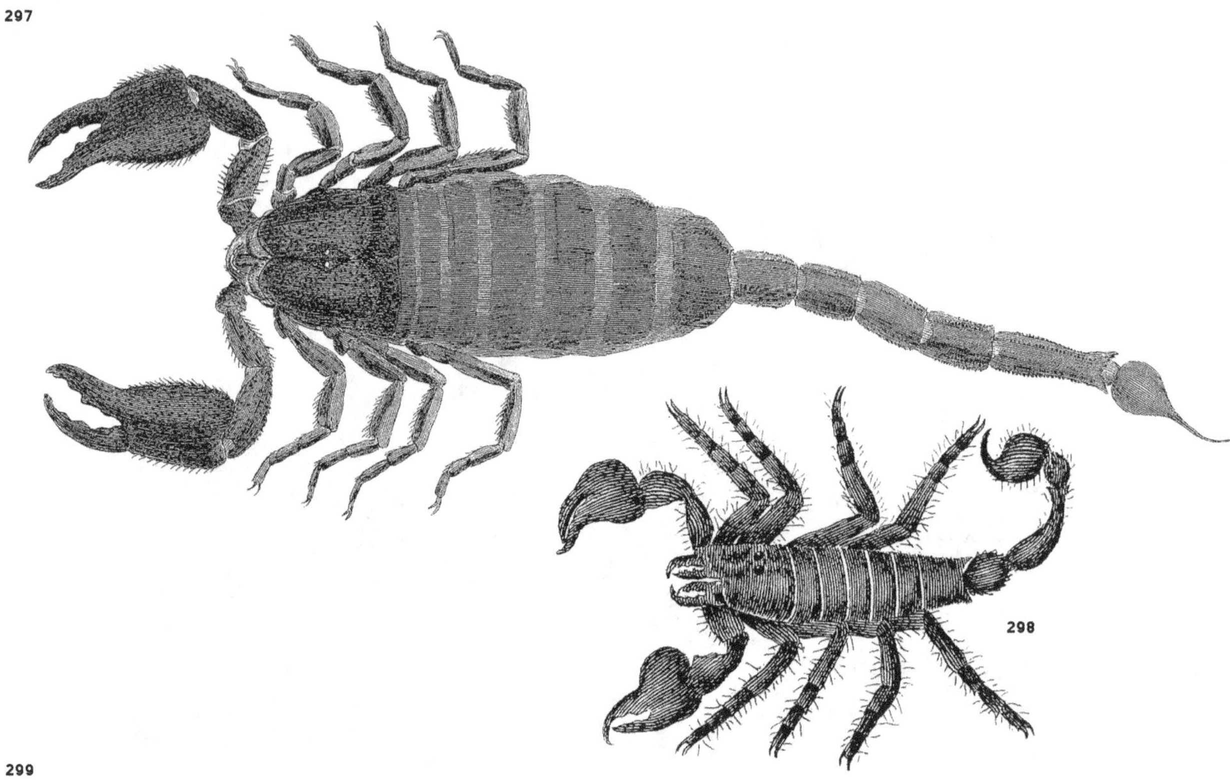

298

299

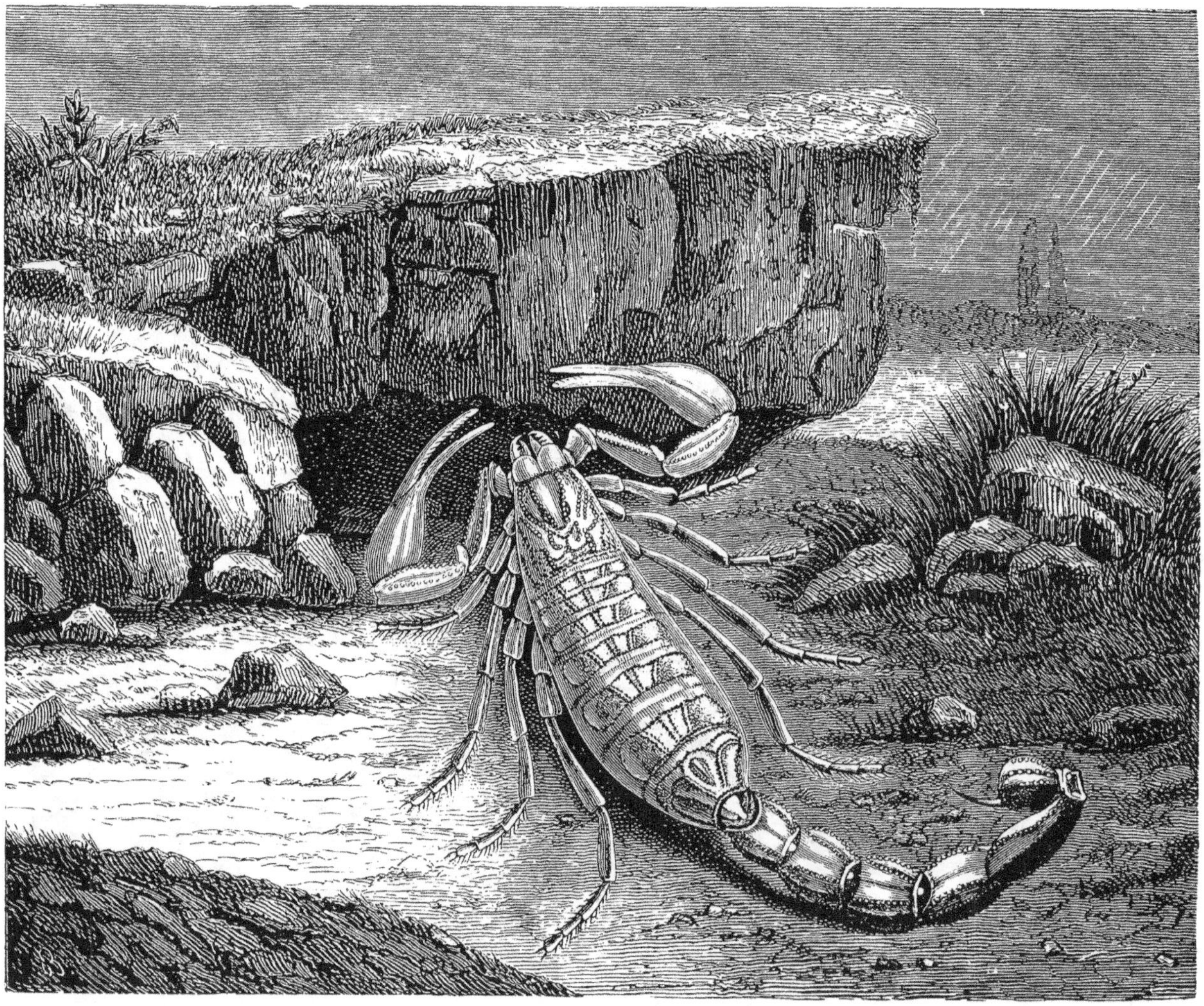

INSECTS

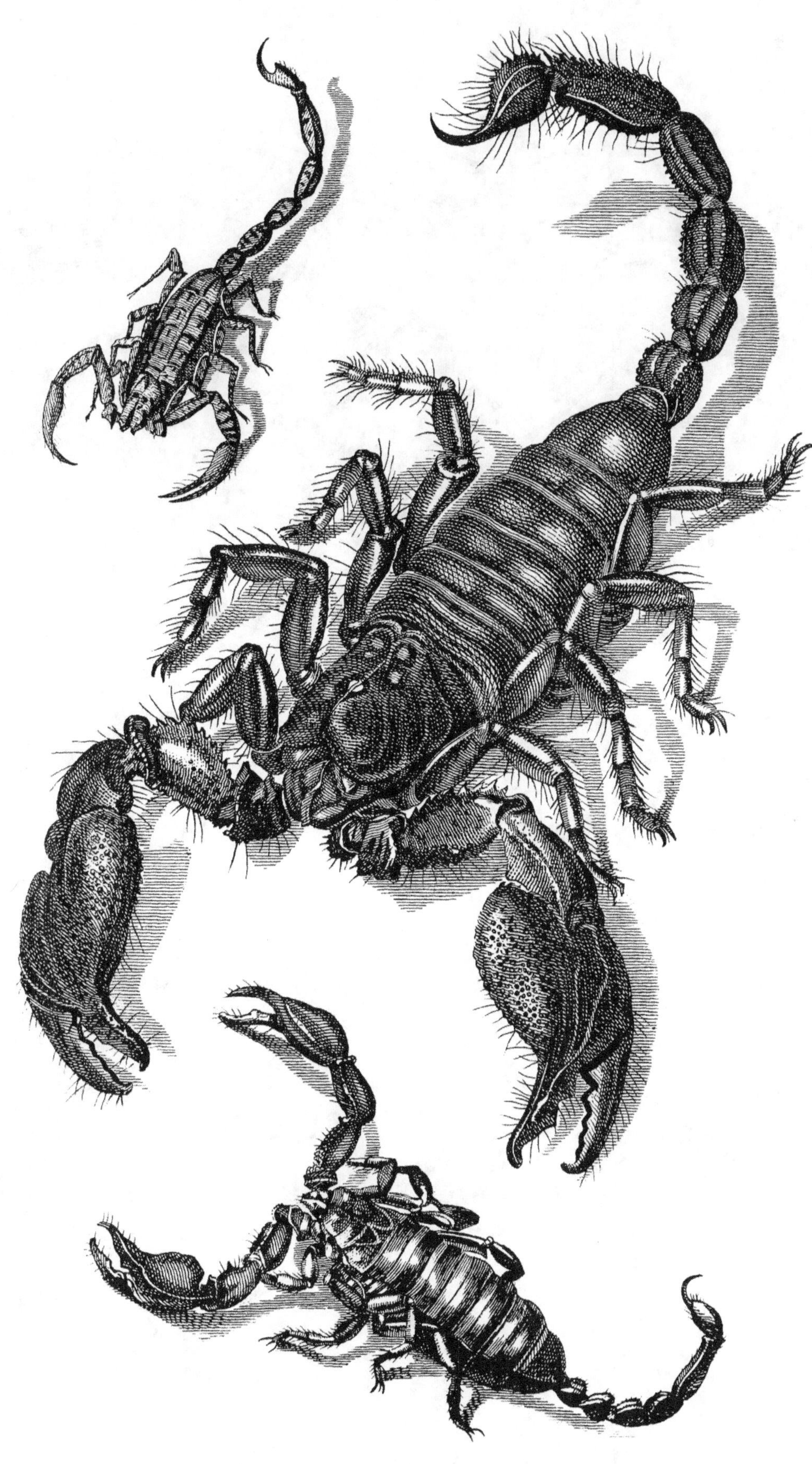

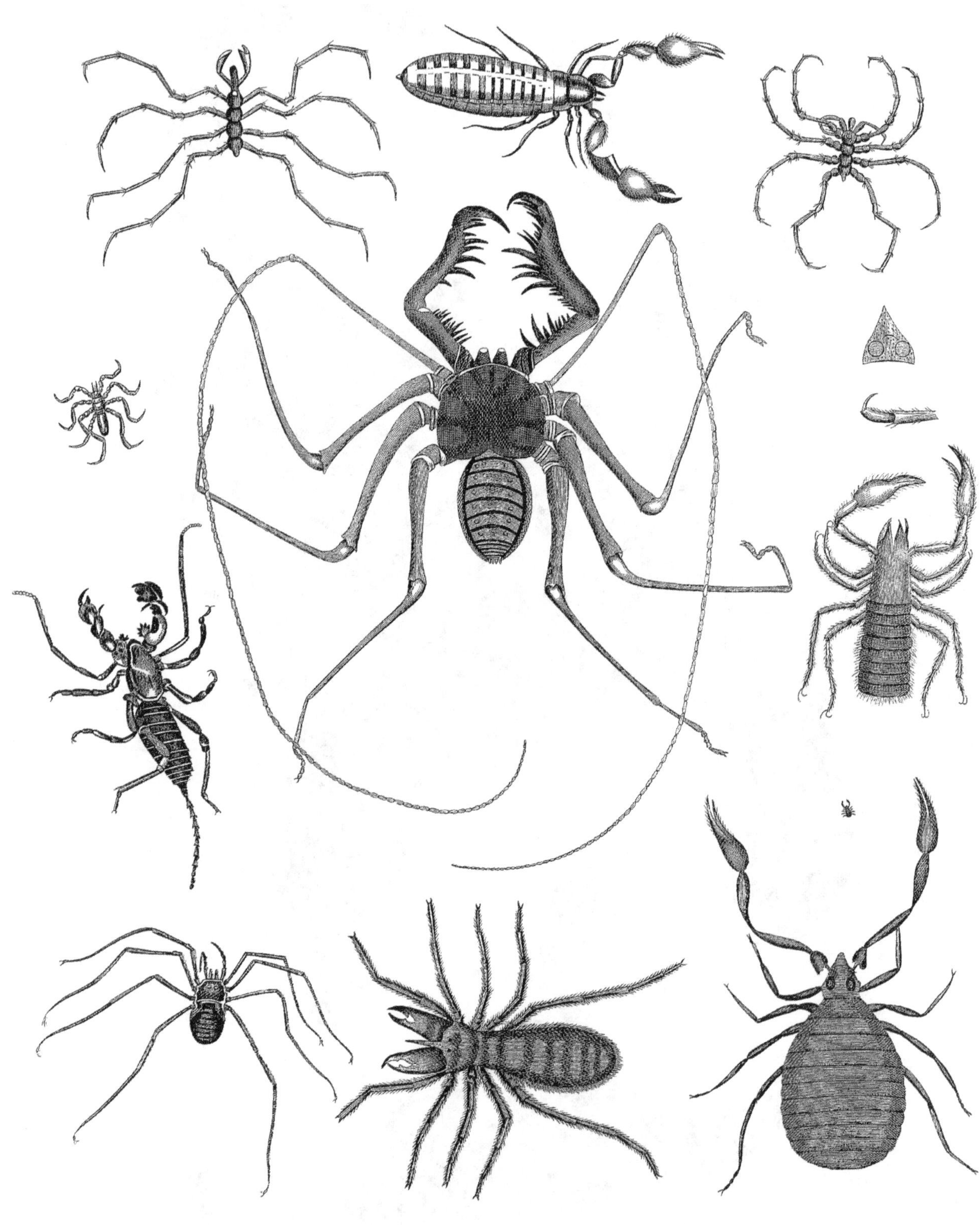

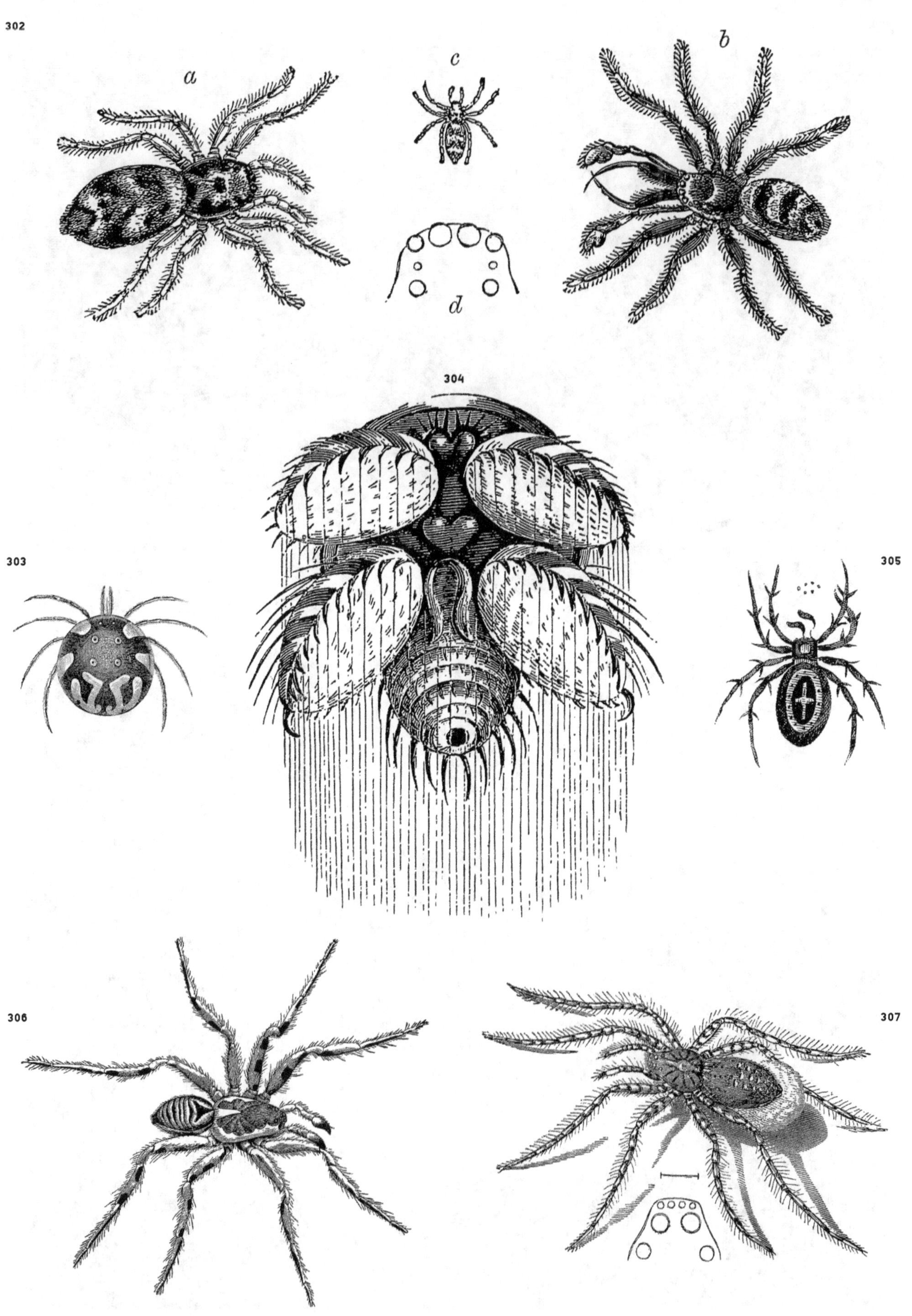
302
a
c
d
b
304
303
305
306
307
INSECTS

INSECTS

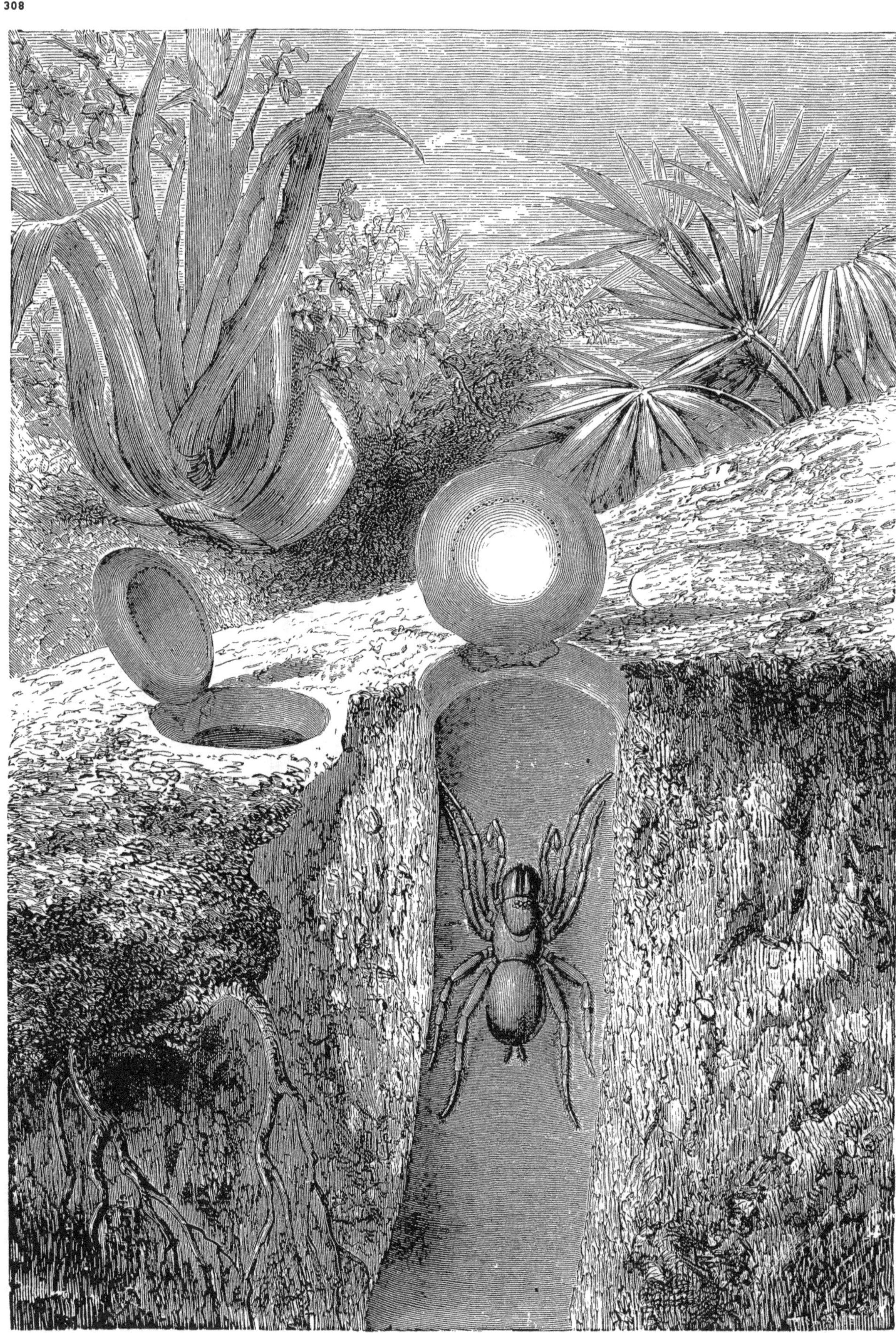

309

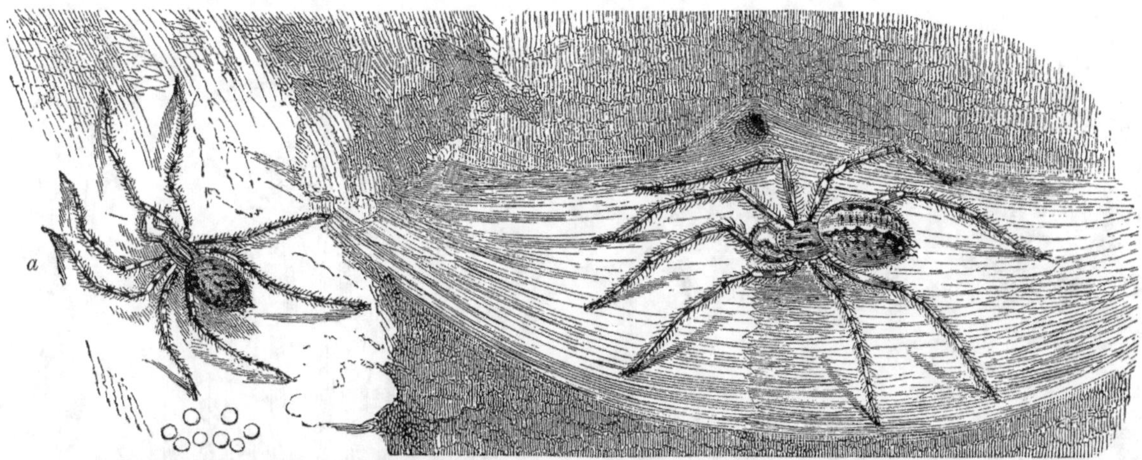

310

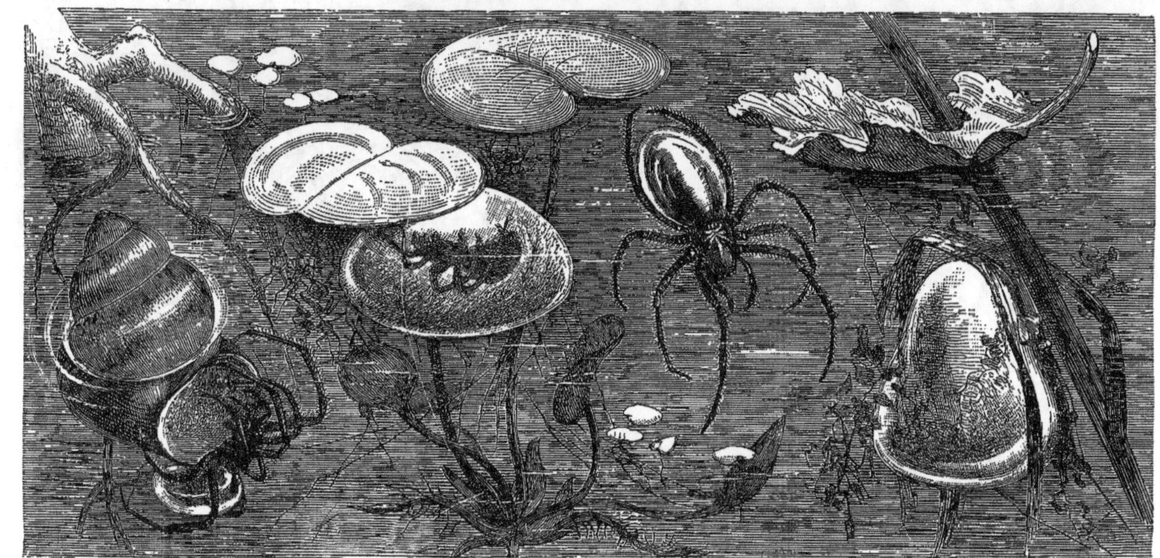

311

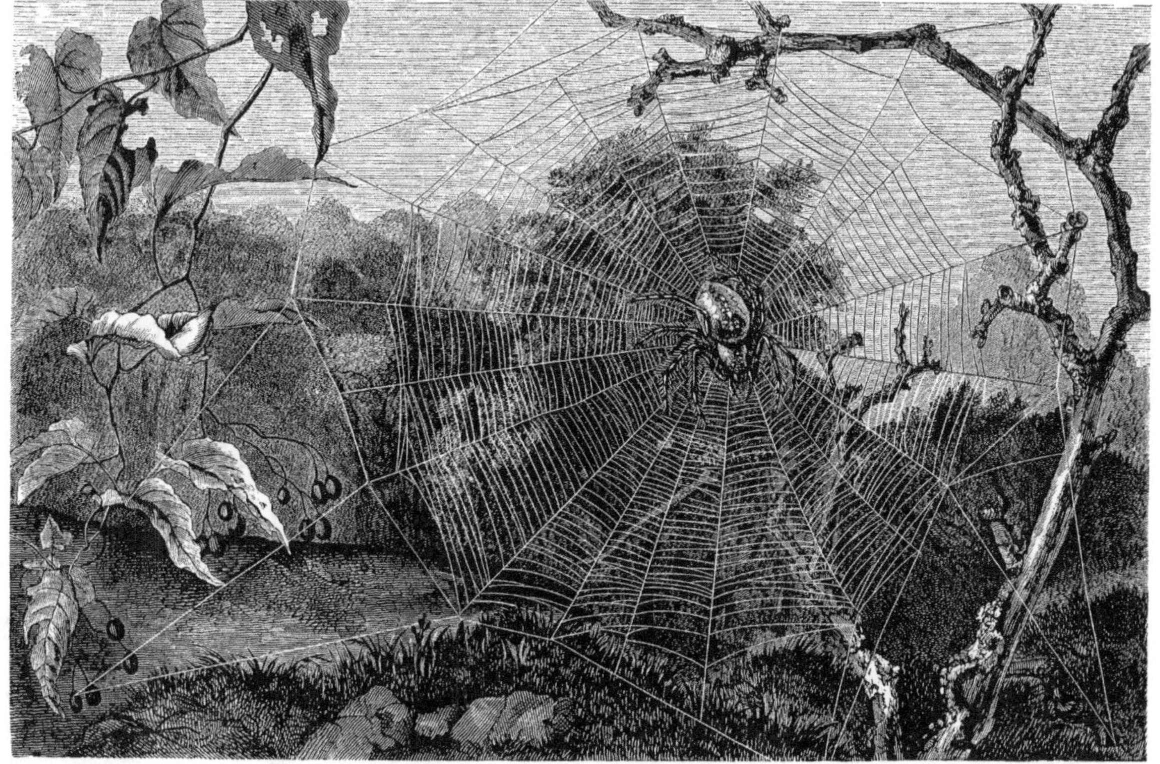

CENTIPEDES, SCORPIONS & SPIDERS

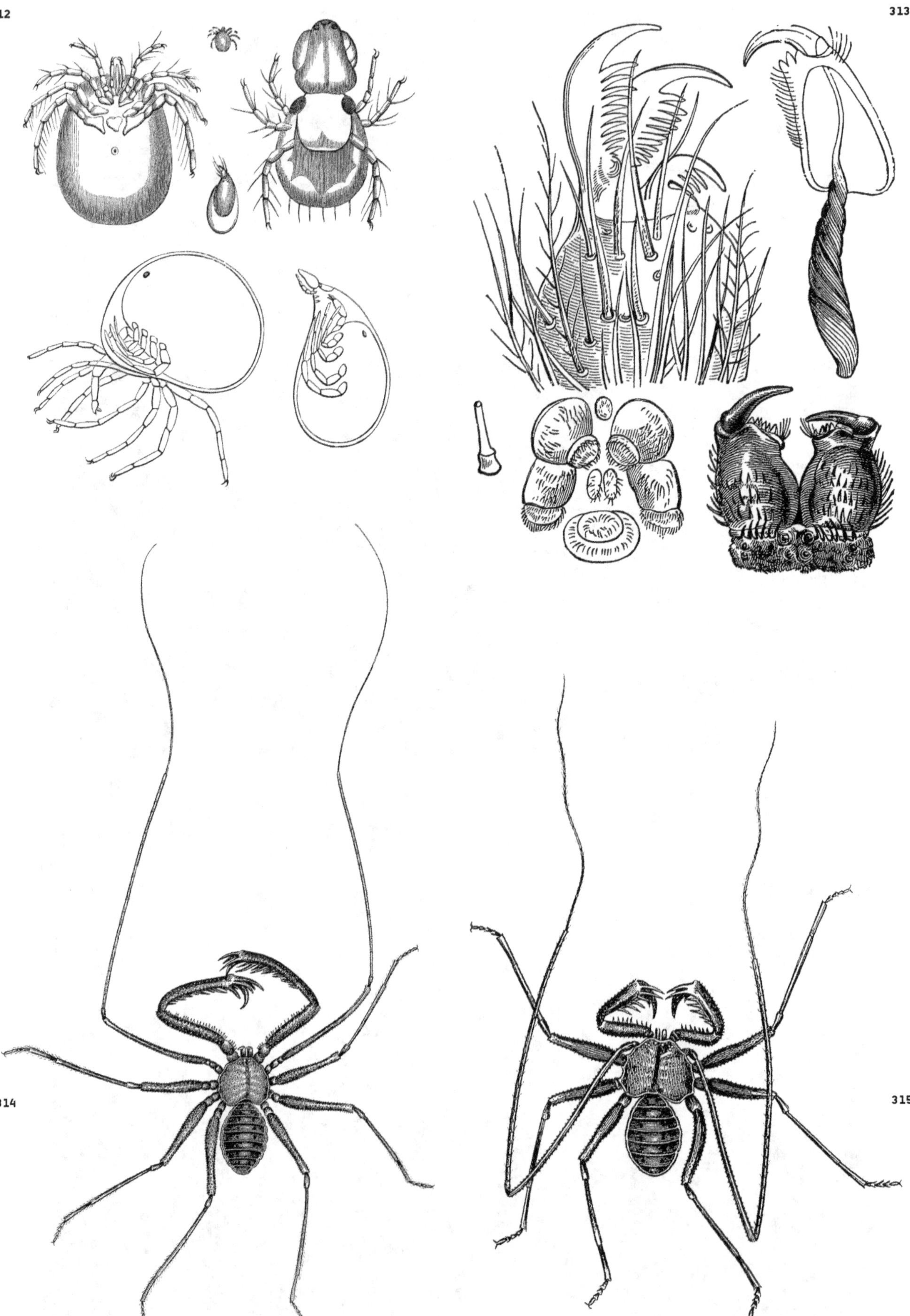

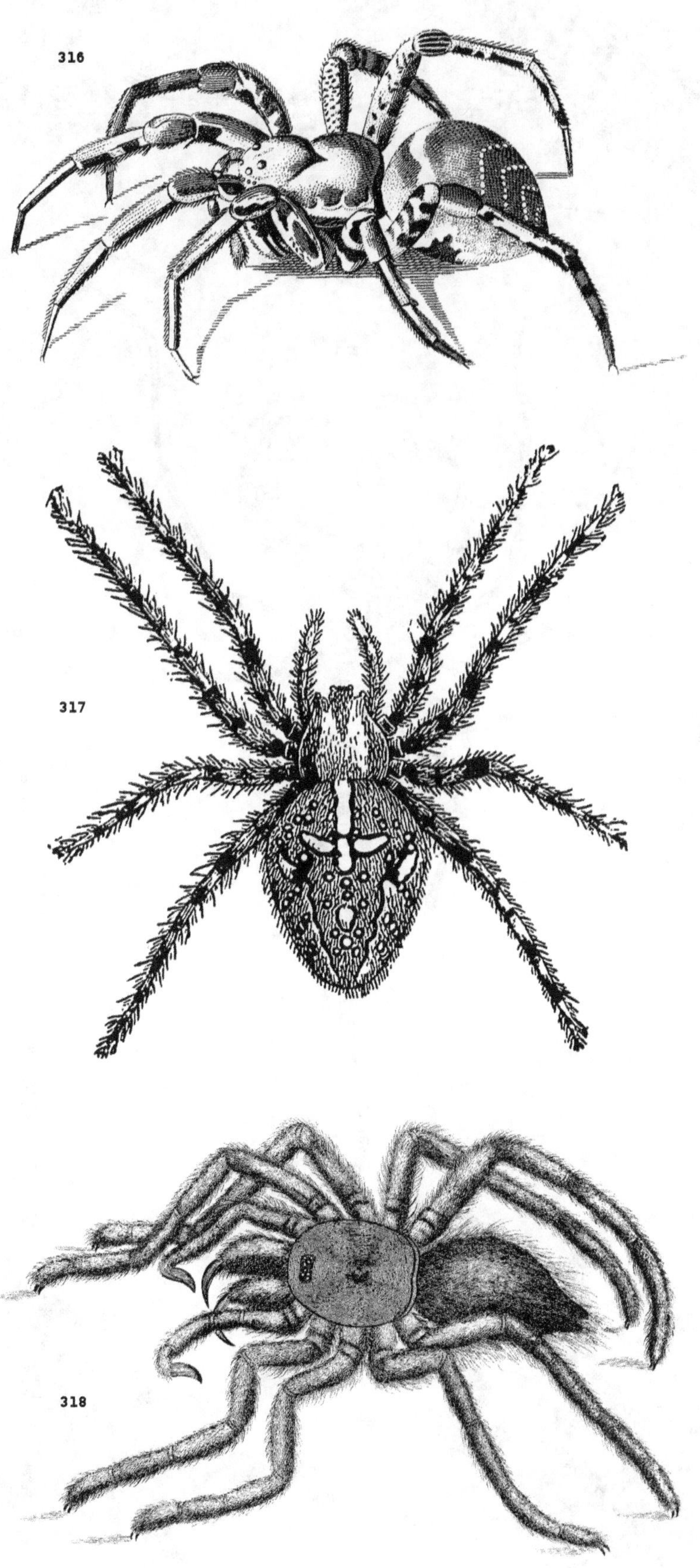

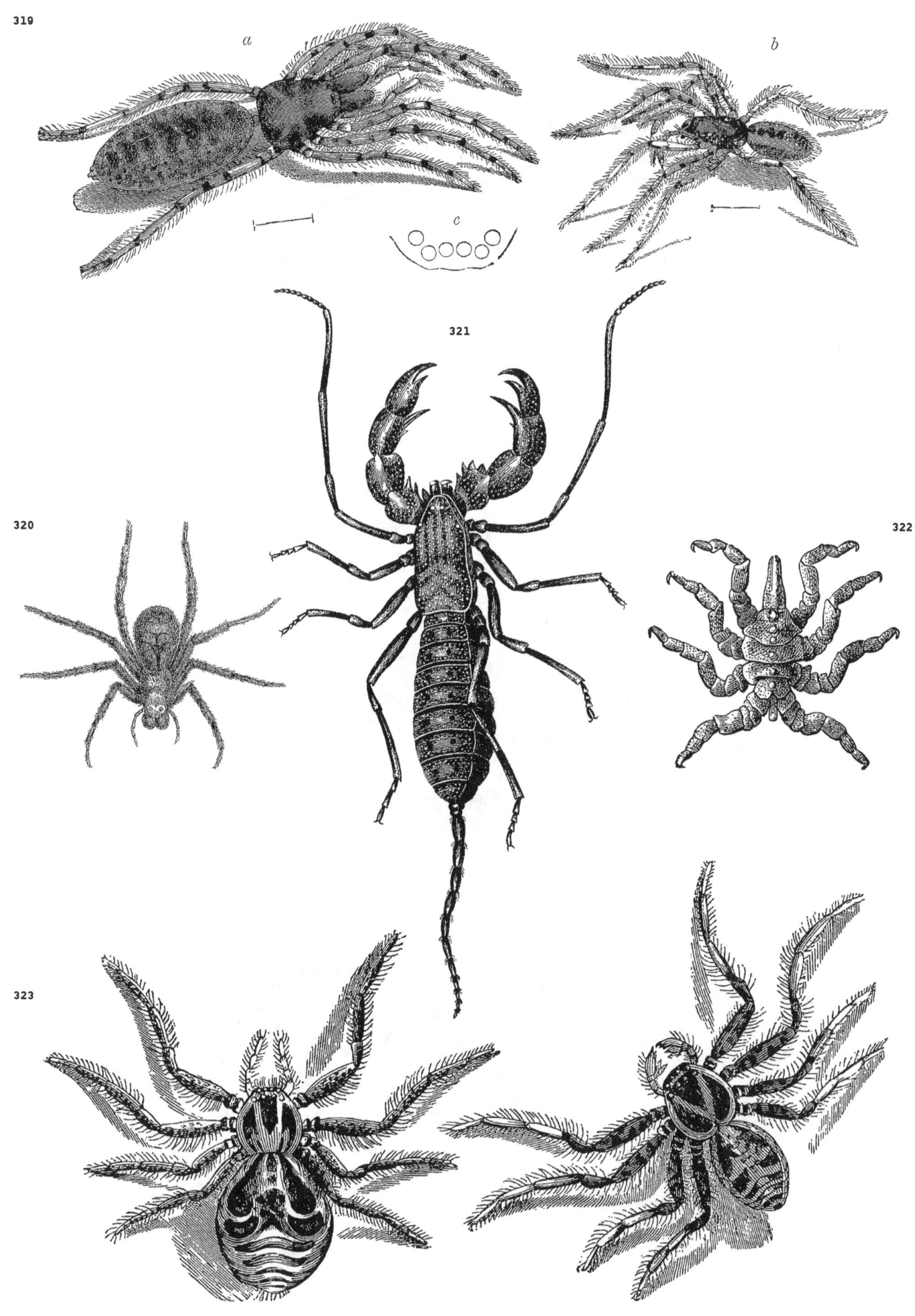
319
a
b
c
321
320
322
323

324

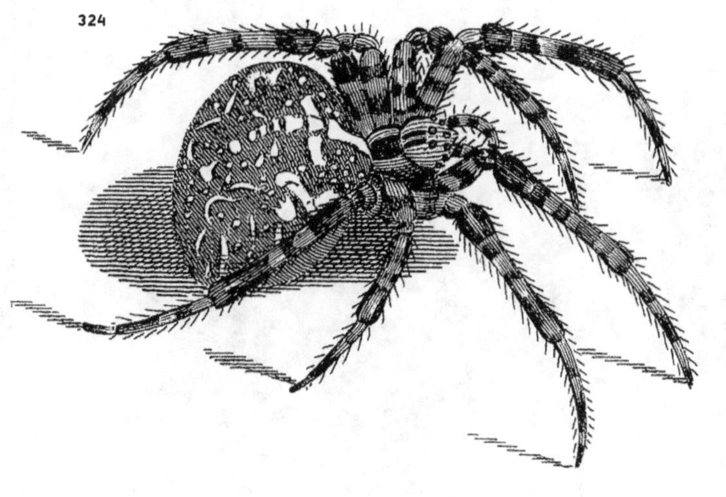

325

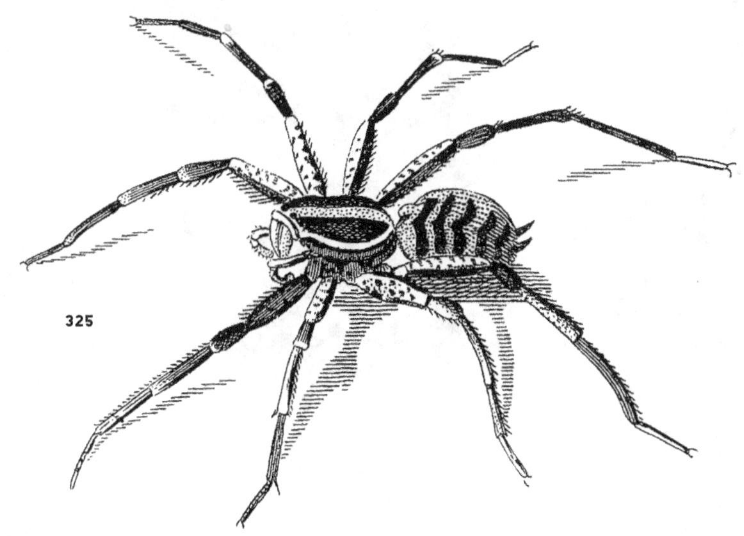

326

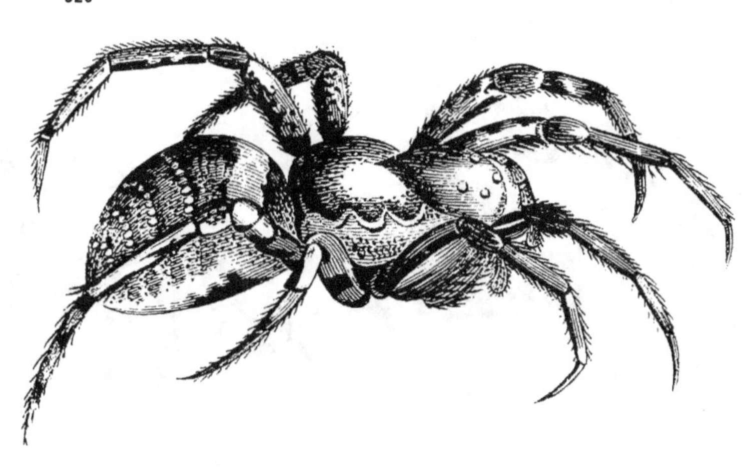

INSECTS

327

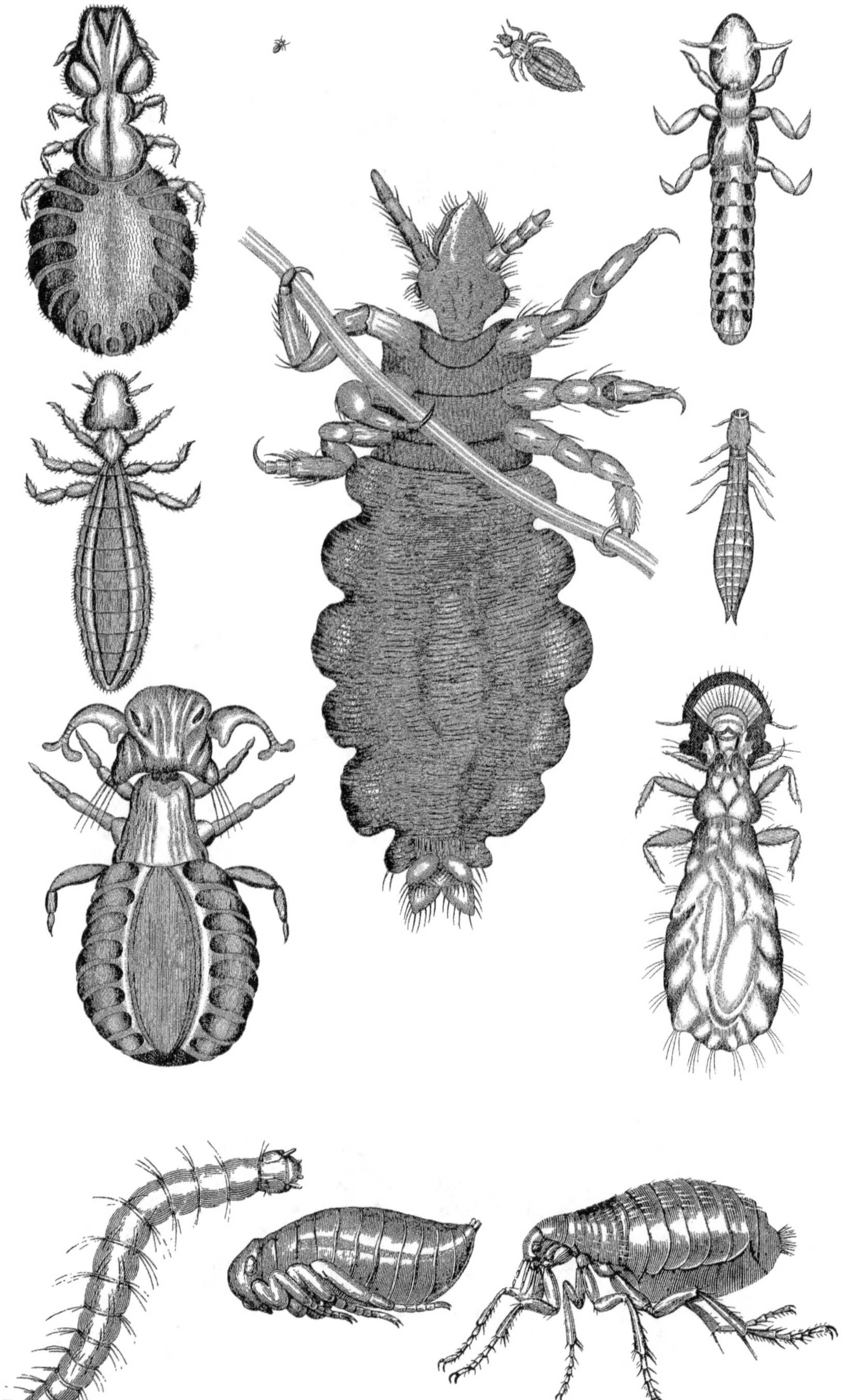

328

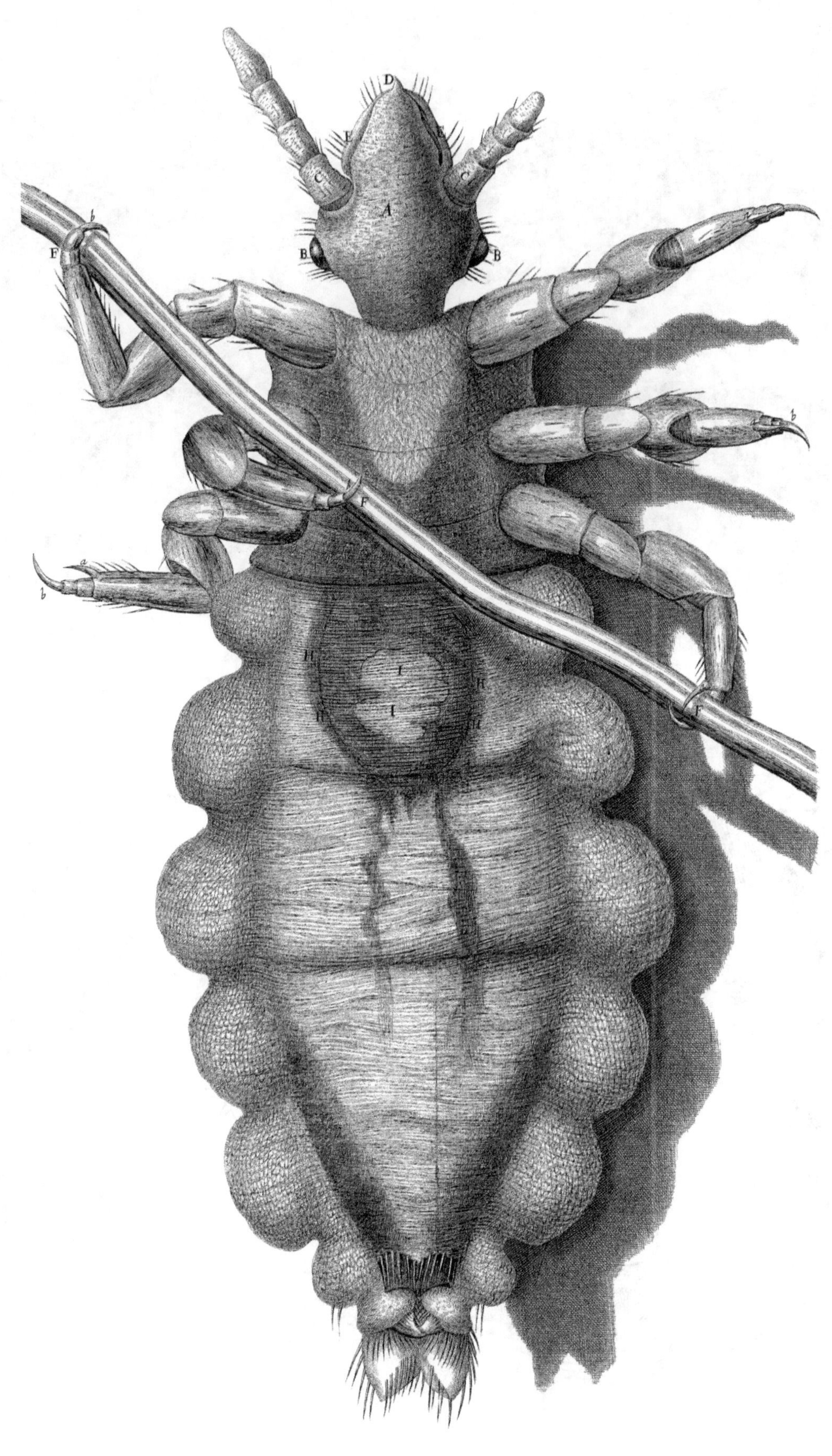

330

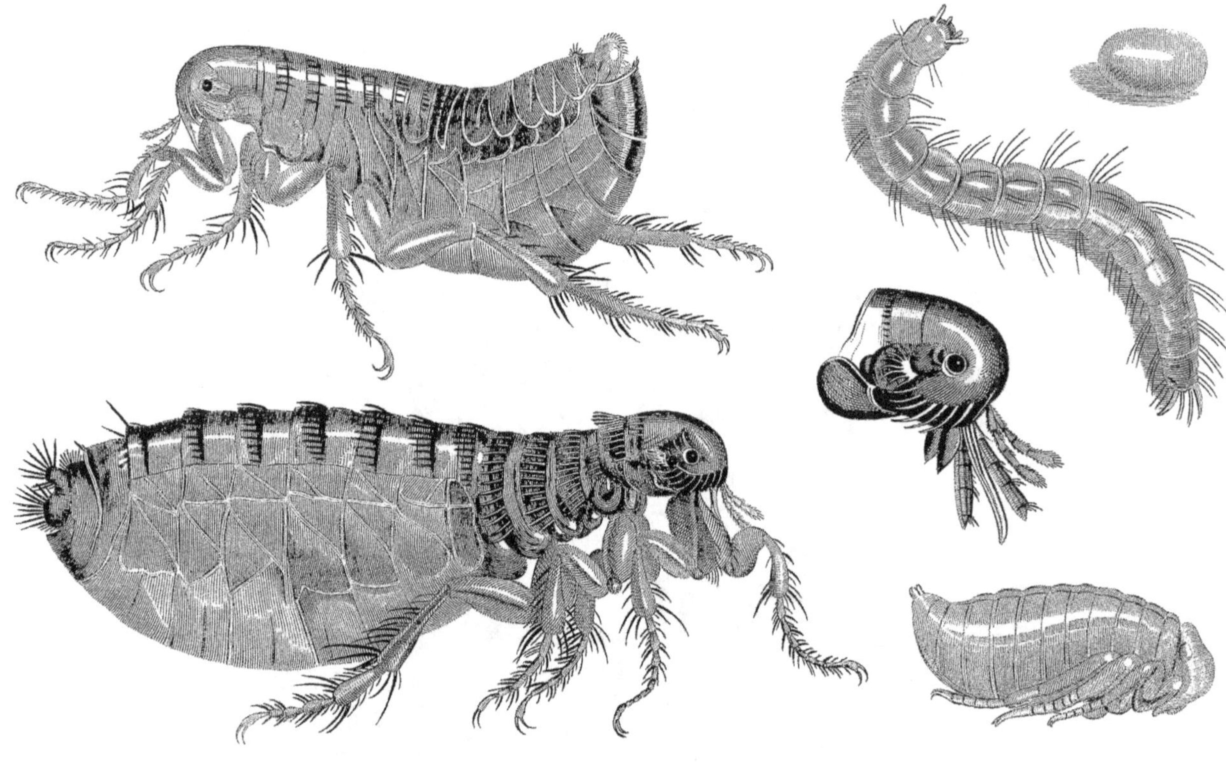

331

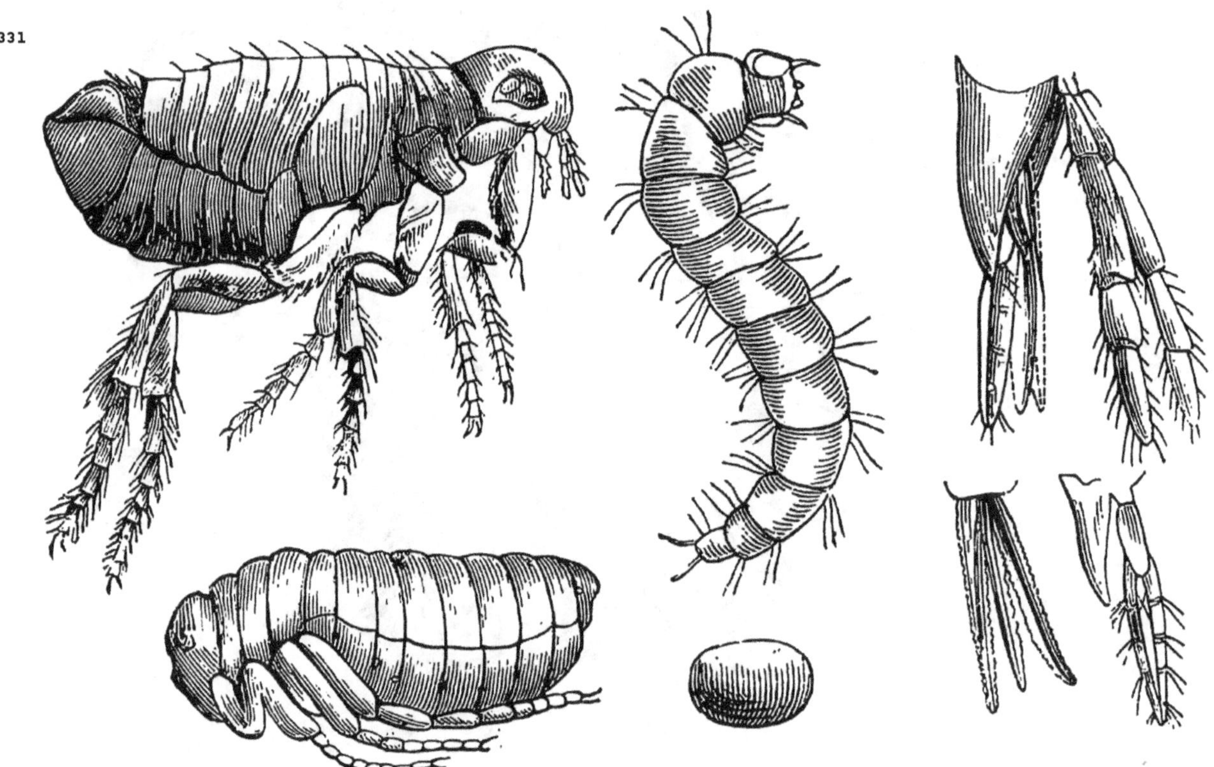

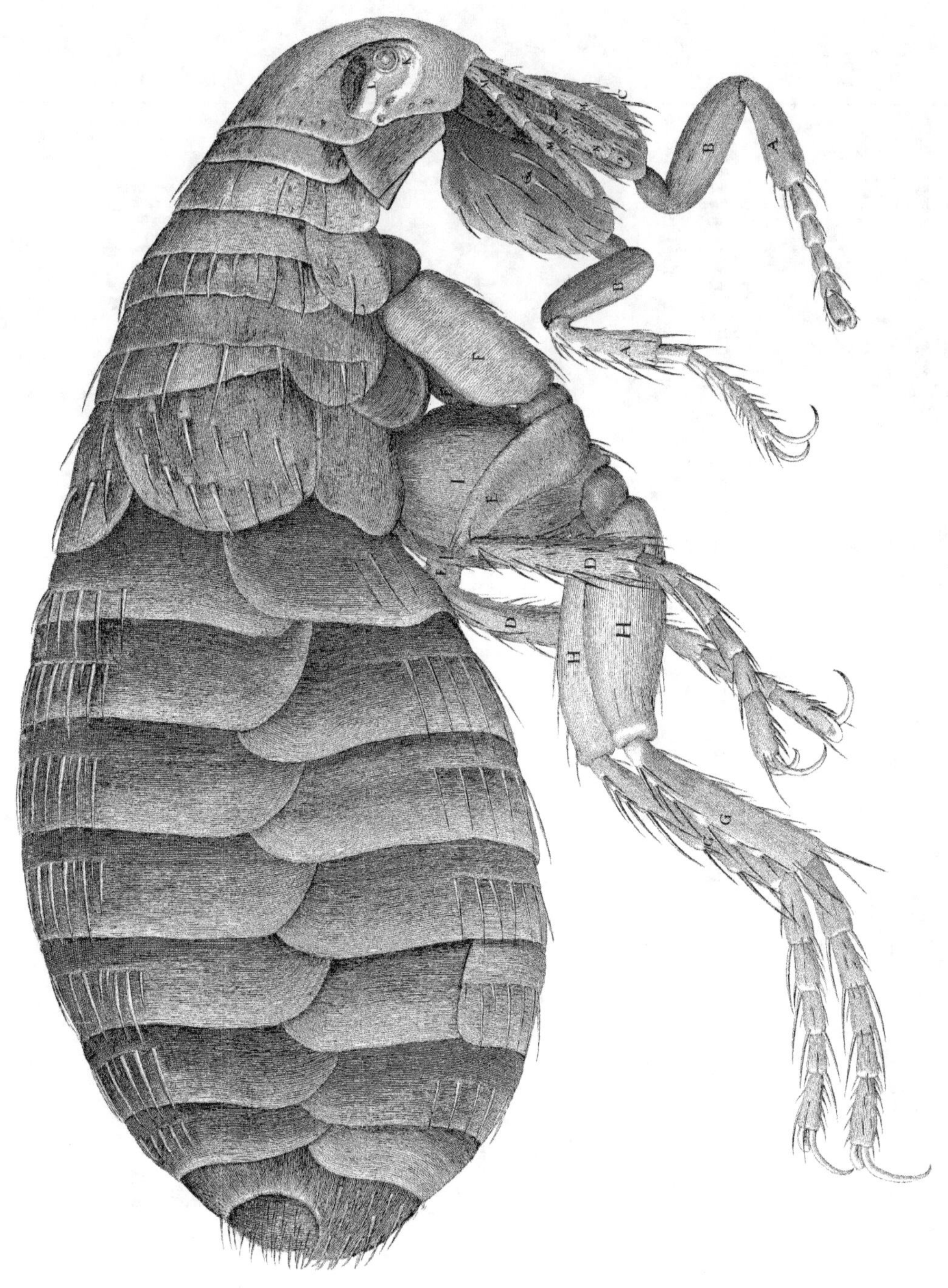

INSECTS

LIST OF ILLUSTRATIONS

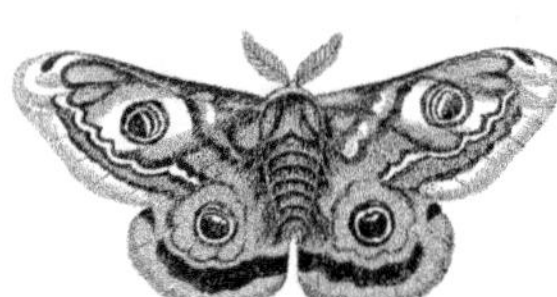

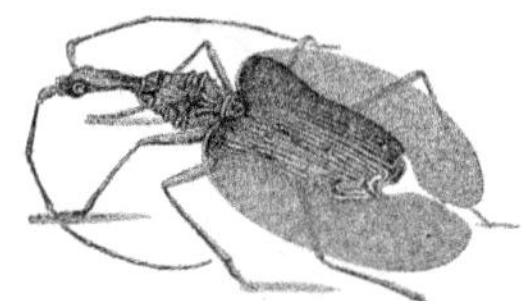

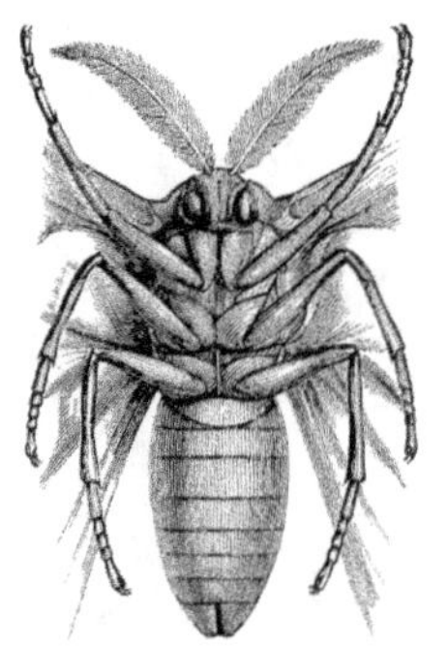

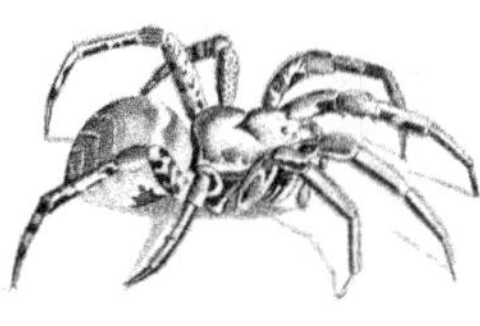

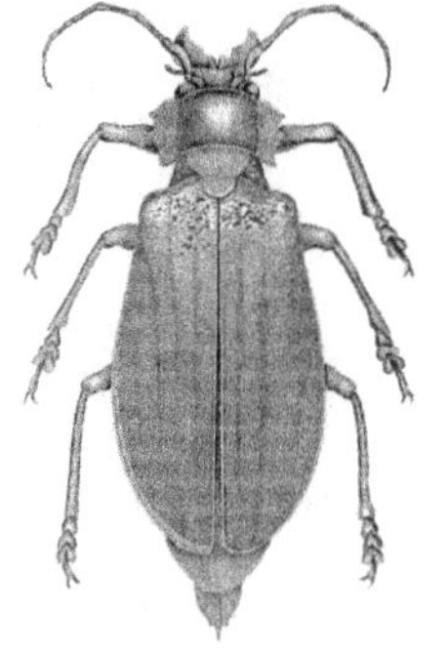

1.   Emperor Moth
2.   Snout
3.   Black-neck
4.   Adult form of moth
5.   Fox Moth
6.   Peach Blossom
7.   Feathered Gothic
8.   The Imperial Moth
9.   Large Yellow Underwing
10. Atlas Moth
11. Tiger Moth
12. Moon Moth
13. Oak Eggar
14. Clouded Magpie
15. Magpie, or Currant Moth
16. The Attacus Promethea (Male)
17. The Attacus Promethea
18. Regal Walnut Moth
19. The Luna Moth
20. Great Angle-Shades
21. Double Spotted Square-Spot
22. Beautiful Double Stripe
23. The Attacus Cecropia
24. Pine Beauty
25. The Attacus Cecropia
26. Emperor Moth
27. Buff-Tip
28. Lappet Moth
29. Wood Leopard
30. Four-horned Ceratomia
31. Kentish Glory
32. Apatela Americana
33. Silver-spotted Hepiolus
34. Swallow Tailed Moth
35. Puss Moth
36. Goat Moth
37. Scaree Kitten
38. Winter Moth
39. The Moth and Larva of Attacus Pavonia Major
40. Lobster Moth
41. Carolina Sphinx
42. Elephant Hawk Moth
43. The Five-spotted Sphinx
44. Ghost Moth
45. Moth of Sphinx Ligustri (Privet Moth)
46. Moths of the first division
47. Moths of the first and second division
48. Moths of the third, seventh and tenth divisions
49. 1, The Lanthorn Fly in its pupa state; 2, The same half evolved; 3, Its mature state; 4, The Fulgora diadema; 5, The Fulgora candelaria; 6, The Fuchia coccinea plant
50. The Moths and Caterpillars of Cucullia Verbasci
51. Moth of Chaerocampa Nerii
52. Larva of the Death's Head Sphinx Moth
53. The Death's Head Moth
54. Larva, or Caterpillar
55. Moths with wings incomplete, just after emergence
56. Chrysalides
57. Mouth of the Privet Hawk Moth (Sphinx Ligustri) Magnified - 1, The Larva; 2, The Perfect Insect
58. The Digestive Organs of the Silkworm and Silkworm Moth. Left, Caterpillar; Right, Moth
59. Terminal parts of the attennae in different genera - 1, Papilio machaon; 2, Argynnis paphia; 3, Thecla W. album; 4, Hesperia Sylvanus
60. Ends of the feet of lepidoptera - 1, Papilio machaon; 2, Heliconia; 3, Sphinx ligustri
61. Sections of the Larva, Pupa, and Moth of Sphinx Ligustri
62. Membranous Feet of Caterpillars 1, Papilio Machaon; 2, Vanessa urticar; 3, Charaxes Jasius; 4, Thecla W. Album
63. Species of Sphynx
64. The Caterpillars of Ennomos illustraria
65. The Lobster Moth
66. The Puss Caterpillar and the Male Moth
67. The Lackey Moth (Clisiocampa neustria)
68. Caterpillar of a Looper
69. Larva of the Silkworm
70. Lime Moth
71. Privet Moth and Larva
72. Pale Tussock Moth, with its Caterpillar and Pupa
73. Erebus Strix
74. Privet Hawk Moth
75. 1, Corn Moth with Larva; 2, Larva of Clothes Moth; 3, Honeycomb, with 4, Larva of the Wax Moth; 5, Pupa; 6, Wax Moth
76. Development of Gipsy-Moth
77. Pepper Moth, with Larva and Pupa
78. 1, Purple-Barred Yellow; 2, Lime-Speck
79. Dark Spinach Moth and Larva
80. Black-Arches Moth
81. Common Tiger-Moth
82. Brown-Tail Moth
83. Life-History of Pine-Lappet Moth
84. Hawk-Moths
85. Pine Hawk-Moth with Larvae and Pupa
86. The Metamorphosis of the Marbled White
87. The Metamorphosis of Papilio Machaon
88. The Metamorphosis of Vanessa
89. Caterpillars and butterflies of Thecla Walbum
90. The Turnus Butterfly
91. Lavinia Butterfly
92. Caterpillar and Chrysalis of Papilio Machaon
93. Group of Tropical Butterflies
94. Group of British Butterflies
95. Resplendent Ptolemy
96. 1, 2, Peacock Butterfly; 3, The Caterpillar; 4, The Chrysalis; 5, Meadow-brown; 6, The Caterpillar
97. Chrysalides Slung and Suspended
98. Caterpillars of the cabbage butterfly slinging themselves before the first metamorphosis
99. Butterflies, Wasp and Other Insects, Wenceslaus Hollar, 1644 - 1652
100. The Metamorphosis of Pamphila Aracynthus
101. Species of Chrysomelae
102. Pterphorus Pentadactylus
103. Orneodes Hexadactylus
104. The Aquatic Larva and Nymph of the Caddis Fly (Phryganea Flavicornis)
105. A species of Hemerobius
106. A species of Hemerobius
107. Tremex Columba
108. Cecidomiya with Viviparous Larvae
109. The Seven orders of insects
110. Larvae and pupa of the seven orders of Insects
111. The Pimpla Lunator
112. Ovipositor of the Hylotoma Rosea
113. Stylops Aterrimus. The Male
114. Female and Larva of Stylops Aterrimus
115. A species of Hemerobius
116. Hydropsyche atomaria. Larva, Imago, Shelter, Pupa and Case
117. The Nymph and Larva of Species of the Genus Phryganea
118. Cochineal Insect
119. The Rose Aphis
120. Prickly Poppy with insect and its larvas
121. Locusts of the first division
122. Locusts if the fourth and fifth division
123. Locusts of the Fifth Division
124. Digestive Apparatus of an Herbivorous Insect. The Green Grasshopper (Locusta Viridissima)
125. Anatomy of the mouth of Locusta Viridissima (Great Green Bush-Cricket)
126. Meadow Grasshopper
127. Cixius Nervosus
128. Field Cricket
129. Mole-Cricket, with eggs and larvae
130. 1, Female of Hetrodes spinulosus; 2, male and female of Meconema varium
131. European Cicadas - 1, Cicada orni; 2, C. plebja and larva
132. Migratory Locust of South-East Europe and its Larvae
133. 1, Manticora Maxillosa; 2-6, Curious Species of the Mantis, or Soothsayer
134. Insect Life in Summer
135. The Larva and Nymph of the Gnat
136. Larvae of a Dipterous Insect
137. The Metamorphosis of Gymnosoma Rotundata
138. Larva and Pupa of an Ephemera
139. Metamorphosis of Volucella Zonaria. Larva, Nymph and Adult
140. Lophyrus Pini
141. The Spectacle Fly
142. Great Horse-Fly
143. Leptataena Cervi
144. Melophagus Ovis
145. White ants and their development
146. Life-History of the Sheep Bot-Fly
147. Development of Horse Bot-Fly
148. Ox Warble-Fly and its Development
149. Army Worm-Fly
150. Group of Flies and their Grubs
151. House Fly
152. Chloros Taeniopus
153. Tsetse Fly
154. Common Forest-Fly
155. Female of Stratiomys Chamoeleon
156. Lace-Wing Flies
157. Life-history of the common Ant-Lion
158. Green Saw-Fly
159. Anterior magnified view of the Blue Fly
160. Robert Hooke, Micrographia. Engraving of a magnified blue fly
161. The Metamorphosis of Sesia Apiformis
162. The New York Bee
163. Chinese Bee
164. The Virginian Bee
165. The Respiratory Apparatus of the Bee
166. The Surinam Bee

167.   Common Bee
168.   Domestic Bees. Right, Female; Worker, Centre; Left, Male
169.   Teleas Laeviusculus and its eggs
170.   Sirex Gigas
171.   Rose Gall-Wasp and its Gall
172.   South African Wasp and its Nest
173.   A Portion of Honeycomb
174.   The Nervous System of a Full-Grown Bee-A Drone
175.   Microgaster Nemorum and its larve feeding upon a large caterpillar
176.   Life-history of the Hornet- a, b, adult; c, Portion of brood-cells; d, Larva; e, Pupa
177.   Pelopaeus Spirifex and its nest
178.   1, Pompilus Natalensis; 2, Pompilus Trivialis; 3, Larva of latter on garden spider; 4, Priocnemis variegatus; 5, Agenia punctum, with its two cells
179.   Hairy-Legged Flower-Bee
180.   Group of Solitary Bees
181.   Common Humble-Bee
182.   Cerceris Arenaria
183.   Ammophila Sabulosa
184.   Cynips Terminalis. Left, Female; Right, Male
185.   The Legless Larvae of the Bee
186.   Nymphs or Pupae of the Bee
187.   Head of a Hornet (Vespa Crabro)
188.   Head of Hive Bee
189.   Hind Legs of a Female and Worker Bee
190.   Under Surface of a Bee
191.   The Sting and Venom Glands of the Bee
192.   The Respiratory Organs (Branchiae) of the Aquatic Larvae of Cloe Bioculata and Ephemera Vulgata
193.   Nymph of the Libellula and the perfect insect emerging
194.   Dragonfly in adult form
195.   Life-history of dragonflies
196.   Vine-Phylloxera
197.   The Fish Scale
198.   The Skip Tail
199.   Different species of Cimex
200.   The Gigantic Cerambix of Cayenne
201.   Chalcophora Mariana
202.   The West Indian Fire-Fly
203.   Calosoma Sycophanta
204.   Lucanus Capreolus
205.   The Calopus Pigmaeus
206.   Scarites gigas
207.   The Metamorphosis of Acanthophorus Serraticornis
208.   Catadromus tenebrioides
209.   Dioctes Lehmannii
210.   Cychrus vidua
211.   Larva of Calosoma Sycophanta
212.   Oryctes Nasicornis
213.   Tefilus Megerlei
214.   Anthia thoracica
215.   The Metamorphosis of Oncideres Vomicosus
216.   Cypholoba Ranzonii
217.   The Metamorphosis of Lina Populi
218.   Hyperion Schroteri
219.   Procerus Tauricus
220.   Necydalis major
221.   Mormolyce phyllodes
222.   Homalosoma Vigorsii
223.   Damaster blaptoides
224.   Carabus Adonis
225.   A species of Curculio
226.   A species of Curculio
227.   Stag beetle
228.   A species of Curculio
229.   Rhynchites Bacchus
230.   Apoderus longicollis
231.   Ceratorrhina smithi
232.   Tomicus Typographus
233.   Sitones Lineatus and allied species
234.   Mantichora mygaloides
235.   Male of Geotrupes typhoeus
236.   Various insects of the family Scarabaeidae
237.   Three beetles of the order Scarabaeus
238.   Scarabaeus Sacer
239.   Dyticus latissimus
240.   The Sacred Beetle (Ateuchus Sacer)
241.   The Eggs and Immature and Adult Forms of Phyllium Siccifolium
242.   Calandra Granaria
243.   Forest floor with various insects
244.   Calandra Oryzae
245.   Digestive Apparatus of a Carnivorous Insect. The Water Beetle (Dytiscus Marginalis)
246.   Silpha atrata and larva
247.   The Metamorphosis of Calandra Palmarum
248.   Epomis Croesus
249.   Megacephala Senegalensis

250.   Scolytus Destructor
251.   Eight-spot Tiger Beetle
252.   Agra Megaera
253.   Apoderus Coryli
254.   Staphylinus versicolor
255.   Enceladus gigas
256.   Cychrus vidua
257.   Calosoma Indicum
258.   The Incomplete Metamorphosis of Thrips Cerealium. Left, The Adult Insect; Right, The Larva
259.   Corotoca Melantho and Larva
260.   Palm-Weevil
261.   Metamorphosis of Sitaris Humeralis
262.   1, Xenos peckii - male; 2, Female
263.   Musk-beetle; 2, Spondylis buprestoides
264.   Polyphylla fullo, Male
265.   Tiger-Beetles
266.   Carnivorous Beetles and Their Prey
267.   Meligethes aeneus
268.   Oil-Beetles and Larvae
269.   British Rove-Beetles
270.   1, Rhagium indagator, with larva and pupa-case; 2, Rhagium bifasciatum
271.   Churchyard Beetle and Larva
272.   Great Black Water-Beetle - 1, Larva; 2, Male; 3, Female with egg-cocoon
273.   Dytiscus marginalis - 1, Male; 2, Female; 3, Eggs; 4, Pupa; 5, Larva attacking tadpole; 6, Hydrocharis caraboides; 7, Its Larva; 8, Acilius sulcatus, Female
274.   Toxotus-meridianus, males and female
275.   Pine-Weevil, With Larva and Pupa
276.   Strangalia armata and larva
277.   Prionus coriarius, female; and Ergates faber, male
278.   Clerus Formicarius, with larva and pupa
279.   Agriotes Lineatus and its larva
280.   The Red Ant. Left, Male; Centre, Worker; Female, Right
281.   The Adult Female of Diplolepis bedeguaris
282.   The Adult Female of Chalcis Minuta
283.   Myrmecocystus Mexicanus
284.   1, Honey-pot Ant; 2, Parasol-ants; 3, Dwellings of husbandmen ants
285.   Different Insects in an Ant-Hill (Termes Lucifugum). 1, Workman; 2, Soldier; 3, Larva 4, Nymph with small wings; 5, Nymph with Long Wings; 6, Male; 7, Little Female; 8, Large Female
286.   A Female Termes From the African Coast
287.   Geophilus Grappling with Earth-worm
288.   Common English Centipede
289.   Centipede Devouring a Beetle Larva
290.   A Centipede
291.   Millipede of the genus Spirostreptus
292.   Flat Millipede
293.   Scolopendra Morsitans
294.   Millipede, Iulus sabulosus
295.   The Development of Julus Terrestris
296.   Various species of Scorpion
297.   A scorpion
298.   A scorpion
299.   The Scorpion (Scorpio occitanus)
300.   Three species of scorpion; American, Africa and European
301.   Ten Species of Phalangium
302.   Jumping Spiders - a, Female; b, Male; c, female; d, arrangement of eyes
303.   Hydrachna geographica
304.   A Spider's Spinnerts (Greatly magnified)
305.   Albin
306.   Italian Tarantula Spider
307.   Female of Wolf-Spider Carrying her cocoon
308.   Mygale fodiens, and its nest
309.   House Spiders - a, Male; b, Female; arrangement of eyes shown on the left hand of figure
310.   Water-Spiders, with nests
311.   The Garden Spider (Epeira diadema)
312.   The Metamorphosis of Hydrancha globula
313.   Anatomy of common Cross Spider
314.   Tar. Reniforme
315.   Tar. Reniforme
316.   Tarantula
317.   Common Cross Spider
318.   Tarantula
319.   Field Spiders - a, Female; b, Male; c, arrangement of eyes
320.   Tarantula
321.   Tar.Caudata
322.   Shore-Spider
323.   A side-walking spider - Female, left; Male, Right
324.   Diadema
325.   Palustris
326.   Mygale
327.   Species of Pediculus
328.   The Metaporphoses of the Common Flea (Pulex Irritans)
329.   Pediculus Capitis
330.   Common Flea in its several states, magnified
331.   Common Flea and its Structure
332.   A flea, 1665, by Robert Hooke.

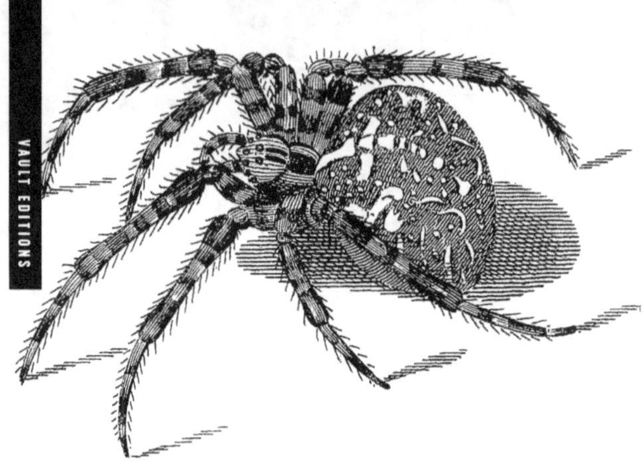

LEARN MORE

At Vault Editions, our mission is to create the world's most diverse and comprehensive collection of image archives available for artists, designers and curious minds. If you have enjoyed this book, you can find more of our titles available at vaulteditions.com.

REVIEW THIS BOOK

As a small, family-owned independent publisher, reviews help spread the word about our work. We would be incredibly grateful if you could leave an honest review of this title wherever you purchased this book.

JOIN OUR COMMUNITY

Are you a creative and curious individual? If so, you will love our community on Instagram. Every day we share bizarre and beautiful artwork ranging from 17th and 18th-century natural history and scientific illustration, to mythical beasts, ornamental designs, anatomical illustration and more. Join our community of 100K+ people today—search @vault_editions on Instagram.

DOWNLOAD YOUR FILES

STEP ONE

Enter the following web address in your web browser on a desktop computer.

www.vaulteditions.com/pages/ins

STEP TWO

Enter the following unique password to access the download page.

inse63483972sxda

STEP THREE

Follow the prompts to access your high-resolution files.

TECHNICAL ASSISTANCE

For all technical assistance, please email: info@vaulteditions.com

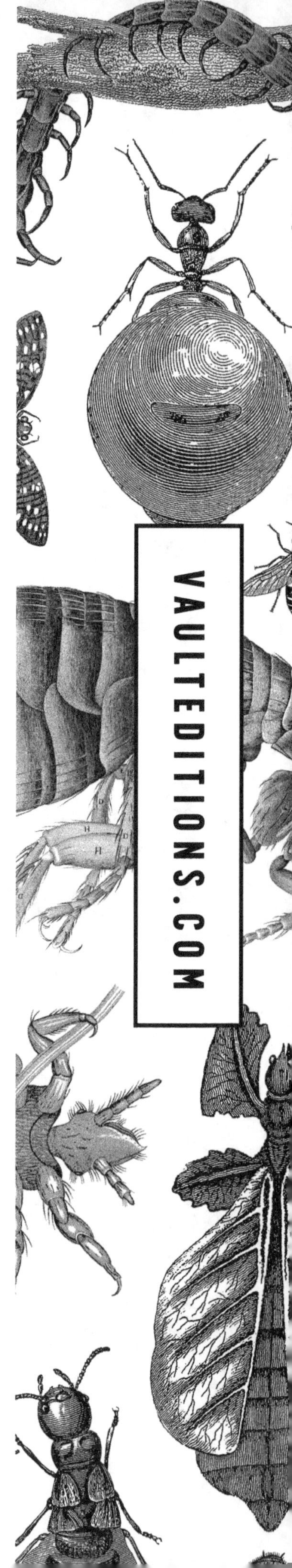

www.ingramcontent.com/pod-product-compliance
Lightning Source LLC
Chambersburg PA
CBHW080520030726
47592CB00012B/3410